P9-CCQ-405

HOOVER ELEMENTARY SCHOOL
INSTRUCTIONAL MATERIAL CENTER
WAYNE COMMUNITY SCHOOL DISTRICT

973.9
Rub
Rubel, David
The United States
in the 20th Century

973.9
Rub

AUTHOR
Rubel, David
TITLE
The United States in the 20th Century
16.95

| DATE DUE | BORROWER'S NAME | ROOM NUMBER |
|---|---|---|
| JUN 6 1997 | [illegible] | 100 |
| MAR 17 1999 | Corey N. | 110 |
| APR 19 1999 / MAR 24 1999 | Emily | 109 |

HOOVER ELEMENTARY SCHOOL
INSTRUCTIONAL MATERIAL CENTER
WAYNE COMMUNITY SCHOOL DISTRICT

WITHDRAWN
DO NOT RETURN
Wayne-Westland
COMMUNITY SCHOOLS

SCHOLASTIC TIMELINES

# ★ THE UNITED STATES ★ in the 20th Century

Editor: Sarah B. Weir
Contributing Editors: Thomas J. Cahill, Sarah Hovde, Lawrence Sprung, Dirk Standen
Copy Editor: Ron Boudreau

Art Director: Tilman Reitzle
Features Design: Bernhard Blythe, Yin Ling Wong
Photo Research: Diane Hamilton, Kamau High, Khara Nemitz
Proof reader: Paul Lipari

We would like to thank Maurice Berger, Senior Fellow of the Vera List Center for Art and Politics, New School for Social Research, for his assistance in the Arts and Entertainment section.

PHOTO CREDITS

AP/Wide World Photos: Cover 1, C2, C5, C6, C7, C9, C11, C12, C13, C14, 11, 19, 24, 34, 36, 41, 51, 54, 58-59, 61 (left), 64, 65, 68, 69, 70, 72, 73 (left), 74, 75 (right), 76-77, 78 (right), 80, 81, 83 (center), 84, 85 (left), 86, 88, 89 (both), 93, 95, 96, 99, 101 (right), 103, 104, 105 (left), 106, 107, 109 (right), 110, 111, 112, 113 (left), 114-122, 123 (right), 125, 127, 128, 130, 131 (left), 132-134, 135 (left), 137-141, 143-163, 165, 166, 168, 169 (right), 170-171, 173-177

All other images are from the Library of Congress except for the following: NASA: C4, 129, 164; Apple Computer, Inc.: C10; Veterans of Foreign Wars: C15, 8-9, 30, 131 (right, center); Girl Scouts of America: 33; Phillips Collection: 37; The National Baseball Hall of Fame and Museum: 42; Institute for Intercultural Studies, Inc., 53; Schomburg Center for Research in Black Culture: 56, 135; National Archives: 101 (left); Roy Lichtenstein: 123 (left); New York Mets: 136; *Ms.*: 142; Sophia Smith Collection/Smith College: 143 (left); The Names Project:167; Alaska Department of Fish and Game: 169 (left); *Earth Times*: 172

Illustrations copyright ©1995 by Scholastic Inc.
Copyright ©1995 by Scholastic Inc.
All rights reserved. Published by Scholastic Inc.

No part of this publication my be reproduced in whole or in part, or stored in a retrieval system, or transmitted in any form or by any means, electronic, mechanical, photocopying, recording, or otherwise, without written permission of the publisher. For information regarding permission, write to Scholastic Inc., 555 Broadway, New York, New York 10012.

Library of Congress Cataloging-in-Publication Data

Rubel, David.
Scholastic timelines : the United States in the 20th century / David Rubel.
p. cm.
"An Agincourt Press book."
Includes index.
ISBN 0-590-27134-2
1. United States—History—20th century—Chronology—Juvenile literature. 2. History, Modern—20th century—Chronology—Juvenile literature. I Title.
E741.R83 1995 94-45702
973.9'02'02—dc20 CIP
AC

12 11 10 9 8 7 6 5 4 3 2 1 5 6 7 8 9/9 0/0

Printed in the USA
First Scholastic printing, October 1995

1900 1910 1920 1930 1940

# THE UNITED STATES in the 20th Century

David Rubel

973.9

An Agincourt Press Book

NEW YORK • TORONTO • LONDON • AUCKLAND • SYDNEY

1950 1960 1970 1980 1990

1900
1910
1920
1930
1940

# Contents



1950 1960 1970 1980 1990

# How to Use

Politics

**POLITICS** includes government affairs and world events.

Life in the Twentieth Century

**LIFE** includes daily life, social movements, fads, and fashions.

Arts & Entertainment

**ARTS AND ENTERTAINMENT** includes the fine arts, literature, radio and television, and popular music.

Science & Technology

**SCIENCE AND TECHNOLOGY** includes inventions, discoveries, and medicine.

## Events

Within each chapter, individual entries summarize important historical events. The events are listed in chronological order, moving from the earliest events to the most recent as you read across the page. So that you can look things up more easily, these events have been divided into four categories: Politics, Life, Arts and Entertainment, and Science and Technology. The subject of each entry is shown in bold, colored type. You can read across the page to learn about one particular category, or you can read up and down to compare events in different categories during the same general time period. Some entries are cross-referenced to events that happened earlier in the century. When you see a date in brackets, such as [December 7, 1941], you should refer back to that date for important information about an earlier, related event.

## Timeline

The timeline that runs along the bottom of every page covers the entire twentieth century. The span of years highlighted in blue corresponds to the years of the era about which you are reading. The vehicle shown was an important means of transportation during that time. Can you recognize it? (The answers appear at the end of the index.)

1900 1910 1920 1930 1940

# This Book

## Chapters

Each chapter in this book covers a different era. Historians use eras to refer to a period of years that, looking back, had a particular, unifying theme. Unlike a decade or a century, an era does not cover a specific number of years. For example, the Great Depression was marked by economic hardship in the United States. It began with the stock market crash of 1929 and ended when the industrial production needed for World War II helped improve the economy.

HISTORICAL ERA

## Features

Every right-hand page has a feature that spotlights a person, an event, or a trend of special importance. The features describe the people and conditions that helped shape each era.

## Introduction

A TIMELINE PRESENTS history as a series of chronological events. ***Scholastic Timelines: The United States in the 20th Century*** **highlights individual events and shows how one event leads to another. Because the book is divided into four categories, it also illustrates the relationships among events happening during the same period of time. For example, this book shows how the Japanese attack on Pearl Harbor in 1941 led to the United States' entrance into World War II. Meanwhile, when men left their jobs in factories to fight abroad, many women entered the workforce for the first time.**

**By understanding how this book is organized, you can look up events and learn about the twentieth century in many different ways.**

## Glossary

You can look up difficult words and historical terms in the glossary at the back of the book.

## Index

You can use the index at the back of the book to look up specific people, places, and events in history.

1950 1960 1970 1980 1990

# The

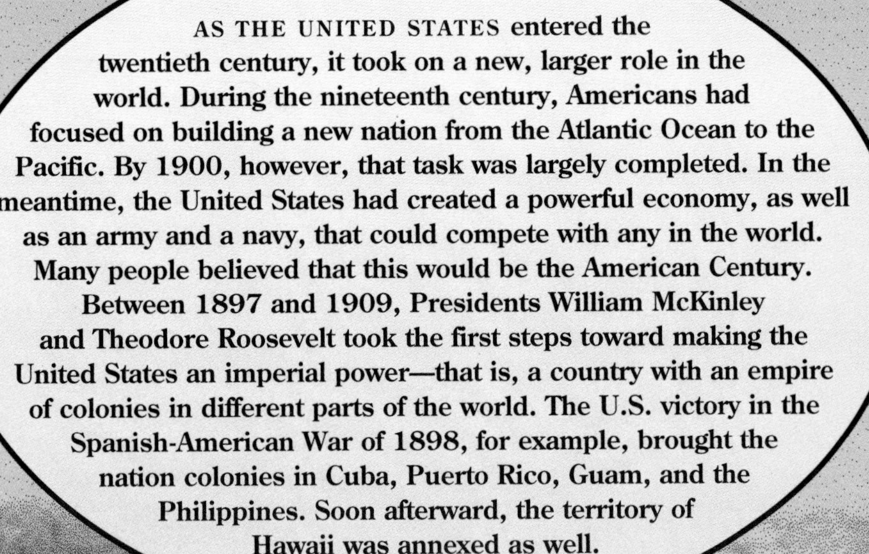

AS THE UNITED STATES entered the twentieth century, it took on a new, larger role in the world. During the nineteenth century, Americans had focused on building a new nation from the Atlantic Ocean to the Pacific. By 1900, however, that task was largely completed. In the meantime, the United States had created a powerful economy, as well as an army and a navy, that could compete with any in the world. Many people believed that this would be the American Century.

Between 1897 and 1909, Presidents William McKinley and Theodore Roosevelt took the first steps toward making the United States an imperial power—that is, a country with an empire of colonies in different parts of the world. The U.S. victory in the Spanish-American War of 1898, for example, brought the nation colonies in Cuba, Puerto Rico, Guam, and the Philippines. Soon afterward, the territory of Hawaii was annexed as well.

★

# New Century

## Politics

**March 20, 1900** Secretary of State John Hay announces that the foreign powers with an interest in China have accepted his **OPEN DOOR POLICY**. All the Western nations agree to trade with China on an equal basis. Hay's purpose is to prevent U.S. competitors from dividing up China for themselves.

**April 12, 1900** Congress adopts a plan for governing Puerto Rico, which the United States obtained from Spain during the 1898 Spanish-American War. The **FORAKER ACT** ends military rule and empowers the president to appoint a governor for the colony. But Puerto Ricans, who are given very little say in these matters, must wait until 1916 before Congress grants them U.S. citizenship.

**April 30, 1900** Congress makes **HAWAII** a territory of the United States. Sanford B. Dole, who had been president of the independent Republic of Hawaii, becomes the new colonial governor. In 1893, Dole had led American sugar planters in a revolution that overthrew Queen Liliuokalani.

## Life in the New Century

**April 30, 1900** Engineer John Luther **"CASEY" JONES** refuses to leap to safety as his speeding Cannonball Express hurtles toward a stalled freight train in the Vaughan, Mississippi, station. Instead, he keeps trying to brake his passenger train until the last possible moment. Jones is killed, but his sacrifice saves many lives.

**June 3, 1900** The **INTERNATIONAL LADIES' GARMENT WORKERS UNION** is founded on Manhattan's Lower East Side. Most members are Jewish immigrant women, who begin organizing to improve conditions in the sweatshops where they work.

**September 18, 1900** Reformers in Minneapolis, Minnesota, hold the first **DIRECT PRIMARY ELECTION** in the United States. In a direct primary, the voters themselves, and not the party leadership, choose the party's candidates. Progressives believe that direct primaries will produce more independent and fewer corrupt office holders.

## Arts & Entertainment

**1900** **HARRY HOUDINI** gains fame with daring escapes from shackles and straitjackets, notably one performed at London's Scotland Yard. Houdini later thrills the world by performing these same escapes underwater in a trunk. The immigrant son of a Hungarian rabbi, Houdini also works to expose crooked mystics who use magic tricks to convince believers they have supernatural powers.

**HARRY HOUDINI • Although he proved many mystics to be frauds, Houdini promised his wife he would contact her after his death.**

**1900** Chicago newspaperman L. Frank Baum publishes ***THE WONDERFUL WIZARD OF OZ***. His story of the little girl Dorothy Gale and her dog, Toto, begins the popular series of Oz books, which serve as the basis for a 1903 Broadway musical and the famous 1939 motion picture starring Judy Garland.

## Science & Technology

**1900** The U.S. Navy purchases the first **MODERN SUBMARINE** from John Holland. Named for its designer, the *Holland* uses gasoline engines to move about on the water's surface like a ship. When it submerges, however, the *Holland* switches to battery-powered electric motors because it cannot burn fuel underwater.

**1900** Eastman Kodak introduces the **BROWNIE BOX CAMERA** at the low price of one dollar. This easy-to-operate cardboard-boxed camera makes photography popular with amateurs. It comes loaded with a hundred-exposure roll that users mail back to Kodak for processing. Kodak's slogan is, "You press the button, and we do the rest."

MAY 31, 1900 In South Africa, the British seize Johannesburg, ending the army-against-army phase of the **BOER WAR**. Although the vastly outnumbered Boers no longer have the strength to engage in open battles, they continue to fight using guerrilla warfare. The war between the British and the Boers, who are white South Africans of Dutch descent, began in 1899 over gold mining in the Transvaal.

JUNE 13, 1900 Germany approves the **SECOND FLEET ACT**, which will double the size of its navy within twenty years. Navy Secretary Alfred von Tirpitz believes that Germany needs a strong navy in order to play a decisive role in world politics. Germany's huge buildup begins the arms race leading up to World War I.

JUNE 1900 Following raids on Christians in the countryside, Chinese nationalists known as Boxers surge into Peking. Named for a ritual they believe makes them bullet-proof, the Boxers hope to drive all "foreign devils" from their country. The **BOXER REBELLION** becomes an international crisis on June 18 when the Chinese Empress Dowager orders all foreigners killed.

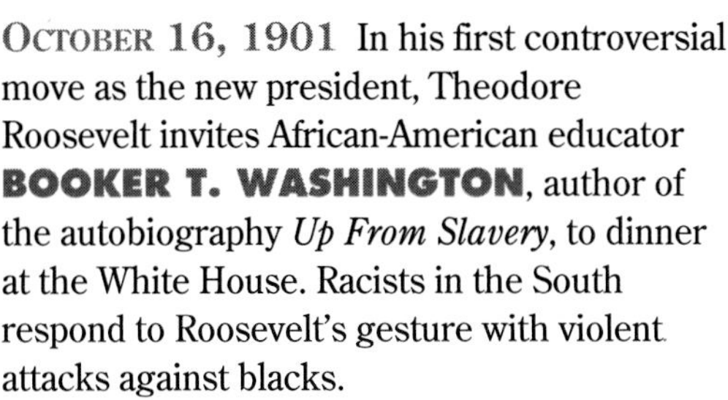

OCTOBER 16, 1901 In his first controversial move as the new president, Theodore Roosevelt invites African-American educator **BOOKER T. WASHINGTON**, author of the autobiography *Up From Slavery*, to dinner at the White House. Racists in the South respond to Roosevelt's gesture with violent attacks against blacks.

# BOOKER T. WASHINGTON



## *Equality Through Education*

**BORN A SLAVE IN 1858, Booker T. Washington grew up very poor in Virginia. Three years after receiving his freedom at the end of the Civil War, ten-year-old Booker went to work in a salt mine, where his day began every morning at four o'clock. Still, he was determined to get an education, and he regularly walked several miles to attend school at night.**

**One day, Washington heard about a school where black students worked and studied at the same time. Several years later, he made the five-hundred-mile trip from his home to the Hampton Institute, where he arrived in rags with no money. At first, the school refused to admit him. But when he begged for a chance, he was given one. In time, Washington founded his own school: the Tuskegee Institute in Alabama.**

**As Tuskegee grew into a large and famous college, Washington emerged as a leading spokesman for African Americans. He believed that the only way African Americans could improve their situation was through education and job training. Because Washington believed that earning a living was more important than fighting discrimination, his views were popular among white people. However, many leading African Americans thought that Washington was encouraging blacks to accept second-class status.**

**Students at Tuskegee Institute were taught how to farm as well as how to read, write, and do arithmetic. Most of the Tuskegee buildings were built by the students, and they raised the food they ate on school farms.**

## Politics

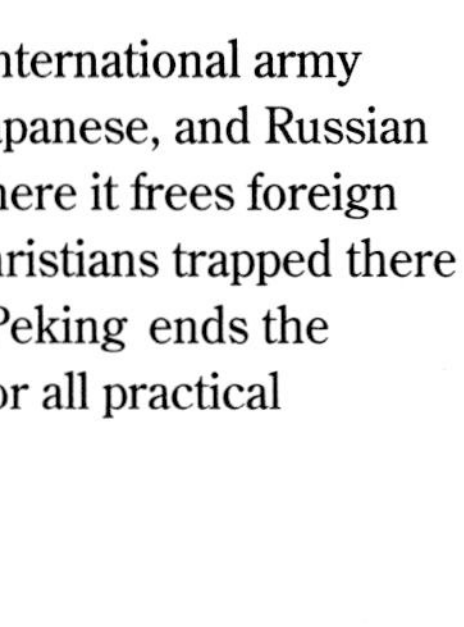

AUGUST 14, 1900 An international army of U.S., British, French, Japanese, and Russian troops reaches Peking, where it frees foreign diplomats and Chinese Christians trapped there since June 20. The fall of Peking ends the **BOXER REBELLION** for all practical purposes.

**BOXER REBELLION • An army of international soldiers drives the rebel Boxers from the Chinese imperial palace in Peking.**

NOVEMBER 6, 1900 Republican William McKinley defeats Democrat William Jennings Bryan in the **1900 PRESIDENTIAL ELECTION**. McKinley's new vice president, Theodore Roosevelt, a former New York governor, became famous during the Spanish-American War as leader of the Rough Riders. McKinley credits his reelection to approval of the expanding U.S. role in world affairs.

## Life in the New Century

1901 **MILTON HERSHEY** begins construction of a factory town outside Harrisburg, Pennsylvania, designed exclusively for making chocolate. His model community includes housing for workers and schools for their children. Hershey chose this site because nearby dairy farms produce enough milk to make his factory the largest manufacturer of milk chocolate in the world.

1901 Social worker Lizzie Black publishes ***THE SETTLEMENT COOKBOOK***, using the slogan, "The way to a man's heart is through his stomach." Her recipes are taken from the chalkboard of a Milwaukee center where volunteers help recent immigrants adapt to American life. The cookbook becomes so popular that royalties from its sales pay for the construction of a new settlement house.

## Arts & Entertainment

1901 Chicago architect **FRANK LLOYD WRIGHT** names his new type of architecture the "prairie house"style because of its resemblance to the prairie landscape. Wright's Robie House (1909), the best example of his prairie style, has a low roof and wide walls that match the flatness of the Midwest. Wright had been working for years to develop the first uniquely American style of home architecture.

1902 British writer **RUDYARD KIPLING** publishes the *Just So Stories*, set in colonial India. These short stories encourage children in England and the United States to learn about distant places and cultures.

1902 Binney & Smith introduces the first **CRAYOLA CRAYONS**. The multicolored wax markers were developed by Edwin Binney and named by his mother after *craie*, the French word for *chalk*. The inexpensive Crayolas soon become a familiar part of American childhood, with an ever-increasing number of colors.

## Science & Technology

JANUARY 10, 1901 Australian mining engineer Anthony F. Lucas makes the first great oil strike in Texas on his Spindletop claim near Beaumont. The **SPINDLETOP GUSHER** produces sixty million barrels of oil by 1925 and leads to an oil boom in Texas, where 491 petroleum companies are chartered.

DECEMBER 12, 1901 At his antenna station in Newfoundland, Canada, Italian inventor Guglielmo Marconi receives the first **TRANSATLANTIC RADIO MESSAGE**: the letter *S*, sent in Morse code by a British telegraph operator. Many scientists had previously believed that the curvature of the earth would prevent the transmission of wireless signals across great distances.

1901 Major William C. Gorgas of the Public Health Service leads a project in Havana, Cuba, to combat **YELLOW FEVER**. Gorgas succeeds by nearly wiping out Havana's mosquitoes, which army doctor Walter Reed has proved carry the deadly disease. Three years later, Gorgas is sent to Panama, where his work controlling yellow fever makes building the Panama Canal possible.

MARCH 2, 1901 In the aftermath of the Spanish-American War, Congress passes the **PLATT AMENDMENT**, in which the United States offers to remove its troops from Cuba if Cuba agrees not to borrow money or make treaties without U.S. government approval. Cuba must also allow the United States to intervene militarily in its affairs and establish naval bases on Cuban soil.

MAY 27, 1901 In the **INSULAR CASES**, the Supreme Court rules that the Constitution does not necessarily "follow the flag." In *Downes v. Bidwell*, for instance, the Court rules that native residents of new U.S. possessions do not automatically receive the same rights as residents of the states. As a result of these decisions, native Hawaiians [April 30, 1900] are denied such civil rights as a trial by jury.

SEPTEMBER 2, 1901 In a speech at the Minnesota State Fair, Vice President Theodore Roosevelt outlines his thoughts on foreign policy. Quoting a proverb, he says, "Speak softly and carry a big stick; you will go far." When Roosevelt takes over as president, his aggressive stance and forceful tactics become known as **BIG STICK DIPLOMACY**.

MAY 12, 1902 The United Mine Workers union leads a **STRIKE OF ANTHRACITE COAL COMPANIES** in Pennsylvania. The miners want higher wages, shorter hours, and recognition of their union. As winter nears and coal prices skyrocket, President Roosevelt, responding to public pressure, threatens to take over the mines. The owners agree to negotiate, and the miners return to work.

# TEDDY ROOSEVELT

## Strong As a Bull Moose

THEODORE ROOSEVELT WAS ONE of the most popular presidents in U.S. history. When he took office in 1901 at the age of forty-two, he was the youngest chief executive ever. But his youthful energy suited the optimism and expansionism of his time. Roosevelt once said, "I am as strong as a bull moose and you can use me to the limit."

Although the mature Roosevelt was a vigorous, athletic man, he had been a frail and sickly child. Illnesses kept him out of school so often that his wealthy parents hired a tutor to educate him at home. As he got older, Roosevelt overcame his weakness through determination and constant physical exercise. As president, he often sparred with professional boxers in the White House gymnasium. Once an opponent hit him so hard that he was permanently blinded in his left eye, but he kept this secret from the public.

In 1898, Roosevelt had helped lead a volunteer cavalry regiment to fight in Cuba during the Spanish-American War. Known as the Rough Riders, Roosevelt's men were glorified by U.S. newspapermen after they courageously charged up San Juan Hill during the battle of Santiago. His fame as a war hero helped him capture the New York state governor's race that same year.

## Politics

SEPTEMBER 6, 1901 Leon Czolgosz, an anarchist, shoots President McKinley at point-blank range while McKinley is visiting the Pan American Exposition in Buffalo, New York. At first, he appears to recover; then his condition worsens, and he dies on September 14. **McKINLEY'S ASSASSINATION** makes forty-two-year-old Vice President Theodore Roosevelt the youngest president ever.

SEPTEMBER 7, 1901 The Boxer Rebellion [June 1900] formally ends when the Chinese government signs the **BOXER PROTOCOL**, which compels China to make payments to the nations whose citizens were attacked and accept Secretary of State John Hay's Open Door Policy [March 20, 1900]. Hay's active role in the negotiations increases U.S. influence in China, the rest of Asia, and throughout the world.

NOVEMBER 18, 1901 With the signing of the **HAY-PAUNCEFOTE TREATY**, Britain gives up its right to build a shipping canal across Central America. In return, the United States promises to allow ships from all nations to use any canal that it might build. Such a canal across Central America could shorten some voyages between the Atlantic and Pacific Oceans by up to eight thousand miles.

## Life in the New Century

NOVEMBER 18, 1902 Brooklyn toy store owner Morris Michtom takes a Clifford Berryman cartoon of President Roosevelt refusing to shoot a bear cub and displays it in his store window next to a stuffed bear. Michtom calls the bear, which looks like the one in the cartoon, "Teddy's bear." Cute, cuddly **TEDDY BEARS** soon become an international fad that has never ended.

**TEDDY BEAR • Morris Michtom wrote to Theodore Roosevelt for permission to use the president's name in selling his stuffed bear. Roosevelt replied that he doubted his name would help, but Michtom was welcome to use it.**

## Arts & Entertainment

1903 Jack London publishes his adventure classic ***THE CALL OF THE WILD***, which is based on his own experiences in Alaska during the Klondike Gold Rush of 1897–1898. London's stories of rugged individualism find an eager audience among young men.

1903 Edwin S. Porter directs ***THE GREAT TRAIN ROBBERY*** for Thomas Edison's film company. This twelve-minute western is the first major film with a dramatic plot. Before *The Great Train Robbery*, most motion pictures were about daily life, famous people, or news events. Porter's development of quick-cut editing, in particular, enabled him to build his story to an exciting climax.

NOVEMBER 27, 1904 The **GEORGE M. COHAN** musical *Little Johnny Jones* opens at Broadway's Liberty Theater. The play features the hit songs "Give My Regards to Broadway" and "I'm a Yankee Doodle Dandy." During his theatrical career, Cohan will write, direct, produce, and star in a number of successful shows with patriotic themes. These efforts win him a special congressional medal in 1940.

## Science & Technology

1902 In Brant Rock, Massachusetts, Reginald Fessenden begins construction of the first **AM RADIO STATION**. *AM* stands for *amplitude modulation*. Radio waves have an amplitude and a frequency. Information can be sent using radio waves by modulating, or changing, one or the other.

JULY 4, 1903 President Theodore Roosevelt sends the first **MESSAGE AROUND THE WORLD** using the newly laid Pacific communications cable. This cable links San Francisco with Honolulu and then Honolulu with Manila in the Philippines. Roosevelt's message takes twelve minutes to travel around the world and reach him again.

1903 Eighteen years after Gottlieb Daimler built the first gasoline-powered model in Germany, Milwaukee draftsman William Harley and mechanic Walter Davidson go into business to make motorcycles in the United States. Their powerful **HARLEY-DAVIDSON** machines soon become the nation's top seller.

**MAY 31, 1902** Lord Kitchener's brutal tactics bring an end to the Boer War [May 31, 1900] when the exhausted Boers agree to the **PEACE OF VEREENIGING**. Kitchener's methods included burning farms and placing Boers in concentration camps, where twenty thousand died. As a result of the peace treaty, the Boers lose their independence and become subjects of the ever-expanding British Empire.

**JULY 1, 1902** Congress passes the **PHILIPPINE GOVERNMENT ACT**, which creates a commission to govern the Philippines, another territory obtained from Spain as a result of the U.S. victory in the 1898 Spanish-American War. However, Filipinos are specifically denied U.S. citizenship.

**JULY–AUGUST 1903** At its second congress in Brussels, Belgium, the exiled **RUSSIAN SOCIAL DEMOCRATIC WORKERS' PARTY SPLITS**. On one side, the Mensheviks believe in a gradual, step-by-step approach to Communist revolution. Meanwhile, the Bolsheviks, under the fiery leadership of Vladimir Lenin, urge an immediate overthrow of the repressive Russian tsar.

**OCTOBER 1–13, 1903** The pennant-winning Pittsburgh Pirates of the National League meet the Boston Red Sox, champions of the three-year-old American League, in the first **WORLD SERIES**. Boston's five-games-to-three victory in the best-of-nine series earns some much-needed respect for the upstart league.

# The Wright Brothers

## *First Flight*

On the morning of December 17, 1903, near the village of Kitty Hawk, North Carolina, brothers Orville and Wilbur Wright did something that humans had never done before: They flew in a heavier-than-air machine. On their first attempt, with Orville at the controls, the plane traveled 120 feet in the air, staying aloft for twelve seconds. On their third attempt, they kept the plane in the air for fifty-nine seconds, traveling 852 feet in that time.

Only a few people witnessed the Wright brothers' flying experiments, which did not attract much publicity. As a result, many people who heard about the flight did not believe it had really happened. Inventors in Europe and the United States had been trying to build engine-powered flying machines for years. Who would believe that two bicycle mechanics from Dayton, Ohio, could succeed where so many others had failed?

The Wright brothers were not scientists, but they were mechanics. Observing that hawks controlled their flight by changing the position of their wings, Orville and Wilbur designed an aircraft with wings that could twist. These wings allowed the plane to turn, roll, and fly up and down. By 1905, their airplanes could remain in the air for thirty minutes at a time. In 1909, the War Department contracted with the Wright brothers to produce the first U.S. Army planes.

**The first Wright brothers plane had no seat for the pilot. Instead, he had to guide the plane while lying down between the wings.**

## Politics

AUGUST 12, 1903 The South American nation of Colombia rejects the **HAY-HERRÁN TREATY**. This agreement would have allowed the United States to build a canal across the province of Panama in Central America. The refusal enrages many Panamanians, who feel betrayed by the Colombian government. The Colombians, however, believe the United States should have made a more generous offer.

NOVEMBER 3, 1903 **PANAMANIANS REVOLT AGAINST COLOMBIA** and declare their independence. The United States quickly recognizes the newly formed government of Panama and immediately sends a warship, which prevents Colombian troops from landing and regaining control of the country.

NOVEMBER 18, 1903 The United States and Panama sign the **HAY-BUNAU-VARILLA TREATY**, which closely resembles the Hay-Herrán treaty recently rejected by Colombia [August 12, 1903]. The new treaty grants the United States permanent rights to a ten-mile-wide canal zone in Panama for ten million dollars plus a yearly fee. Roosevelt's ambitious Panama Canal project begins the next year.

## Life in the New Century

1903 W.E.B. Du Bois publishes ***THE SOULS OF BLACK FOLK***, a collection of essays that challenge Booker T. Washington's approach to black-white relations. A Harvard graduate, Du Bois believes African Americans can succeed without sacrificing their separate identity as people of color. While Washington advocates working within the system, Du Bois argues that action is necessary for results.

MAY 23, 1904 Competition between steamship lines reduces the one-way fare for a transatlantic crossing to ten dollars, which is about one week's wages for the average U.S. worker. About one million **IMMIGRANTS** will make the journey this year, most from southern and eastern Europe.

1904 When an ice cream stand at the busy Louisiana Purchase Exhibition in St. Louis, Missouri, runs out of plates, its workers begin using rolled Syrian waffles from a nearby bakery to hold their melting ice cream. The result are the first **ICE CREAM CONES**.

**IMMIGRATION • Eastern European immigrants travel to New York aboard the S.S. *Amsterdam*.**

## Arts & Entertainment

DECEMBER 27, 1904 A musical version of James M. Barrie's ***PETER PAN*** opens in London at the Duke of York Theatre. The play, also written by Barrie, appeals to both children and adults and becomes one of the world's longest-running shows.

1905 American **ISADORA DUNCAN** opens an unconventional dancing school for children in Berlin. She emphasizes free and spontaneous expression instead of classical ballet training. Her modern dance technique attempts to combine music and poetry with the "forces of nature."

## Science & Technology

OCTOBER 27, 1904 The **NEW YORK CITY SUBWAY** opens to the public. Work first began in 1900 on the Interborough Rapid Transit Broadway line, which runs from the Brooklyn Bridge to West 145th Street in upper Manhattan. A one-way fare costs five cents.

1904 Health officials in New York trace a typhoid epidemic on Long Island to a cook named Mary Mallon, who worked in the homes where the disease first appeared. Nicknamed **TYPHOID MARY**, she carries the highly infectious disease but is immune to it herself. Mallon escapes, however, and continues to spread the disease until she is tracked down and permanently hospitalized in 1915.

**February 8, 1904** During a dispute over territory in China, the Japanese launch a surprise attack on the Russian naval base at Port Arthur, Manchuria. The outbreak of the **RUSSO-JAPANESE WAR** shocks western Europe, which had dominated Asia militarily during the nineteenth century. When Russia fails to take strong action, popular unrest against the tsar builds [July–August 1903].

**March 14, 1904** The Supreme Court uses the **NORTHERN SECURITIES CASE** to issue its most important antitrust decision. It rules that the Northern Securities Company, which controls nearly all western railroads, violates the Sherman Antitrust Act (1890) and must be dissolved. The decision is a victory for President Roosevelt, whose "trust-busting" campaign makes him hugely popular.

**November 8, 1904** Promising a Square Deal for every American citizen, President Roosevelt routs New York judge Alton B. Parker, the Democratic candidate, in the **1904 PRESIDENTIAL ELECTION**. Roosevelt's landslide victory encourages him to look for ways to make life fairer for the average person.

**February 1, 1905** President Roosevelt makes Gifford Pinchot the first chief of the Bureau of Forestry. At Roosevelt's request, vast areas of forest are preserved for public use and protected from private development. An outdoorsman himself, the president becomes known as the **GREAT CONSERVATIONIST** for his commitment to protecting the nation's natural resources.

# Ragtime

## The Birth of Popular Music

**When Americans danced into the twentieth century, they moved to a ragtime beat. Ragtime had two main sources: southern black banjo music and white minstrel shows. Although the white performers in minstrel shows made fun of blacks, their music definitely had African-American roots.**

**Ragtime music probably got its name from its jazzy, "ragged" beat. Among the most popular ragtime songwriters were Scott Joplin, called the King of Ragtime, and Irving Berlin. Joplin was an African American from Missouri, but Berlin was a Russian Jewish immigrant who grew up on New York City's Lower East Side, where he worked as a singing waiter.**

**Musical critics found it difficult to accept the popularity of ragtime, which they considered inferior to classical European music. But the public paid them no attention, and songs like Joplin's "Maple Leaf Rag" and Berlin's "Alexander's Ragtime Band" remained all the rage until the 1920s.**

**New technologies broadened ragtime's appeal, making it the first truly popular music. New printing techniques made sheet music affordable, and Thomas Edison's new phonograph allowed people to play recordings of the music in their own homes.**

**Scott Joplin**

## Politics

**December 6, 1904** President Roosevelt announces the **ROOSEVELT COROLLARY** to the Monroe Doctrine. In 1823, President James Monroe warned European colonial powers to stay out of the Western Hemisphere. Now Roosevelt says that the United States will occasionally take over the affairs of Latin American countries. His speech is an example of Big Stick Diplomacy [September 2, 1901].

**January 21, 1905** When the Dominican Republic, a tiny Caribbean nation, stops paying its debts to European bankers, President **ROOSEVELT TAKES CONTROL OF THE DOMINICAN TREASURY**. In this first, controversial application of the Roosevelt Corollary [December 6, 1904], the president shifts control of the loans to U.S. banks and sets up a new payment schedule.

**January 22, 1905** On **BLOODY SUNDAY**, Tsar Nicholas II orders Russian troops to fire on demonstrators outside the Winter Palace in St. Petersburg. Hundreds of factory workers are killed or wounded. The unarmed marchers, led by Russian Orthodox priest Georgy Gapon, had intended to present a petition of grievances to the tsar. Strikes and violent protests follow the massacre.

## Life in the New Century

**April 17, 1905** In ***LOCHNER V. NEW YORK***, the Supreme Court strikes down a state law limiting bakers to sixty hours of work each week. In a famous dissent, Justice Oliver Wendell Holmes, Jr., voices concerns about the workers' health, but the majority of justices believes that not enough evidence exists to restrict the right of an employer and an employee to make a contract.

**June 27, 1905** Charismatic labor leader William "Big Bill" Haywood helps found the **INDUSTRIAL WORKERS OF THE WORLD** at a meeting in Chicago. Members of this militant union, known as the Wobblies, hope to organize all workers into one big union. Unlike the more conservative trade unions, the IWW accepts any worker regardless of skills, race, or gender.

**July 11–13, 1905** W.E.B. Du Bois and a group of his supporters gather in Niagara Falls and launch the **NIAGARA MOVEMENT**. Its goals include equal opportunity for blacks in political and economic life as well as an end to segregation. Du Bois and his colleagues have to meet on the Canadian side of the border because no hotels on the U.S. side will allow African Americans to register.

**1905** The first **NICKELODEON** opens in Pittsburgh. Within six years, eight thousand more nickelodeon movie theaters open around the country showing short films to twenty-five million people a week. Named for their five-cent admission price, nickelodeons are especially popular among recent immigrants, who do not need to know English to enjoy the silent films.

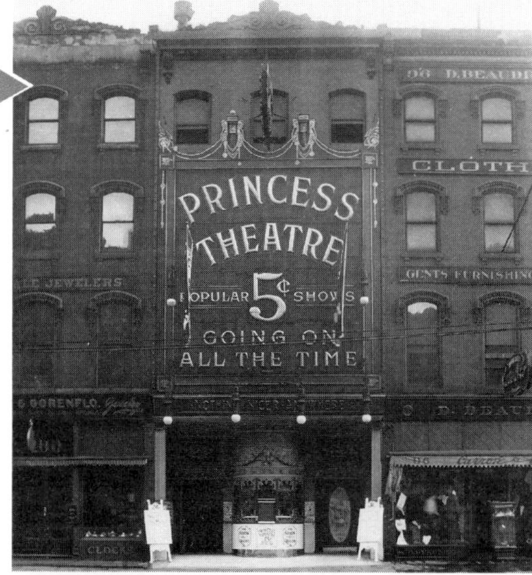


**NICKELODEON • Nickelodeons, such as Detroit's Princess Theatre, often showed advertisements, short films on good manners, and lyrics for singalongs.**

**1905** Pioneering photographer **ALFRED STIEGLITZ** opens the "291" gallery at his 291 Fifth Avenue brownstone in New York City to promote new styles in modern art. At 291, Stieglitz displays the works of such artists as John Marin, Marsden Hartley, and his future wife, Georgia O'Keeffe.

**1904** Russian physiologist Ivan Pavlov wins the Nobel Prize for his research on the **CONDITIONED REFLEX**. By ringing a bell each time he served a dog food, Pavlov trained the dog to salivate when it heard the bell, whether or not there was food.

**1905** Albert Einstein introduces his **SPECIAL THEORY OF RELATIVITY**, from which he derives the famous equation $e = mc^2$. Einstein's theory suggests that time is relative and that inside a spaceship time would slow down as the ship's speed approaches the speed of light. The Swiss physicist's ideas challenge concepts accepted as fact since the publication of Isaac Newton's *Principia* in 1687.

JUNE 27, 1905 Aboard the Russian ship **POTEMKIN**, an officer kills a member of the crew who protests his rations of spoiled meat. The enraged crew mutinies, kills the captain, and seizes control of the battleship. Landing at the Russian port of Odessa, the crew joins in the revolutionary movement, and this event becomes a rallying point for the Revolution of 1905 [January 22, 1905].

SEPTEMBER 5, 1905 At a New Hampshire meeting, President Roosevelt convinces the Russians and Japanese to sign the **TREATY OF PORTSMOUTH**, ending the Russo-Japanese War [February 8, 1904]. Roosevelt's negotiating strategy adds to his international prestige and that of the nation. For his efforts in bringing the two exhausted sides together, he wins the 1906 Nobel Peace Prize.

JUNE 29, 1906 Congress passes the **HEPBURN ACT**, which gives the federal government the power to control railroad rates. Although President Roosevelt has been responding to public outrage against the railroad monopolies, he hopes that the Hepburn Act will sidetrack the populist campaign for a governmental takeover of the railroads.

APRIL 18, 1906 A hugely destructive **EARTHQUAKE DEMOLISHES SAN FRANCISCO**. The fires that follow last for three days, destroy two-thirds of the city, and leave half a million people homeless.

**Helen Keller published her autobiography, *The Story of My Life*, in 1902, while she was a student at Radcliffe. The book, which became a worldwide best-seller, was eventually translated into fifty languages. A sentence from the book in Braille is shown below.**

## Helen Keller

**GRADUATING FROM prestigious Radcliffe College in Cambridge, Massachusetts, has always been a thrill for any young woman. But it was a particularly special achievement for one twenty-four-year-old graduate in the Class of 1904. Unlike any other student in her class, Helen Keller was both blind and deaf.**

**Born in 1880, Keller lost her sight and hearing when she was just nineteen months old as the result of a serious illness. Unable to speak or communicate with the world around her, she grew moody and uncontrollable. Her parents hired a private tutor for Helen when she was six years old. The teacher, Anne Sullivan, would transform Helen's life.**

**Slowly, Sullivan calmed Keller's wild behavior. Then she began to teach Helen the names of everyday objects using sign language. By holding Helen's hands as she signed, Sullivan taught Keller how to communicate. Later, Keller also learned how to read and write in Braille.**

**After her college graduation, Keller devoted herself to helping blind and deaf people. She particularly fought to improve their educational opportunities. The strength Keller showed in overcoming her handicaps inspired others to rethink their attitudes toward the disabled.**

I l e f t the w e l l - h ou s e e a g er to l(ea)r n .

# The Pro

THE PROGRESSIVE ERA took its name from a group of early twentieth-century reformers who worked tirelessly to make life better for all Americans, not just those with money and power. These "progressives" spoke out early and often on behalf of the country's working poor. At first, few people listened, but the conditions they described were so awful that more and more Americans became convinced that things had to change.

Progressives were particularly disturbed by the evils of industrialism, which became widespread as the U.S. economy shifted from farms to factories. In magazines and newspapers, crusading journalists exposed many of the ways in which Big Business took advantage of the average American. Some reformers criticized trusts, or monopolies, that kept prices artificially high, while others attacked conditions in factories, where small children often worked twelve-hour days using dangerous equipment.

Laws passed during the Progressive Era set new government standards for food quality, placed tough restrictions on child labor, improved conditions in unsafe factories, weakened the power of corrupt politicians, and granted women the right to vote.

★

# gressive Era

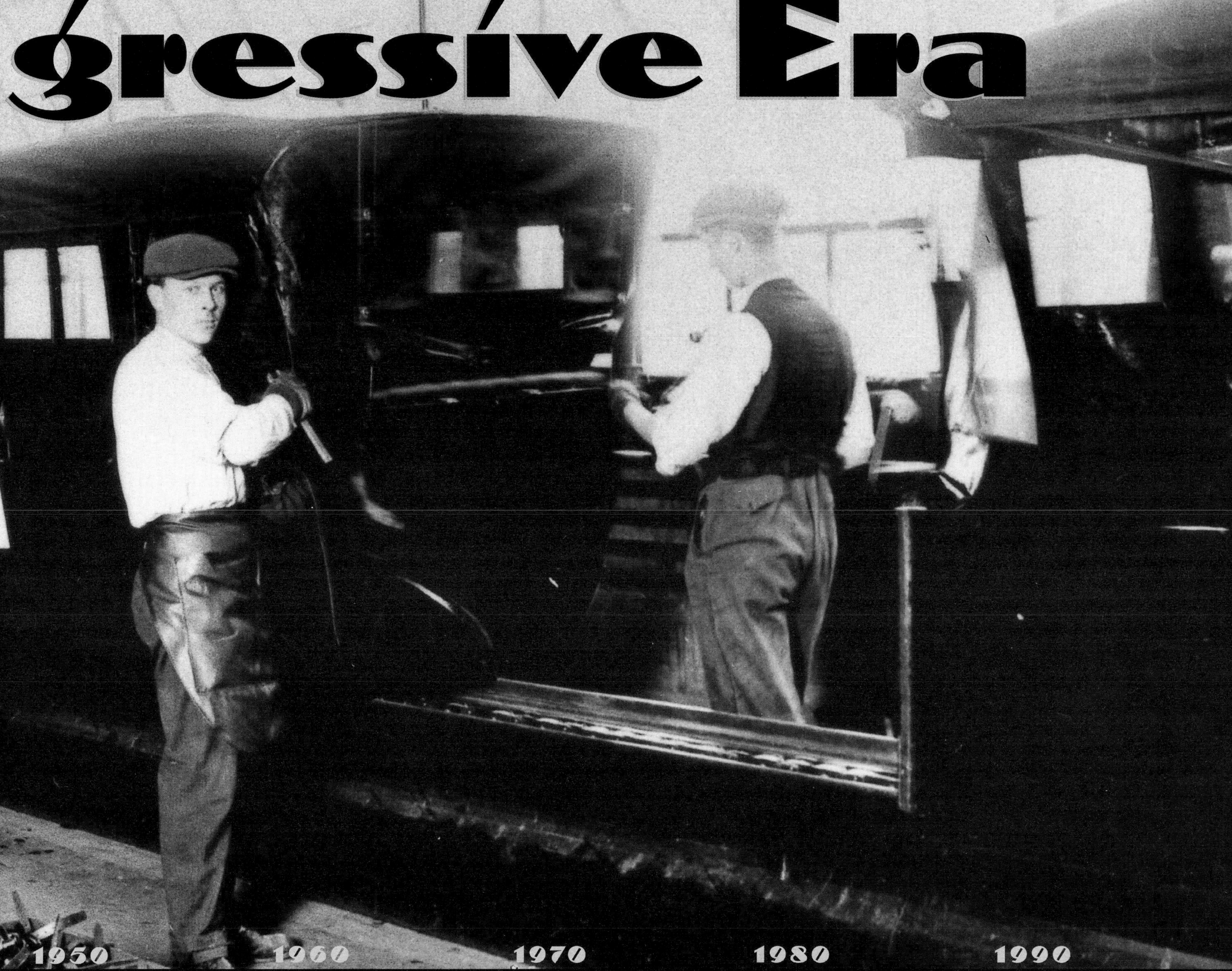

## Politics

June 30, 1906 Under severe public pressure, Congress passes the **PURE FOOD AND DRUG AND MEAT INSPECTION ACTS**. These pieces of Progressive legislation respond to charges by muckraking journalists that the U.S. food supply is not fit to eat.

**MOHANDAS K. GANDHI • Gandhi *(center)* poses outside his law office in South Africa.**

September 11, 1906 While living in South Africa, Indian lawyer Mohandas K. **GANDHI** leads a nonviolent protest against the discrimination Indians face there. The campaign lands Gandhi in jail, but the techniques of peaceful resistance he develops will prove useful when he returns home in 1915 and begins working to free India from British rule.

## Life in the Progressive Era

August 13–14, 1906 During the night, a **SHOOTING SPREE IN BROWNSVILLE, TEXAS**, kills a white civilian. The mayor and other white citizens accuse black soldiers stationed nearby of participating in the attack. Although they deny the charges, 167 black soldiers are dishonorably discharged by President Roosevelt for maintaining a "conspiracy of silence" to protect the guilty among them.

October 11, 1906 The San Francisco Board of Education orders Asian children to attend segregated schools. President Roosevelt calls the segregation "wickedly absurd" and pressures the school board to cancel the order, which it does on March 13, 1907. However, **CALIFORNIANS' FEAR OF ASIAN IMMIGRANTS**, whom they call the Yellow Peril, continues to grow.

## Arts & Entertainment

April 14, 1906 "The men with the muckrakes are often indispensable to the wellbeing of society," President Theodore Roosevelt admits in a Washington speech, "but only if they know when to stop raking the muck and to look upward." Roosevelt believes that these Progressive journalists, or **MUCKRAKERS**, should write about positive subjects as well.

1906 Children's author Edward Stratemeyer founds the Stratemeyer Literary Syndicate, which will publish the **HARDY BOYS AND NANCY DREW MYSTERIES**. After developing successful formulas for these adventure series, Stratemeyer hires anonymous writers to fill in the details.

1906 New Orleans pianist Ferdinand **"JELLY ROLL" MORTON** writes the ragtime hit "King Porter Stomp." With typical flair, the charismatic Morton takes credit for having invented the newly popular "jass" music in 1902. Other musicians dispute this claim, but Morton is recognized as one of the great jazz pioneers. His recordings with the Red Hot Peppers influence the Jazz Age of the 1920s.

## Science & Technology

December 24, 1906 On Christmas Eve in Brant Rock, Massachusetts, Reginald Fessenden broadcasts the **FIRST MUSIC EVER TO COME OUT OF A RADIO**. He plays "O Holy Night" and reads from the Bible.

September 12, 1907 Steaming into New York harbor, the luxury liner ***LUSITANIA*** completes its maiden voyage in record time. It took the *Lusitania*, the largest steamship in the world, just five days to cross the Atlantic from Ireland. The British ship, owned by the Cunard Line, can hold two thousand passengers as well as its six-hundred-member crew.

1907 A Cincinnati surgeon creates Ovorono, the first **UNDERARM DEODORANT** for women. Ads for Ovorono promote its use "within the curve of a woman's arm" to avoid mentioning armpits. Ovorono is not marketed to men, however, because they are expected to smell as nature intended.

FEBRUARY 20, 1907 President Theodore Roosevelt signs the **IMMIGRATION ACT OF 1907**, which taxes each immigrant four dollars upon arrival in the United States. The new law also gives the president the power to exclude "undesirable" people, particularly Asians. In mid-March, President Roosevelt bans many Japanese laborers from entering the country.

OCTOBER 21, 1907 On Wall Street, the **PANIC OF 1907** begins when depositors start withdrawing all their money from the Knickerbocker Trust Company. When this "run" on the bank forces the Knickerbocker to close, the government turns to the country's leading banker, J.P. Morgan, for help. Stock prices keep dropping until Morgan arranges for money to stabilize the situation.

NOVEMBER 3, 1908 Running as President Roosevelt's handpicked successor, Republican William Howard Taft easily wins the **1908 PRESIDENTIAL ELECTION**. He beats Democrat William Jennings Bryan, who had already lost two presidential races. Although Roosevelt would have surely won reelection, he felt obliged to honor a 1904 campaign promise that he would not run again.

FEBRUARY 4, 1908 In ***MULLER V. OREGON***, the Supreme Court upholds a law limiting the workday of women to ten hours. The decision reverses the Lochner case [April 17, 1905], which held that laws limiting work were unconstitutional. The justices' minds are changed by lawyer Louis D. Brandeis, who cites sociological research by Progressives that shows the dangers of working long hours.

# Muckrakers

## *The Crusade for Social Reform*

One magazine portrayed muckrakers as medieval Crusaders.

THE TYPE OF NEWS THAT WAS reported changed during the early years of the twentieth century. The people who practiced this new kind of journalism were called muckrakers because they found news by raking through the "muck" of dishonest business practices. Muckrakers were the first real investigative journalists. Their speciality was exposing the cheating and corruption of people in powerful places.

One of the first and most important muckrakers was Lincoln Steffens, who wrote a series of articles called "The Shame of the Cities" between 1901 and 1906. These articles uncovered corruption in city governments all over the country. One article revealed that the Minneapolis police department took bribes from criminals. Following Steffens's example, other writers began to investigate bribery in the nation's largest corporations and even the U.S. Senate.

Muckraker Upton Sinclair took on the U.S. food industry. In his 1906 novel, ***The Jungle***, Sinclair described in realistic detail the revolting working conditions in Chicago meat-packing plants. He wrote about how garbage, including dead rats, was sometimes packed in cans along with the meat. The public outrage caused by Sinclair's book led directly to passage of the Pure Food and Drug and Meat Inspection Acts, which established quality standards and a system of government inspection.

President Roosevelt was so disgusted by the description of the meat-packing process in *The Jungle* that he temporarily became a vegetarian.

## Politics

MAY 31, 1910 The **SOUTH AFRICA ACT** unites four self-governing British colonies into the independent Republic of South Africa. It also grants the white minority political control over more than five million Indians and black natives. The Natives Land Act (1913) further separates races by reserving almost ninety percent of the land for whites only.

AUGUST 22, 1910 Building on its gains from the Russo-Japanese War, **JAPAN FORMALLY ANNEXES KOREA**. The Japanese, now the leading military power in Asia, restrict the Koreans' freedom of speech and force them to study the Japanese language and culture in their schools.

AUGUST 1910 Former president Theodore Roosevelt tours the West, speaking about a **NEW NATIONALISM**. Roosevelt's ideas are loosely based on *The Promise of American Life*, an influential 1909 book by Progressive thinker Herbert Croly. Croly and Roosevelt both believe that the government should protect the people as a whole against "selfish individualism."

## Life in the Progressive Era

MAY 10, 1908 The first **MOTHER'S DAY** celebrations are held in Grafton, West Virginia, and Philadelphia, Pennsylvania. This special day for mothers developed out of a May 1907 church service arranged by Anna M. Jarvis on the anniversary of her mother's death. In 1911, the federal government recognizes Mother's Day, the second Sunday in May, as a holiday. The first Father's Day is held on June 19, 1910.

DECEMBER 26, 1908 Knocking out Tommy Burns, Jack Johnson becomes the **FIRST BLACK HEAVYWEIGHT BOXING CHAMPION**. Burns, a Canadian, was the first white boxer willing to fight Johnson, who had lost only three fights in his entire career. Outraged whites immediately begin the search for a Great White Hope who can win back the title.

FEBRUARY 12, 1909 White Progressives and members of the former Niagara Movement [July 11–13, 1905] found a group that becomes the **NATIONAL ASSOCIATION FOR THE ADVANCEMENT OF COLORED PEOPLE**. W.E.B. Du Bois, the only African American officer on the NAACP board, becomes editor of the organization's journal, *Crisis*.

## Arts & Entertainment

JULY 8, 1907 The lavish **ZIEGFELD FOLLIES** opens at the Roof Garden Theater in New York. The show plays in various theaters on Broadway through 1929. Produced by Florenz Ziegfeld, this vaudeville spectacular features beautiful chorus girls who dance between appearances by such comedy greats as Will Rogers, W.C. Fields, and Fanny Brice.

**ZIEGFELD FOLLIES • Florenz Ziegfeld modeled his own follies on the Folies-Bergères of Paris, which mixed music, comedy, dance, and some scantily clad women.**

1907 Working in Paris, Spanish painter **PABLO PICASSO** completes *Les Demoiselles d'Avignon*, his first in the new Cubist style. Cubism reduces its subjects to flat, one-dimensional slabs of color. Picasso challenges established forms of art and inspires artists in Europe and the United States to experiment with Cubist techniques.

## Science & Technology

JULY 30, 1908 A U.S. car wins the first **AROUND-THE-WORLD AUTOMOBILE RACE**. Sponsored by the *New York Times* and the French newspaper *Le Matin*, the thirteen-thousand-mile race began in New York and ended in Paris. Stops along the way included San Francisco; Tokyo, Japan; Moscow, Russia; and Berlin, Germany. The U.S. team completes the course in 169 days.

OCTOBER 1, 1908 The Ford Motor Company introduces its new **MODEL T**. "I will build a motorcar for the multitudes," Henry Ford had said, and the Model T, priced at $850, is just that. Their relatively low price makes Ford's cars, called Tin Lizzies, available to people of moderate incomes.

JANUARY 21, 1911 Wisconsin senator **ROBERT LA FOLLETTE** founds the National Progressive Republican League to push for Progressive legislation and more open government. Unhappy with President Taft, other Progressive Republicans back La Follette for president in 1912.

MAY 15, 1911 The Supreme Court orders the **BREAKUP OF THE STANDARD OIL COMPANY** for violating the Sherman Antitrust Act (1890). The Sherman law made it illegal for one company to monopolize an entire industry and control its prices. The size and wealth of Standard Oil allowed its founder—John D. Rockefeller, Sr.—to drive smaller oil companies out of business.

OCTOBER 10, 1911 Chinese troops seize control of Wuchang, triggering a general **REVOLT AGAINST THE IMPERIAL MANCHU GOVERNMENT OF BOY EMPEROR PU YI**. Hawaiian-educated Sun Yat-sen becomes president of the new Chinese republic, but the government is still dominated by powerful regional warlords.

AUGUST 7, 1909 In Philadelphia, the U.S. Mint ceremonially replaces the Indian head penny with the new **LINCOLN PENNY**. The Indian head reappears in 1913 on the face of the new Buffalo nickel.

# Motoring
## America Hits the Road

**BEFORE HENRY FORD introduced his Model T in 1908, cars were rich people's toys, built for reckless racing and not daily transportation. The inexpensive Model T, however, made cars affordable to the masses.**

**Originally known as "horseless carriages," automobiles had several advantages over the horse-drawn type. For one, cars did not get sick or injured or tired. For another, they needed fuel only when they were running. Cars could go faster and longer than any horse, and they were much cleaner as well. Before automobiles took over, city streets were regularly littered with droppings and even the carcasses of dead horses.**

**Ford's Model T and other popular cars, such as the Stanley Steamer and the Oldsmobile, changed the way Americans lived. Now that people could drive to work, towns began to expand and suburbs were created. Many new types of businesses appeared, such as repair shops and service stations. The highways that branched out across the nation also gave Americans a new sense of freedom and adventure. With a Model T, a tool kit, and enough gas, Americans could now vacation in places where there were no railroad stations, such as the new national parks.**

**At first, there were no speed limits on the nation's roads. In 1906, one newspaper reported that more Americans had been killed in speeding accidents during the last five months than in the entire Spanish-American War.**

**In the early days of motoring, automobile companies discouraged women from driving. Some steering wheels were even inscribed "Men and Boys Only."**

## Politics

**1911** The term ***BANANA REPUBLIC*** is coined when U.S. planter Samuel Zemurray supports a military coup in Honduras in exchange for special privileges. Zemurray provides Honduran general Manuel Bonilla with money, guns, men, and even a ship. When Bonilla takes over, he allows Zemurray to expand his banana plantations, which greatly increases the profits of his export business.

**June 18–22, 1912** At their convention, **REPUBLICANS SPLIT BETWEEN TAFT AND ROOSEVELT**, who has decided that Taft is doing a poor job. Progressives had hoped to nominate Robert La Follette [January 21, 1911], but his health has been failing. Roosevelt, however, declares himself "fit as a bull moose." When Taft wins the nomination, Roosevelt forms the Bull Moose party.

ROBERT PEARY • Peary aboard the steamship *Roosevelt.*

## Life in the Progressive Era

**1909** Wind-blown faces with "automobile wrinkles" become fashionable as cars increase in popularity. Fashion designers create special **MOTORING CLOTHES** for women, including gloves and long veils to keep a lady's hat in place. In 1927 safety issues become a concern when a long scarf worn by dancer Isadora Duncan catches in the rear wheels of a convertible and snaps her neck, killing her.

**April 1910** At a Washington Senators home game, President William Howard Taft throws out the **FIRST BALL OF THE NEW BASEBALL SEASON**, starting a presidential tradition.

## Arts & Entertainment

**1908** Scottish writer Kenneth Grahame publishes ***THE WIND IN THE WILLOWS***, which quickly becomes a classic of children's literature. Grahame's fanciful animal tales began as bedtime stories for his son, Alistair, and continued in the form of letters once Alistair went away to school. In 1929, A.A. Milne, the author of *Winnie-the-Pooh*, turns Grahame's book into a popular play.

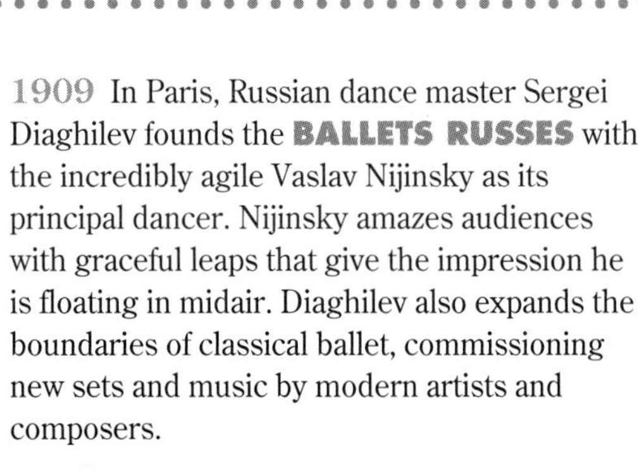

**1909** In Paris, Russian dance master Sergei Diaghilev founds the **BALLETS RUSSES** with the incredibly agile Vaslav Nijinsky as its principal dancer. Nijinsky amazes audiences with graceful leaps that give the impression he is floating in midair. Diaghilev also expands the boundaries of classical ballet, commissioning new sets and music by modern artists and composers.

## Science & Technology

**1908** German physicist Hans Geiger builds the first machine capable of measuring radioactivity. The **GEIGER COUNTER** registers radiation by giving off static-like clicks through a speaker.

**1908** Cleveland janitor James M. Spangler patents the electrically driven suction-sweeper known as the **VACUUM CLEANER**. He subsequently sells the rights to his invention to leather merchant W.H. Hoover, whose name soon becomes synonymous with vacuums.

**April 6, 1909** After spending a lifetime trying, navy engineer Robert E. Peary finally reaches the **NORTH POLE** and achieves his goal of being the first person to stand on "the roof of the world." Peary's rivals argue, however, that bad weather and shifting ice make his claim a difficult one to prove.

AUGUST 14, 1912 President **TAFT SENDS THE MARINES TO NICARAGUA** to help the conservative government there put down a rebellion. The Nicaraguan conservatives have been particularly friendly to U.S . business interests. Democratic candidate Woodrow Wilson promises to replace Taft's money-based Dollar Diplomacy with a foreign policy based on morality.

NOVEMBER 5, 1912 With Taft and Roosevelt splitting the Republican vote, Democratic candidate Woodrow Wilson wins the **1912 PRESIDENTIAL ELECTION** with his New Freedom program. A bigger surprise, however, is the performance of Socialist party leader Eugene V. Debs, who receives nearly one million votes.

FEBRUARY 25, 1913 The **SIXTEENTH AMENDMENT** takes effect, making income taxes legal. On October 3, as part of the Underwood Tariff bill, Congress approves a graduated income tax for individuals earning more than $3,000 per year. Progressives hail the new income tax as the fairest way for the government to raise money, but rich Americans soon find ways to avoid the new tax law.

APRIL 1910 The **NATIONAL URBAN LEAGUE** is founded in New York City to assist southern blacks who have been moving north in search of jobs. The Urban League, which eventually becomes the largest civil rights group in the world, soon begins to organize black city dwellers in the South and West as well.

# CHILD LABOR

UNTIL THE TWENTIETH century, poor parents expected their children to work. On family farms, children always had chores that kept them busy. And in the cities, parents apprenticed their children to skilled workers, such as carpenters and bricklayers, who taught them a trade. However, as industry grew rapidly during the late nineteenth century, more and more children began to work long hours in factories, mines, and garment-industry sweatshops.

Most of these children had to work under terrible conditions. Boys and girls working in cotton mills sometimes lost fingers when their hands got caught in the spinning machinery. Other children were forced to work all night in glass factories, where the intense heat and glare damaged their eyes. It was not unusual for children to work as many as fifteen hours a day. Of course, there was no time for school.

In 1904, the National Child Labor Committee was formed to educate the public about the hardships of child labor. The group encouraged politicians to pass laws regulating the hours and conditions under which children could work. In 1912, they convinced the federal government to set up the U.S. Children's Bureau, which gathered and published information on child labor. However, child labor was not dramatically reduced until the 1930s.

**Entire families were hired together to work in mines or cotton mills. They were paid so little that they could survive only if everyone worked.**

## Politics

APRIL 19, 1913 Anti-Japanese feelings in California [October 11, 1906] pressure Governor Hiram W. Johnson to sign the **WEBB ALIEN LAND-HOLDING ACT** The Webb Act bans foreign citizens from owning farmland in the state. President Wilson complains that this law damages U.S. relations with Japan, but his protests are ignored.

**JACK JOHNSON • Boxer Jack Johnson fought 114 professional fights, losing only 7.**

## Life in the Progressive Era

MAY 18, 1910 The return of **HALLEY'S COMET SPARKS A PANIC** of people who fear the end of the world is near. Con artists make a fortune selling "comet pills" to gullible people who believe that the comet's tail is made of poisonous gas. Many miners refuse to work on the day the earth travels through the comet's tail because they do not want to die underground.

JULY 4, 1910 Former champion Jim Jeffries, dubbed the Great White Hope, comes out of retirement to fight **JACK JOHNSON** [December 26, 1908]. Johnson's successful defense of the heavyweight title sparks race riots in which ten people die. To ease tensions, newsreels of Johnson's victory are banned in most major cities.

MARCH 25, 1911 A fire at the **TRIANGLE SHIRTWAIST COMPANY** in Manhattan kills 146 garment workers. The victims, mostly immigrant women, are trapped inside the burning sweatshop. Factory owners had locked the doors to keep the women at their machines. The tragedy spurs the International Ladies' Garment Workers Union [June 3, 1900] to take a more active role in worker safety.

## Arts & Entertainment

OCTOBER 29, 1911 In his will, the late newspaper publisher Joseph Pulitzer leaves money for the establishment of several awards. Beginning in 1917, **PULITZER PRIZES** are awarded by the trustees of Columbia University for outstanding achievements by Americans in fiction, poetry, history, and journalism.

1911 Frances Hodgson Burnett publishes the ***THE SECRET GARDEN***. Her popular children's novel describes the joys two cousins find in the privacy of a hidden English garden. Burnett was born in England, but she emigrated to Tennessee with her parents in 1865, when she was sixteen. She published her first hugely successful children's book, *Little Lord Fauntleroy*, in 1886.

1911 **IRVING BERLIN** composes his first hit song, "Alexander's Ragtime Band," and begins his long career as one of the world's most popular songwriters. The twenty-three-year-old Berlin, whose family emigrated from Russia to the United States in 1893, had been working as a singing waiter. Although he has little formal musical training, Berlin keeps American toes tapping for decades.

## Science & Technology

SEPTEMBER 10, 1909 Austrian psychiatrist Dr. **SIGMUND FREUD** begins a lecture tour of the United States. In his talks, he describes his controversial theories about human psychology, the study of which he has pioneered. Freud explains that people have unconscious motives that affect their behavior and that children have sexual feelings.

1909 Paul Ehrlich discovers the first bacteriological cure for a disease, thus beginning the medical practice of chemotherapy. The treatment, called **DR. EHRLICH'S MAGIC BULLET**, cures syphilis without major side effects. Despite Ehrlich's success, some people criticize his work because syphilis is a sexually transmitted disease. They argue that curing syphilis encourages sin.

1909 The Sharp-Hughes Tool Co. of Houston, Texas, begins to manufacture **DRILLING EQUIPMENT FOR OIL RIGS**. Founded by Howard Hughes, Sharp-Hughes specializes in rotary bits that drill through rock rather than pound it. Sharp-Hughes Tool soon realizes profits of one million dollars a year. When Hughes dies in 1924, control of the company passes to his son, also named Howard.

MAY 31, 1913 The **SEVENTEENTH AMENDMENT** is ratified, providing for the direct election of U.S. senators by the voters of each state. Previously, senators had been elected by state legislatures, which often favored influential businessmen. Direct election is one of the many voting reforms championed by Progressives, including recall petitions, the secret ballot, and women's suffrage.

APRIL 10, 1914 In Vera Cruz, **MEXICAN TROOPS ARREST U.S. SAILORS** from the warship *Dolphin*. Although the Mexicans quickly release the sailors and apologize, President Wilson uses the incident to help topple the Mexican dictator Victoriano Huerta. Admiral Henry T. Mayo insists that the Mexicans salute the U.S. flag. When they refuse, President Wilson orders the occupation of Vera Cruz.

JUNE 28, 1914 A young **SERBIAN NATIONALIST KILLS AUSTRIAN ARCHDUKE FRANZ FERDINAND** and his wife, Sophie, in the Bosnian capital of Sarajevo. The political assassination of the heir to the Austro-Hungarian empire enrages the Austrians, who deliver a harsh ultimatum to Serbia on July 23.

NOVEMBER 10, 1911 Steel magnate Andrew Carnegie donates $125 million to start the **CARNEGIE CORPORATION**, which he dedicates to the "advancement and diffusion of knowledge." In his essay "The Gospel of Wealth," Carnegie wrote that a rich man should return his wealth to the community. John D. Rockefeller, Sr., follows Carnegie's example, creating the Rockefeller Foundation in 1913.

# THE *TITANIC* SINKS!

**ON APRIL 10, 1912, the *Titanic* began her maiden voyage from Southampton, England, to New York City. The event was newsworthy because the *Titanic* was the largest and most luxurious passenger liner ever built. She was constructed using the most modern technology, and her owners bragged that a series of watertight compartments made her unsinkable.**

**Four days into the journey, shortly before midnight, the *Titanic* struck an iceberg that cut a huge gash along her hull. The damage was so great that not even the watertight compartments could save her. Water began pouring into the engine room, but the passengers and crew were so confident that they had trouble believing the *Titanic* was actually sinking.**

**The captain of the *Titanic* hoped to break the record for the fastest crossing of the Atlantic Ocean.**

**During the next two hours, while the orchestra played popular songs to calm the passengers, the crew loaded and launched the lifeboats. Unfortunately, the *Titanic*'s designers were so sure the ship was unsinkable that they had not bothered to include enough lifeboats for everyone.**

**The *Titanic* finally sank to the bottom of the frigid North Atlantic at 2:20 A.M. More than fifteen hundred people died in the disaster, including Isidor and Ida Straus, a wealthy elderly couple who gave up their lifeboat seats so that younger people could live.**

**The *Titanic* disaster led to the first international rules requiring ships to carry enough lifeboats to hold all the people aboard. Ships were also required to maintain twenty-four-hour radio watches. The night that the *Titanic* sank, the *Californian* was less than twenty miles away, but she had no radio operator on duty to hear the *Titanic*'s frantic calls for help.**

## Politics

JULY 28, 1914 Serbia accepts all but two Austrian demands, and those two it agrees to negotiate. But Austria-Hungary is not satisfied. With the secret support of its ally Germany, **AUSTRIA-HUNGARY DECLARES WAR ON SERBIA**. Meanwhile, Serbia's ally Russia readies some of its troops for war.

JULY 30–AUGUST 1, 1914 One escalation after another leads to the **OUTBREAK OF WORLD WAR I** in central Europe. First, Austria-Hungary responds to the Russian troop movements by mobilizing some of its own forces along the Russian border. This provokes Russia to call out its entire army. Germany and Russia's ally France also mobilize.

**WORLD WAR I • Entrenched soldiers fire across No Man's Land. This was the name given to the dangerous ground between two lines of trenches.**

## Life in the Progressive Era

JANUARY 12, 1912 **TEXTILE WORKERS IN LAWRENCE**, Massachusetts, begin a two-month strike against American Woolen, which has just reduced their pay without warning. Organizers with the Industrial Workers of the World [June 27, 1905] lead the strikers, most of whom are immigrants. Several die in clashes with the police, but they win concessions, for which the IWW receives credit.

## Arts & Entertainment

1912 Mack Sennett founds the Keystone Company, which will produce the slapstick **KEYSTONE KOPS** films. These early, silent comedies rely on physical comedy and stunts, most of which are quite dangerous. The bumbling Keystone Kops always seem to be falling on top of one another.

1912 Universal Pictures hires Mary Pickford away from D.W. Griffith's Biograph Company, beginning the film industry's **STAR SYSTEM**. Universal intends to promote the personalities of its stars. Pickford, for example, is marketed as "America's sweetheart." Pickford then leaves Universal at the height of her stardom to found United Artists in 1919 with Griffith, Douglas Fairbanks, and Charlie Chaplin.

MAY 29, 1913 Igor Stravinsky's ballet ***THE RITE OF SPRING*** debuts at the Théâtre des Champs-Elysées in Paris. The performance by the Ballets Russes [1909] provokes a near-riot among audience members outraged by the unconventional music. Stravinsky's wild, disjointed style begins a new era in classical music.

## Science & Technology

1909 Belgian-born U.S. chemist Leo H. Baekeland develops the first completely synthetic plastic, which he names **BAKELITE**. The waterproof material becomes increasingly popular with U.S. industry because it can be easily shaped and does not conduct electricity. Bakelite starts as a liquid, then hardens as it cools.

1909 The General Electric Company markets the first **ELECTRIC TOASTER**, which is made of wires wrapped around strips of mica. Charles Smith improves on this model, patenting the first pop-up toaster in 1919. Unlike the original, Smith's toaster grills bread on both sides.

MARCH 16, 1910 At Daytona Beach, Florida, race car driver **BARNEY OLDFIELD** sets a new land speed record, reaching a speed of 131 miles per hour on Daytona's hard sand beach.

AUGUST 3, 1914 **GERMANY DECLARES WAR ON FRANCE**. Using a twenty-year-old plan developed by former chief of staff Alfred von Schlieffen, the Germans launch a surprise invasion from the north through neutral Belgium. The Schlieffen plan thus avoids the imposing defensive line built by France along the French-German border.

AUGUST 4, 1914 Great Britain has no interest in Serbia, nor does it have a treaty obligation to defend either Russia or France. However, it does have a mutual defense treaty with Belgium. Therefore, the German invasion through Belgium forces the **BRITISH TO DECLARE WAR ON GERMANY**. The United States declares itself neutral on August 5.

SEPTEMBER 26, 1914 The **FEDERAL TRADE COMMISSION ACT** sets up a five-member panel to investigate and stop unfair business practices that might violate the nation's antitrust laws.

MAY 5–JULY 22, 1912 Native American **JIM THORPE** amazes the world with his athletic accomplishments at the Olympic Games in Stockholm, Sweden, where he wins gold medals in the pentathlon and decathlon. He loses the medals, however, when he later admits to having played semiprofessional baseball in 1909. At that time, the Olympics had an amateurs-only rule.

# THE ARMORY SHOW

## Shock of the New

ON FEBRUARY 17, 1913, an important new exhibition of modern art opened at the Sixty-ninth Regiment Armory in New York City. Although two-thirds of the paintings on display were by Americans, it was the work of several European artists that captured the country's attention. More than three hundred thousand people saw the Armory Show, which later traveled to Boston and Chicago. Everywhere, the reaction was the same: shock, scorn, and bewilderment.

About this time, American artists were still trying to re-create the way their subjects looked in "real" life. But the European painters were not realists. Instead, they exaggerated shapes and used unusual colors. As a result, most Americans did not know what to think when they saw works by Henri Matisse, Paul Cézanne, and Pablo Picasso for the first time.

**One critic ridiculed Marcel Duchamp's *Nude Descending a Staircase* as "an explosion in a shingle factory."**

In Chicago, stuffed figures of Matisse and sculptor Constantin Brancusi were hanged by outraged art students. However, despite the uproar, the Armory Show played a key role in opening American eyes to new forms of art.

**At the time of the Armory Show, the leading U.S. artists belonged to the realistic Ash Can School. *Stag at Sharkey's* by George Wesley Bellows shows the artist's interest in the toughness of city life.**

## Politics

OCTOBER 15, 1914 Congress passes the **CLAYTON ANTITRUST ACT**, which strengthens the Sherman Act of 1890. The new law focuses on such unfair business practices as cutting prices below cost in order to bankrupt smaller competitors. Labor leaders hail the clause in the act stating that unions are not an illegal attempt to prevent workers from contracting freely with employers.

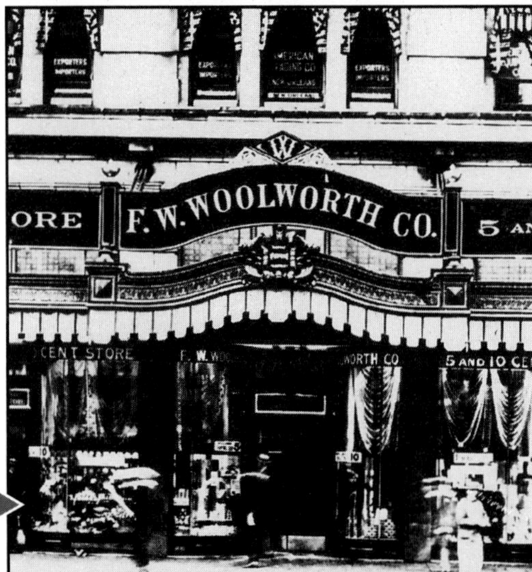


WOOLWORTH COMPANY • Frank W. Woolworth founded his first five-and-dimes in Utica, New York, and Lancaster, Pennsylvania, in 1879. The store in Utica failed.

NOVEMBER 22, 1914 At Ypres in northwest France, where British and French troops have been fighting the Germans, heavy rains bog down the soldiers. As winter approaches, the **ARMIES SETTLE INTO A NETWORK OF OPEN TRENCHES**, where they remain for the rest of the war. During the next four years, hundreds of thousands of men die along this front fighting for tiny gains of ground.

## Life in the Progressive Era

1912 Frank W. Woolworth merges four chains of retail stores with his own "five-and-dimes" to form the **F.W. WOOLWORTH COMPANY**. With 596 stores, the Woolworth Company becomes the largest retail chain in the world. Its stores offer a large selection of goods at affordable prices. Woolworth dies in 1919, leaving an estate worth sixty-seven million dollars.

1912 In *The Montessori Method*, Italian educator Maria Montessori explains her unique system for teaching very young children. The book becomes a best-seller in the United States, and the method becomes the basis for **MONTESSORI SCHOOLS** all over the country. Montessori herself was the first woman ever to receive a medical degree in Italy.

## Arts & Entertainment

DECEMBER 1913 **ERECTOR SETS** are the most popular Christmas gift this year. The collection of girders, nuts, and bolts is also the first toy to be advertised extensively in national magazines. The toy's slogan is "Hello, Boys! Make lots of toys!" American children continue their building spree with Tinkertoys (1914) and Lincoln Logs (1916), which are developed by Frank Lloyd Wright's son John.

1913 A craze for the **TANGO** sweeps the country, much to the dismay of prudish government authorities. One New York City official argues that its Latin steps "stimulate too much abandon, too much freedom." Because the tango requires couples to hold each other close, the dance is banned in Boston, where the legislature nearly approves six-month prison sentences for couples who tango in public.

1913 Jesse Lasky, Samuel Goldwyn, and Cecil B. DeMille film *The Squaw Man* in a barn one block from the intersection of Hollywood and Vine in Hollywood, California. The filmmakers choose to film in **HOLLYWOOD** instead of New York, where most other film companies are located, because of the mild weather, the sunshine, the different types of terrain available, and the low land prices.

## Science & Technology

JULY 12, 1910 Aircraft pioneer Glenn Curtiss drops oranges from a plane onto the deck of a ship to demonstrate the **POTENTIAL OF AIR ATTACKS**. If those oranges had been bombs, the ship would have been sunk. Curtiss's demonstration helps convince the navy to award Curtiss the first contract to build naval seaplanes.

DECEMBER 14, 1911 Norwegian explorer Roald Amundsen becomes the first person to reach the **SOUTH POLE**. Amundsen and his four companions managed to survive the difficult Antarctic conditions by eating seal blubber and feeding one of the sled dogs to the remainder of the pack. Sadly, three months later, the members of a British expedition led by Robert Scott die of starvation.

1911 Searching for the cause of an Indonesian disease, Polish researcher Casimir Funk discovers thiamine, later known as vitamin $B_1$. Funk concludes that certain diseases, such as scurvy, are caused by the lack of certain chemicals in a person's diet. Funk calls these necessary chemicals "vital amines," which he shortens to ***VITAMINS***.

MAY 7, 1915 Off the coast of Ireland, a German U-boat sinks the passenger liner **LUSITANIA** [September 12, 1907]. Nearly 1,200 people are drowned, including 128 Americans. Although the Germans point out that the ship had been carrying arms and ammunition, the attack without warning turns American public opinion strongly against Germany.

FEBRUARY 21, 1916 The Germans launch a major offensive against the French stronghold of **VERDUN**. They hope to wear down the French slowly, through increasing casualties rather than overwhelming force. Although little territory changes hands during the year, French casualties at Verdun exceed 540,000, while the Germans lose 430,000.

MARCH 9, 1916 Mexican rebel **PANCHO VILLA** leads a raid across the border into Columbus, New Mexico, killing seventeen Americans. President Wilson orders General John J. Pershing to "capture Villa dead or alive." Pershing pursues Villa for a entire year without success until Wilson finally recalls him.

MARCH 3, 1913 In Washington, D.C., five thousand **SUFFRAGISTS** led by Alice Paul march down Pennsylvania Avenue on the day before Woodrow Wilson's inauguration. The women have gathered to demand the right to vote, but their march ends in a brawl when male bystanders attack the marchers. Forty people are hospitalized before the cavalry can restore order.

# Scouting

**BRITISH GENERAL Robert Baden-Powell founded the Boy Scouts in 1908 following the success of his book *Scouting for Boys*. In that book, Baden-Powell wrote about camping skills, first aid, personal health, and self-discipline, all of which appealed to young boys at the time. As scouting grew in England, it also spread to the United States, where there were more than three hundred thousand Boy Scouts by 1919.**

**Baden-Powell's goal was to develop good citizens by teaching boys to be responsible and self-reliant. The Boy Scouts stressed loyalty, helpfulness, thriftiness, and cheerfulness. Required skills included making fires, cooking, tying different kinds of knots, performing basic first aid, and being able to save money in a bank account.**

**Interest in scouting among British girls led Baden-Powell to found the Girl Guides in 1910. American Juliette Low, who met Baden-Powell while traveling in England, organized the first troop of U.S. Girl Guides in 1912 in her hometown of Savannah, Georgia. Three years later, she founded the national Girl Scouts of America. Much like their male counterparts, Girl Scouts devoted themselves to self-reliance and serving their communities.**

A troop of Girl Scouts attends a rally in New York City's Central Park in 1920.

## Politics

APRIL 24, 1916 In Dublin, the Irish Republican Brotherhood declares Irish independence from Great Britain in the **EASTER UPRISING**. British forces quickly crush the revolt and begin daily executions of the surviving rebels. Although there was little popular support at first for the rebels, the executions prompt the Irish to rally behind the demands for self rule.

CHARLIE CHAPLIN • Chaplin played his Little Tramp character in *The Gold Rush* (1925).

JUNE 1, 1916 The Senate votes to confirm President Wilson's nomination of **LOUIS D. BRANDEIS** [February 4, 1908] to the Supreme Court. The first Jewish justice, Brandeis is also one of the most liberal jurists ever to sit on the bench. He tilts the balance of the Court in favor of Progressive legislation.

## Life in the Progressive Era

1913 Designer **COCO CHANEL** begins to reinvent women's fashion at her small hat shop in Deauville, France. Offering sweaters, open-collared shirts, and skirts made out of comfortable cloth, Chanel ignores the current trend toward frilly outfits and huge hats. Within five years, Chanel's simple designs revolutionize women's fashion, freeing women to dress more practically.

JANUARY 5, 1914 Fearing labor trouble, **HENRY FORD RAISES HIS WORKERS' STARTING PAY** to five dollars a day. Ford's action doubles the company's minimum wage and pioneers higher wages across the U.S. economy. Ford believes that raising workers' standard of living will create an even-larger market for his automobiles.

## Arts & Entertainment

1914 Edgar Rice Burroughs publishes ***TARZAN OF THE APES***, an adventure tale about a baby raised by apes in the African jungle. The story becomes so popular that it spins off twenty-two sequels as well as dozens of films and comic strips. Tarzan makes Burroughs a multimillionaire before his death in 1950 near Tarzana, the Los Angeles suburb named for his creation.

1914 In his second film, *Kid Auto Races at Venice*, **CHARLIE CHAPLIN** uses a bowler hat, a cane, and baggy clothing to create his Little Tramp character. In *The Tramp*, which appears the next year, Chaplin adds a certain sadness and helplessness, which audiences find endearing. Chaplin's silent comedies are so successful that he quickly becomes one of the highest-paid performers in Hollywood.

1914 Marcella Gruelle, the terminally ill daughter of political cartoonist John Gruelle, finds a faceless rag doll. She asks her father to draw a face on it. Meanwhile, her mother restuffs the doll and sews onto its stomach a red heart with the words "I love you." Because the result is still somewhat ragged, the Gruelles call the doll **RAGGEDY ANN**. They later license the doll to a toy company.

## Science & Technology

1912 Paleontologists believe that a skull found on the Piltdown Common in southern England may be the missing link between humans and apes. The **PILTDOWN MAN** fossil appears to combine an orangutan's jaw with a large, human cranium. Forty years will pass before scientists prove that the Piltdown fossil is actually a hoax.

1912 Electrical engineer Gideon Sundback invents the "slide fastener," or **ZIPPER**. Sundback's invention, which he calls the Hookless #2, is adopted by the U.S. Navy for use in windproof flying suits. Later, in 1923, B.F. Goodrich uses the fasteners to produce a new line of rubber shoes called Zipper Boots.

SUMMER 1913 The Ford Motor Company develops the first **MODERN ASSEMBLY LINE** at its Model T plant in Highland Park, Michigan. Henry Ford's highly efficient new methods cut the time it takes to assemble a Model T from thirteen hours to six. The huge savings in labor allows Ford to drop the price of the Model T [October 1, 1908] to $440.

**September 1, 1916** President Wilson signs a federal **CHILD LABOR LAW** that prohibits the interstate sale of goods made by children under fourteen years of age. Regulation of child labor had long been a Progressive goal. The Keating-Owen Act also protects children under sixteen from mine work, workdays longer than eight hours, and night work, but the Supreme Court strikes down these provisions in 1918.

**September 3, 1916** President Wilson signs the **ADAMSON EIGHT-HOUR ACT**, which establishes an eight-hour workday for railroad workers. The bill was rushed through Congress to avoid a railroad strike scheduled to begin on September 4. Passage of the law prevents the strike, but opponents criticize Wilson for playing to union voters during an election year.

**November 7, 1916** Voters in Montana make Jeanette Rankin the **FIRST WOMAN EVER ELECTED TO CONGRESS**. While serving in the House of Representatives, Rankin speaks out on women's issues and opposes U.S. military actions abroad.

**November 19, 1915** Utah executes **JOE HILL**, the Industrial Workers of the World organizer who wrote most of the songs in the IWW's *Little Red Song Book*. Because Hill's murder conviction rested on weak evidence, many claimed he was framed for his radicalism. Before facing the firing squad, Hill wrote a telegram to IWW leader "Big Bill" Haywood: "Don't waste any time in mourning. Organize!"

# Margaret Sanger

## *The Campaign for Birth Control*

Because Sanger worked with poor immigrant women, she advertised her clinic in Yiddish and Italian as well as English.

When Margaret Sanger began her work as a visiting nurse on Manhattan's Lower East Side, birth control was not available to the poor immigrant women who lived there. It was 1910, and obscenity laws made it illegal to distribute written information about birth control.

Constant pregnancy had worn down many of Sanger's female patients and made them sickly. Sanger also saw some women die from home abortions. These daily tragedies convinced her that the key to a woman's freedom lay in her ability to control having children. In 1914, Sanger began distributing the birth-control pamphlet "Family Limitation" through the mail. After the police charged her with issuing obscene materials, she fled to Europe to escape arrest.

After returning to the United States, Sanger and her sister opened the nation's first birth-control clinic on October 16, 1916. Within ten days, the police closed down the clinic in Brooklyn and sent Sanger to a workhouse for thirty days. After her release, Sanger continued to fight for a woman's right to prevent unwanted pregnancies despite the constant threat of arrest. Slowly, public opinion changed to match her own.

## Politics

JANUARY 16, 1917 The British intercept a telegram from German foreign minister Arthur Zimmermann to his ambassador in Mexico. The decoded message reveals a proposal that Mexico attack the United States. The British pass the **ZIMMERMANN TELEGRAM** to President Wilson on February 24. Its March 1 publication in U.S. newspapers leads to public demands for a declaration of war on Germany.

MARCH 8, 1917 (FEBRUARY 23 BY THE OLD RUSSIAN CALENDAR) The **FEBRUARY REVOLUTION** begins when protests over food shortages in Petrograd escalate into riots. Tsar Nicholas II sends troops to restore order, but the soldiers mutiny rather than fire on the crowds. On March 15, the Duma, or Russian parliament, forms a temporary government. That evening, the tsar gives up his throne.

APRIL 2, 1917 Frustrated with continuing U-boat attacks on neutral U.S. ships, President **WILSON ASKS CONGRESS FOR A DECLARATION OF WAR**. "The world must be made safe for democracy," he says. Congress passes the resolution on April 6.

## Life in the Progressive Era

NOVEMBER 25, 1915 At a meeting outside Atlanta, Georgia, William J. Simmons revives the disbanded **KU KLUX KLAN**. Wearing white robes and hoods and riding at night, the Klan had terrorized African Americans in the South in the years following the Civil War. Under Simmons' leadership, the ranks of the KKK's Invisible Empire swell to one hundred thousand during the next six years.

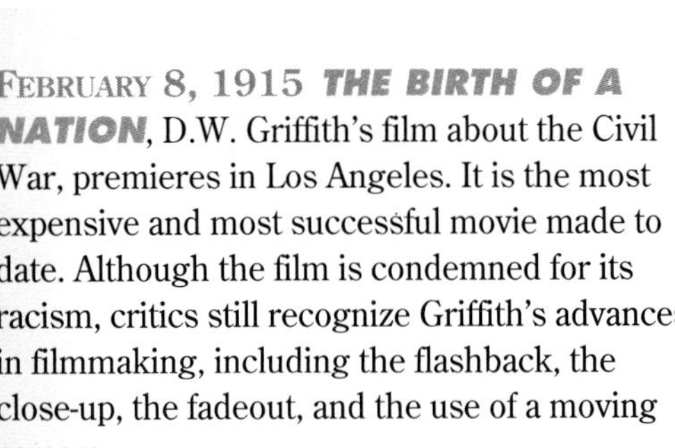

**KU KLUX KLAN • The Klan often rode through black neighborhoods at night, terrorizing the residents. During the 1910s and 1920s, the Klan expanded its enemies to include Jews, Roman Catholics, foreigners, and union organizers.**

## Arts & Entertainment

FEBRUARY 8, 1915 ***THE BIRTH OF A NATION***, D.W. Griffith's film about the Civil War, premieres in Los Angeles. It is the most expensive and most successful movie made to date. Although the film is condemned for its racism, critics still recognize Griffith's advances in filmmaking, including the flashback, the close-up, the fadeout, and the use of a moving camera.

## Science & Technology

1913 Danish physicist Niels Bohr develops the first modern **MODEL OF THE ATOM**. According to Bohr's model, negatively charged particles called electrons circle a nucleus of neutrons and positively charged protons in the same way that planets orbit a sun.

AUGUST 15, 1914 Built at a cost of more than $350 million, the **PANAMA CANAL** opens to shipping. The canal is made possible by a series of gravity-fed locks that raise and lower the canal level. Although open to ships of all nations, the fifty-mile-long canal is controlled and protected by the United States.

SEPTEMBER 1, 1914 When the last **PASSENGER PIGEON** dies in the Cincinnati Zoo, the once-familiar species becomes extinct. Only a century earlier, great migratory flocks of passenger pigeons darkened the North American sky, but the birds were hunted until now all of them are gone.

**APRIL 16, 1917** Bolshevik leader Vladimir **LENIN ARRIVES AT THE FINLAND STATION** in Petrograd, where he calls for another Russian revolution. Lenin had been living in exile in Switzerland until the February Revolution [March 8, 1917], when the Germans arranged his return to Russia in a sealed train car. The Germans correctly believe that Lenin's presence will take Russia out of World War I.

**OCTOBER 15, 1917** A French firing squad executes **MATA HARI** after she is convicted of passing military secrets to the Germans. Throughout the war, the beautiful Dutch dancer pursued love affairs with important military and government officials on both sides.

**NOVEMBER 6, 1917 (OCTOBER 26 BY THE OLD RUSSIAN CALENDAR)** Calling for "peace, bread, and land," Lenin leads the nearly bloodless **OCTOBER REVOLUTION**. The Bolsheviks oust Alexander Kerensky's Provisional Government and establish a government based on Communist-controlled workers' committees, or soviets.

**1915 "WHAT THIS NATION REALLY NEEDS,"** Vice President Thomas Marshall jokes during a long, tiring Senate debate, **"IS A GOOD FIVE-CENT CIGAR."** For a nickel in 1915, you can also see a movie or buy a loaf of bread.

# The Great Migration

**This painting by Jacob Lawrence is part of a series he did to illustrate the Great Migration.**

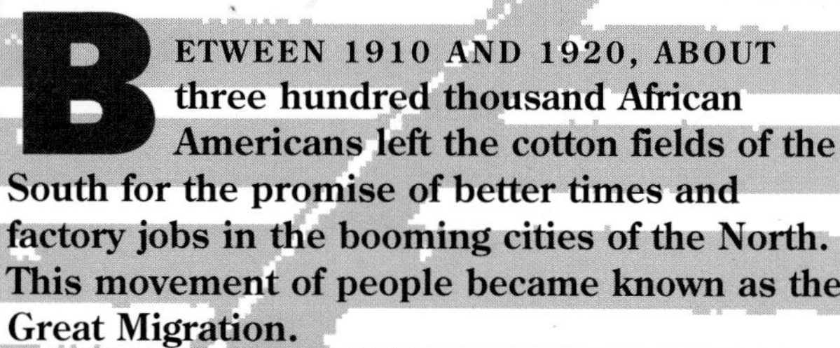

**BETWEEN 1910 AND 1920, ABOUT three hundred thousand African Americans left the cotton fields of the South for the promise of better times and factory jobs in the booming cities of the North. This movement of people became known as the Great Migration.**

**Since the end of Reconstruction, life in the rural South had been barely tolerable for blacks. After the federal soldiers left in 1877, racist white politicians began to pass segregation laws that prevented blacks from eating in the same restaurants as whites, traveling on the same trains, and even voting. Most African Americans tried to make a living as sharecroppers, but low crop prices kept them poor. Lynchings of African Americans by the Ku Klux Klan were common.**

**During World War I, northern factories began to hire more workers to replace those who had joined the army. Seeing an opportunity, many southern blacks headed north, hoping to land a job with decent pay. Some northern factory owners even sent agents south to recruit African-American workers for their companies. Many needed little convincing to take this chance on a better life.**

Politics

JANUARY 8, 1918 In a speech to Congress, President Wilson outlines ideal conditions for peace in Europe. His **FOURTEEN POINTS** are meant to reassure the Central Powers that they will be treated fairly at the end of the war. Wilson's final point calls for the creation of a "general association of nations" to negotiate disputes before they lead to war.

APRIL 21, 1918 German flying ace Baron Manfred von Richthofen dies on the ground when he is trapped inside his red Fokker during an Allied air raid near Amiens, France. The **RED BARON** has been credited with eighty kills.

Life in the Progressive Era

JULY 22, 1916 A **BOMB EXPLODES IN SAN FRANCISCO** during a parade, killing ten people and wounding forty more. Police arrest five labor leaders for the crime, including Tom Mooney, who is well known for his radical antiwar beliefs. Mooney's death sentence is reduced to life imprisonment after some of the testimony in the case is proved false. He is finally pardoned in 1939.

1916 John Dewey's latest book, ***DEMOCRACY AND EDUCATION***, challenges accepted teaching techniques. A Progressive philosopher and educator, Dewey argues that teachers should focus more on problem-solving skills than memorization.

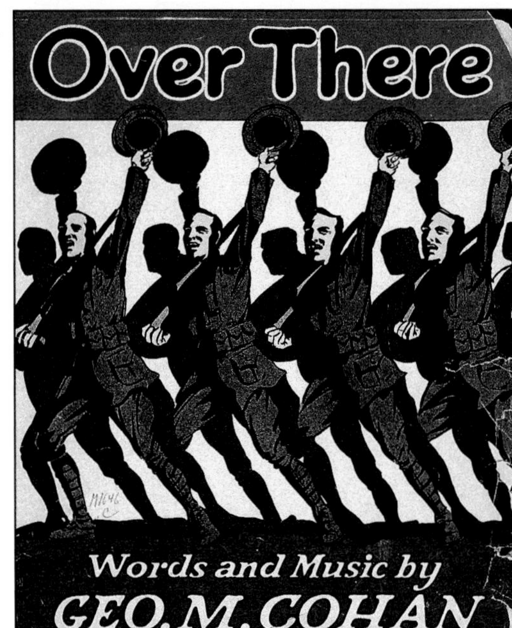


**"OVER THERE" • "Over There" encouraged the war effort with its bugle calls and marching rhythm.**

Arts & Entertainment

MAY 20, 1916 The first cover illustration by **NORMAN ROCKWELL** appears on the *Saturday Evening Post*, which will soon feature ten Rockwell covers a year. Rockwell's idealized scenes of small-town American life strike a chord with *Post* subscribers, many of whom have recently moved to large cities from the country.

APRIL 6, 1917 Showman George M. Cohan [November 27, 1904] writes the patriotic anthem **"OVER THERE"** after reading a newspaper headline announcing the U.S. entry into World War I. President Wilson sends Cohan a note thanking him for the song, which Wilson calls "a genuine inspiration to American manhood."

OCTOBER 27, 1917 Fleeing revolutionary Russia by way of Siberia, sixteen-year-old **JASCHA HEIFETZ** makes his U.S. debut at Carnegie Hall in New York City. Already an experienced performer, Heifetz first began playing the violin at the age of three, and he toured Europe at twelve.

Science & Technology

APRIL 22, 1915 In France during the second battle of Ypres, German troops release clouds of **POISONOUS CHLORINE GAS**. The effectiveness of the gas, the first chemical weapon used on the western front, surprises even the Germans, who were not prepared to take advantage of the resulting panic among Allied troops. The gas burns exposed skin and lung tissue.

1915 In his **GENERAL THEORY OF RELATIVITY**, Albert Einstein suggests that the presence of matter makes space curve. Although confusing, Einstein's theory does account for irregularities on the orbit of the planet Mercury that cannot be explained by Newtonian physics alone. Einstein's theory begins an entirely new era in physics.

SEPTEMBER 15, 1916 The British introduce the latest advance in military technology, the **TANK**, during the Battle of the Somme in France, but its short range and slow speed limit its effectiveness. The British designed the new motorized artillery piece to cross difficult terrain, including barbed-wire fences. The name *tank* was selected at random for secrecy, but somehow it stuck.

SEPTEMBER 14, 1918 A federal judge sentences Socialist party leader **EUGENE V. DEBS** to ten years in jail for violating the Espionage Act. This 1917 law made it a crime to oppose U.S. involvement in World War I, including speaking out against the war. Debs broke the law by making a speech defending the IWW [September 5, 1917], the Bolshevik Revolution [November 6, 1917], and pacifism.

OCTOBER 29, 1918 **GERMAN SAILORS MUTINY IN THE PORT OF KIEL** against Kaiser Wilhelm II. The uprising triggers a democratic revolution in Germany, which is losing the war now that U.S. troops are arriving in force. On November 9, the kaiser resigns his throne, and two days later, a new government under Frederick Ebert signs an armistice ending the fighting on the western front.

JANUARY 15, 1919 Conservative police officers and anti-Communist toughs crush the **SPARTACIST REVOLT** in Berlin and murder its Communist leaders, including Rosa Luxemburg and Karl Liebknecht. Mimicking the events in Russia, the Spartacists had hoped to lead a Communist revolution in Germany.

FEBRUARY 5, 1917 Congress passes a law over the president's veto forcing immigrants to pass a **LITERACY TEST**. The Immigration Restriction League, which championed the law, claims that poor, illiterate immigrants threaten the United States with "race suicide." The country's xenophobia, or fear of foreigners, is further heightened by World War I and the Communist uprising in Russia.

# EUGENE V. DEBS

## THE SOCIALIST CANDIDATE

**BORN IN 1855 IN TERRE HAUTE, Indiana, Eugene Victor Debs left home at the age of fourteen to work for the railroads. During the next twenty years, he became convinced that the beaten-down railway workers could control their lives only if they banded together. In 1893, Debs founded the American Railway Union, and the next year he organized a strike against the Pullman railroad car company for better wages and working conditions.**

**Debs was arrested and sentenced to six months in jail for his part in the strike, which stopped nearly all the rail traffic between Chicago and the West for over two months. During his time in prison, Debs read a lot, and his reading included the works of German socialist philosopher Karl Marx. Debs emerged from prison a strong supporter of the rights of workers and the regulation of big business.**

**In 1900, Debs ran the first of his five campaigns as the Socialist candidate for president. In both the 1912 and 1920 elections, he won close to one million votes. In between campaigns, Debs toured the country, giving lectures about workers' rights. "While there is a lower class," he declared, "I am in it....While there is a soul in prison, I am not free."**

**Debs ran his 1920 presidential campaign from prison, where he was serving a ten-year term for speaking out against World War I.**

**Debs delivers a speech during one of his five presidential campaigns.**

## Politics

**February 6–August 11, 1919** A German constitutional assembly meeting in Weimar writes the new **WEIMAR CONSTITUTION**, establishing the first democratic republic in Germany. Modeled after the most progressive democracies, Weimar Germany grants women the right to vote, sets an eight-hour workday, and allows free speech.

***TEN DAYS THAT SHOOK THE WORLD*** **• Vladimir Lenin addresses an armed crowd of workers, whose councils were called soviets.**

## Life in the Progressive Era

**July 28, 1917** W.E.B. Du Bois and several other officers of the NAACP [February 12, 1909] lead a **SILENT MARCH** down Fifth Avenue in New York City. More than fifteen thousand people show up to protest the ongoing racial violence, including the July 2 race riots in East St. Louis, Illinois, that killed thirty-nine people and injured hundreds more, mostly blacks.

**September 5, 1917** Federal agents stage simultaneous, nationwide raids on meeting halls and offices used by the **INDUSTRIAL WORKERS OF THE WORLD** [June 27, 1905]. The government is looking for evidence of treason among leaders of this most radical labor union. The IWW, which opposes U.S. entry into World War I, has already instructed its members to resist the draft.

## Arts & Entertainment

**December 1918** Drawing for the *New York Evening Globe* sports page, cartoonist Robert LeRoy Ripley collects seven unusual sporting records under the headline **"BELIEVE IT OR NOT!"** The cartoon becomes so popular that Ripley begins drawing others. For subjects, he expands beyond sports to draw on the most bizarre and unusual facts he can find.

**1919** John Reed publishes ***TEN DAYS THAT SHOOK THE WORLD***, his gripping account of the October Revolution [November 6, 1917], which Reed witnessed as a foreign correspondent. After his return to the United States, Reed is charged with treason and flees to Moscow, where he dies of typhus in 1920. Lenin has him buried in the Kremlin, the only American ever buried there.

**1919** Walter Gropius founds the **BAUHAUS** school of architecture in Germany. A follower of the International Style, Gropius encourages the use of glass and metal in construction. As a result, most of the buildings Gropius designs have very box-like shapes. When the Nazi government closes the Bauhaus in 1933, Gropius joins the stream of German artists and intellectuals emigrating to the United States.

## Science & Technology

**1916** Britain introduces "summer time" to save energy during wartime. By turning clocks one hour ahead during the summer, the British will use less fuel to light their homes in the evening, because evening will come one hour later. The United States adopts **DAYLIGHT SAVINGS TIME** in 1918. However, when farmers complain about dark mornings, Congress repeals the law.

**1917** Toward the end of World War I, French physicist Paul Langevin begins using ultrasonic waves to track German U-boats underwater. The process, called **SONAR**, works on the same principle as the echo. By calculating how long it takes the waves to bounce off an object, Langevin can locate that object underwater.

**September 1918** An **INTERNATIONAL INFLUENZA EPIDEMIC** peaks, infecting one out of every four Americans with this life-threatening disease. More than twenty million people, or one percent of the world's population, die from this flu, which first appeared in the United States on August 27. In some cities, people are required to wear masks in public to prevent the spread of the infection.

MARCH 3, 1919 In ***SCHENCK V. U.S.***, Supreme Court justice Oliver Wendell Holmes, Jr., votes to uphold Schenck's conviction under the 1917 Espionage Act. Schenck had been found guilty of distributing antidraft leaflets. Writing for the majority, Holmes explains that freedom of speech can be restricted when there is "a clear and present danger" to the public, such as shouting "Fire!" in a crowded theater.

MARCH 1919 Vladimir Lenin founds the Third Communist International, known as **COMINTERN**, to promote the spread of the Communist revolution worldwide. Centralizing leadership of the international Communist movement in Moscow, the Soviet leader declares that "unreserved support of Soviet Russia is the very first duty of Communists in all countries."

APRIL 13, 1919 In Amritsar, India, **BRITISH TROOPS OPEN FIRE ON TEN THOUSAND INDIANS** demonstrating against laws that allow the British colonial government to imprison Indians without trial. Fifteen hundred unarmed protesters die in the massacre, which inspires Mohandas K. Gandhi [September 11, 1906] to begin his campaign for an end to colonial rule.

MAY 15, 1918 Lieutenant George Boyle of the Army Signal Corps takes off on the first **AIRMAIL** flight. Unfortunately, after leaving Washington, D.C. for Philadelphia, he flies off course and has to make a forced landing in a Maryland cow pasture. The first airmail stamps cost twenty-four cents, while surface mail stamps remain at three cents.

# Babe Ruth

**GEORGE HERMAN "Babe" Ruth was the first sports superstar. His skills as a ballplayer, along with his exuberance and enthusiasm, made him a memorable symbol of the Roaring Twenties.**

**Ruth began his major-league career in 1915 as a pitcher for the Boston Red Sox. Appearing in the 1916 and 1918 World Series, he set a record by pitching 29 2/3 consecutive scoreless innings. Ruth was such a powerful hitter, however, that the Red Sox switched him to the outfield in 1919 so he could play every day. Ruth responded by setting another record: most home runs in a single season. In January 1920, the Red Sox sold the Babe to New York. The $125,000 that the Yankees paid for him was both a staggering sum and a bargain. In his first two seasons with New York, Ruth broke and rebroke his own home-run record.**

**Before Ruth, home runs were rare in baseball. The ball was less lively off the bat, and most players just tried to make contact rather than take a full swing. But Ruth made a habit of holding the bat near the end so that he could extend his powerful arms, and the results were historic. Ruth led the American League in home runs in twelve different years, and his success made him the highest-paid player in baseball. In 1930, after the stock market crash, one sportswriter asked him how he felt about earning more money than President Hoover. "I had a better year," Ruth said.**

**The six-foot, two-inch Ruth had quite an appetite. He would often eat a fifteen-egg omelette and six hot dogs just for breakfast. He also loved to visit nightclubs, flirt with women, drive fancy cars, and spend a lot of money.**

## Politics

JUNE 28, 1919 A defeated Germany signs the **TREATY OF VERSAILLES**. According to its severe terms, Germany gives up its colonies as well as its navy. The Germans are also forced to acknowledge their "war guilt" and pay billions of dollars in damages. President Wilson makes sure that the treaty includes a provision establishing a League of Nations modeled after the last of his Fourteen Points.

OCTOBER 28, 1919 Congress passes the Prohibition Enforcement Act, also known as the **VOLSTEAD ACT**, over President Wilson's veto. The new law bans non-medicinal alcohol beginning January 16, 1920. It enforces the Eighteenth Amendment, ratified on January 29, which made the manufacture, transportation, and sale of intoxicating liquor illegal.

NOVEMBER 19, 1919 Despite an intense public campaign by President Wilson, the **SENATE REJECTS THE TREATY OF VERSAILLES** [June 28, 1919] as well as U.S. membership in the League of Nations. Henry Cabot Lodge, who led the fight against the treaty, demanded some changes, but Wilson refused to compromise and lost everything.

## Life in the Progressive Era

JULY 1, 1918 Food administrator Herbert Hoover begins **SUGAR RATIONING**, limiting Americans to eight ounces of sugar per week. On July 26, Hoover asks his fellow citizens to observe wheatless Wednesdays, meatless Tuesdays, and porkless Saturdays. In the spirit of the war effort, Americans begin calling sauerkraut "Liberty cabbage" and German toast becomes French toast.

OCTOBER 1-9, 1919 Eight Chicago White Sox conspire with gamblers to lose the World Series. Because the Sox were heavily favored, the gamblers make a fortune betting on the Cincinnati Reds. Those banished for taking part in the **BLACK SOX SCANDAL** include "Shoeless" Joe Jackson, the idol of many young fans. "Say it ain't so, Joe," one of them tells Jackson as he enters a courthouse.

FEBRUARY 13, 1920 Chicago American Giants manager Rube Foster organizes eight teams into the **NEGRO NATIONAL LEAGUE**, the first black professional baseball league. Blacks have to play in their own league because white major-league teams will not sign them. The pay on Negro league teams is low, and the playing conditions are usually poor, but the players include many baseball greats.

## Arts & Entertainment

1920 Twenty-three-year-old Ivy League dropout F. Scott Fitzgerald publishes his first novel, ***THIS SIDE OF PARADISE***, which immediately makes him a leading spokesman for the new Jazz Age. Fitzgerald describes the popular book, based on his college years at Princeton University, as "a novel about flappers written for philosophers."

BLACK SOX SCANDAL • Joe Jackson was nicknamed "Shoeless" because, it was said, he grew up so poor that he could not afford shoes.

1920 British civil engineer Hugh Lofting publishes ***THE STORY OF DOCTOR DOOLITTLE*** about a remarkable doctor who can talk to animals. Lofting turned to writing and illustrating after a war injury left him bedridden. Doctor Doolittle becomes such a popular character that Lofting writes a number of sequels.

## Science & Technology

1918 Harlow Shapley calculates the **DIAMETER OF THE MILKY WAY** to be three hundred thousand light years. He also determines the galaxy's shape and the location of our solar system within it.

1918 Asking them "What might this be?" psychiatrist Hermann Rorschach begins to show his patients ink-blot stains with unusual, random shapes. The Swiss analyst finds that these **RORSCHACH TESTS** can reveal valuable details about a patient's subconscious state of mind.

1900 1910 1920 1930 1940

JANUARY 2, 1920 Attorney General A. Mitchell Palmer orders nationwide raids on homes, offices, and meeting places of radicals. Most of the four thousand people arrested during the **PALMER RAIDS** are foreign born. Palmer estimates that at least twenty-seven hundred will be deported. The attorney general calls them "moral perverts" and "misguided anarchists."

MAY 13, 1920 Suffragist Carrie Chapman Catt founds the **LEAGUE OF WOMEN VOTERS** of New York State to distribute unbiased information to millions of new women voters. The League issues reports on candidates, party platforms, and important ballot issues. In later years, the group will sponsor debates and other voter education projects.

JUNE 1920 Harry M. Daugherty predicts that the Republican nomination will not be decided until party leaders "sit down about two o'clock in the morning around a table in a smoke-filled room." When that happens, according to Daugherty, Warren Harding will be selected. After Harding wins, the phrase **"SMOKE-FILLED ROOM"** becomes a popular way to describe how political deals are made.

AUGUST 1, 1920 **MARCUS GARVEY** opens the first national convention of the Universal Negro Improvement Association at Harlem's Liberty Hall. Garvey, who owns the New York–based *Negro World* newspaper, has become famous for his "back to Africa" campaign. Garvey's goals of black unity, pride, and economic independence attract the support of African Americans eager for change.

# PROHIBITION

## The Noble Experiment

**BY THE TIME THE Eighteenth Amendment was ratified in 1919, most southern and western states had already passed prohibition laws. In these "dry" states, making and selling alcoholic beverages were banned.**

**The prohibition movement began during the 1860s, when women began to fight the drunkenness that was rampant in the Wild West. Indirectly, alcoholism greatly affected women, who were often abused by drunken husbands. Women whose families had been destroyed by drink formed groups such as the Women's Christian Temperance Union, which was the first national women's group of any kind.**

**Although the temperance activists finally convinced Congress and two-thirds of the state legislatures to approve a prohibition amendment to the Constitution, they could not stop people from drinking. Hundreds of thousands of "speak-easies," or illegal taverns, opened. They were usually run by mobsters who fought with one another for control of the business. Because the prohibition laws were broken so often, Congress and the states eventually amended the Constitution again in 1933 to permit the sale of alcohol.**

**Many supporters of Prohibition were devout Christians who believed that drinking alcohol was sinful behavior.**

# The Roaring

AMERICANS WERE RICH, they were young, and they had just won a world war. It was time for a party. They called it the Roaring Twenties.

American women, in particular, changed in remarkable ways. Having just won the right to vote, they felt a new sense of equality with men that encouraged them to explore new roles in society. After World War I, American women got married later in life, went to college more often, and entered the work force in greater numbers.

It may seem strange that this party took place during Prohibition, when selling liquor was against the law. But the many illegal bars, or speakeasies, made bootleg whisky easy to obtain. In fact, so many people drank illegally that lawlessness of other kinds became widespread. In Chicago, the Twenties roared with gunfire as rival gangs fought for control of the profitable bootlegging business. Meanwhile, a series of frivolous fads captured the public's attention. College students sat on flagpoles for days on end, while everyone danced to the exciting rhythms of the Jazz Age.

★

# Twenties

## Politics

AUGUST 26, 1920 Ratification of the **NINETEENTH AMENDMENT**, which Congress had narrowly approved in 1919, finally gives American women the right to vote. Voting in their first presidential election this fall, women will help elect Warren Harding.

**NINETEENTH AMENDMENT • At first, politicians found it difficult to predict which candidates the new women voters would support.**

NOVEMBER 2, 1920 Advocating a "return to normalcy," Republican candidate Warren G. Harding wins the **1920 PRESIDENTIAL ELECTION** over Democrat James M. Cox. Once again, Socialist candidate Eugene V. Debs polled nearly one million votes, even though his imprisonment [September 14, 1918] prevented him from campaigning personally.

## Life in the Roaring Twenties

SEPTEMBER 7–8, 1921 Sixteen-year-old Margaret Gorman wins the first **MISS AMERICA PAGEANT** held over two days at the seaside resort of Atlantic City, New Jersey. Local businesses support the contest as a way to extend the tourist season past Labor Day. In 1925, the pageant adds a talent competition to assure that contestants represent femininity "of the most desirable type."

AUGUST 28, 1922 New York radio station WEAF airs the first paid **RADIO COMMERCIAL**, beginning a movement toward private control of the public airwaves. During the next year, WEAF, which will become WNBC, attracts twenty-five regular advertising sponsors.

## Arts & Entertainment

MAY 23, 1921 The all-black musical *Shuffle Along*, which opens today, becomes a smash hit on Broadway. Featuring the popular song "I'm Just Wild About Harry," the play adds to **NEW YORK'S GROWING INTEREST IN AFRICAN-AMERICAN CULTURE**.

FEBRUARY 2, 1922 Sylvia Beach, owner of the Paris bookstore Shakespeare & Co., publishes Irish writer James Joyce's masterful ***ULYSSES***. Virtually every other publisher had rejected Joyce's manuscript because of its coarse language. Five hundred copies of Joyce's epic smuggled into the United States were burned because the U.S. Post Office in New York considered them obscene.

1922 Published this year, T.S. Eliot's controversial work **"THE WASTE LAND"** will become the twentieth century's most influential poem. Eliot's attack on modern life comes to represent the disappointment many Americans and Europeans felt after World War I.

## Science & Technology

NOVEMBER 2, 1920 Station KDKA in Pittsburgh, Pennsylvania, begins the first **REGULAR RADIO BROADCASTS** with its report of the presidential election results. Only a few thousand Americans own radios at this time, but KDKA's programming encourages many more to buy them. In the next year, Americans spend more than ten million dollars on radio sets and parts.

1921 Canadian physicians Charles Best and Frederick Banting isolate the hormone **INSULIN**. Treating diabetics with insulin saves an estimated twenty-five million lives during the next fifty years. Banting receives a 1923 Nobel Prize for his efforts.

1924 Edwin Hubble announces his **DISCOVERY OF OTHER GALAXIES IN THE UNIVERSE**. Using the new one-hundred-inch Mount Wilson telescope, Hubble has been able to resolve the outer edges of the neighboring Andromeda galaxy. Studying variable stars that blink on and off, he calculates that the Andromeda galaxy is nearly one million light years away.

**1920** Clarence Darrow, Upton Sinclair, Helen Keller, and several other social reformers found the **AMERICAN CIVIL LIBERTIES UNION** in New York City. The ACLU's mission is to protect "the rights of man set forth in the Declaration of Independence and the Constitution." Among the first members are undercover FBI agents, who suspect the ACLU is a Communist organization.

**MARCH 1921** Soviet leader Vladimir Lenin announces his **NEW ECONOMIC POLICY** Hoping to end Russian food and fuel shortages, Lenin decides to compromise his principles and allow some private land and shop ownership, but he leaves heavy industry in the hands of the state. Lenin's NEP permits peasants to build large, privately run farms, which become extremely productive and ease the food crisis.

**APRIL 1921** Meeting in Paris, the Allied Reparations Commission sets the amount of **PAYMENTS OWED BY GERMANY** according to the terms of the Treaty of Versailles [June 28, 1919]. Economists agree, however, that the exact figure, approximately thirty-three billion dollars, is impossibly and unfairly high. Within one year, Germany begins to fall behind its payment schedule.

**NOVEMBER 7, 1922** In the Valley of the Tombs of the Kings in Egypt, British archaeologist Howard Carter reaches the sealed entrance to the grave of the boy pharaoh Tutankhamen. The magnificent treasures he finds inside King Tut's tomb tour the world and inspire countless fads in the United States, where **TUTMANIA** reigns.

# Flappers

## A New Generation of Women

**The fashionable young woman of the 1920s wore her hair bobbed, her skirt short, and her stockings rolled down beneath her knees.**

**THE ROARING TWENTIES was the decade of the flapper. Also known as the New Woman, she cast off many of the manners and restrictions of her mother's generation and redefined the meaning of femininity. Her clothing was designed for comfort and freedom, and she enjoyed the fact that the older generation was shocked by the exposure of her arms and legs. Gone were petticoats and corsets. Gone were long, elaborate hairdos. Now the athletic tomboy look was in.**

**Flappers also liked to behave boyishly. They smoked, they drank, and they danced all night. Until the 1920s, women had been expected to stay at home and care for their families, but the flappers rejected all that. They craved adventure, and in order to get what they wanted, they changed people's ideas about what a woman should be. Femininity would never be quite the same.**

## Politics

MAY 19, 1921 Responding to public fears about the flood of immigrants from southern and central Europe, Congress passes the **EMERGENCY QUOTA ACT**, which includes the first general restrictions on immigration to the United States. The new law establishes limits on the number of people who can enter the United States each year from individual countries.

JULY 14, 1921 A Massachusetts jury finds immigrants Nicola Sacco and Bartolomeo Vanzetti guilty of murdering two men during a shoe factory robbery in South Braintree. The case had attracted national attention because there was very little evidence to link **SACCO AND VANZETTI** with the crime. Many believe that their conviction had more to do with their radical politics than with their guilt.

DECEMBER 6, 1921 Rather than go to war with England, Irish Catholics agree to the **ANGLO-IRISH TREATY**, which sets up an independent Irish Free State in the southernmost twenty-six of Ireland's thirty-two counties. The remaining six northern counties remain under British, and therefore Protestant, control.

## Life in the Roaring Twenties

1922 Italian-born Angelo Siciliano changes his name to **CHARLES ATLAS** and wins the World's Most Perfectly Developed Man contest. Claiming dishonestly that he had once been a "ninety-seven-pound weakling," Atlas begins promoting a physical fitness program, which he claims will turn other weaklings into hunks.

1922 **EMILY POST** publishes her best-selling manners guide, *Etiquette in Society, in Business, in Politics and at Home*. Post's goal is to raise the social standards of ordinary Americans to those of the most gracious Europeans. Her simple tips about which fork to use at dinner and how to deal with body odor make her the leading national authority on polite behavior.

MARCH 3, 1923 Recent Yale graduates Henry R. Luce and Briton Hadden begin publishing ***TIME***. Designed for college-educated men and women, the nation's first weekly newsmagazine outlines the week's top news stories while paying particular attention to developing national trends. *Time* itself coins words like *socialite* and *tycoon*, which become part of the national vocabulary.

## Arts & Entertainment

FEBRUARY 12, 1924 Bandleader Paul Whiteman conducts the first performance of George Gershwin's *Rhapsody in Blue*, at New York's Aeolian Hall. The twenty-five-year-old Gershwin plays piano before the capacity crowd. Written in only three weeks, *Rhapsody in Blue* is the **FIRST PIECE OF JAZZ WRITTEN FOR THE CONCERT HALL**.

**GEORGE GERSHWIN • The composer at his piano.**

MAY 15, 1924 Eugene O'Neill's play ***ALL GOD'S CHILLUN GOT WINGS***, about an interracial couple, opens quietly despite threats of violence from the Ku Klux Klan. The Salvation Army and the Society for the Suppression of Vice had also warned the producers not to stage O'Neill's play.

## Science & Technology

JULY 10–21, 1925 The state of Tennessee puts biology teacher John T. Scopes on trial for teaching Charles Darwin's theory of evolution. Scopes had violated a state law passed on March 13 banning the teaching of any theory denying that God created man. With William Jennings Bryan prosecuting and Clarence Darrow defending, the **SCOPES MONKEY TRIAL** captures national attention.

1925 Using techniques he learned while trading furs with the Eskimos, Clarence Birdseye perfects a deep-freezing process that allows him to market **FROZEN FOOD**. Birdseye's innovative General Seafoods Co., which becomes General Foods, revolutionizes American eating habits.

DECEMBER 23, 1921 President Warren **HARDING PARDONS EUGENE V. DEBS** unconditionally for violations of the 1917 Espionage Act. Debs had already served three years of his ten-year sentence [September 14, 1918]. "I either go out a man as I came in," Debs had written from his Atlanta cell, "or I serve my term to the last day."

FEBRUARY 6, 1922 The three-month-long **WASHINGTON CONFERENCE** concludes with an agreement banning the construction of battleships during the next ten years. The treaty, pushed through by Secretary of State Charles Evans Hughes, ends the naval arms race among the United States, Britain, Italy, France, and Japan. The conference also limits submarine warfare and the use of poison gas.

APRIL 7, 1922 President Harding's corrupt interior secretary, Albert G. Fall, secretly grants the Mammoth Oil Company exclusive rights to the government's **TEAPOT DOME** oil reserves in Wyoming. In exchange, he receives various lavish gifts, including a herd of cattle and a "loan" of one hundred thousand dollars. The Senate begins an investigation of the Teapot Dome scandal on April 16.

APRIL 18, 1923 A sellout crowd watches George Herman "Babe" Ruth hit a three-run homer on opening day at the new **YANKEE STADIUM**. Sportswriters call the new ballpark the House That Ruth Built because ticket sales inspired by Ruth's ability and showmanship paid for it. Almost single-handedly, Ruth makes baseball the most popular spectator sport in the country.

# The Harlem Rennaissance

**During the 1920s, for the first time, major publishing houses sought out African-American writers such as Langston Hughes. Meanwhile, white audiences crowded Harlem cabarets, especially the Cotton Club, to hear the wild new music called jazz.**

**IN THE YEARS AFTER World War I, African Americans continued their migration from the country to the cities. Many ended up in the New York City neighborhood of Harlem, where African-American writers, artists, and musicians flourished. This period has come to be known as the Harlem Renaissance.**

**The 1920s was a time of great excitement and hope for African Americans. Because black soldiers had fought and died for their country in Europe, they expected to be treated with some respect when they returned home. African-American artists living in Harlem could not help being influenced by this expectant attitude. Like the soldiers, they often thought about racial justice, and their work expressed a common concern with racial pride. For new subject matter, they began to examine the daily lives of black people.**

**One of the most famous Harlem Renaissance writers, poet Langston Hughes, wrote, "We younger Negro artists who create now intend to express our individual dark-skinned selves without fear or shame....We know we are beautiful."**

## Politics

OCTOBER 31, 1922 Emphasizing the need for order, Italy's **BENITO MUSSOLINI** becomes Europe's first fascist head of state after his Black Shirts march on Rome to break up a general strike. Mussolini calls himself *Il Duce*, which means "the leader" in Italian. Granted emergency powers for one year, he immediately begins a massive public works campaign to rebuild the Italian economy.

NOVEMBER 1, 1922 Turkish reformer Mustafa **KEMAL ENDS THE SEVEN-HUNDRED-YEAR-OLD OTTOMAN EMPIRE**. A year later, Kemal (later Kemal Atatürk) becomes the first president of the Republic of Turkey. Kemal modernizes Turkey by appealing to nationalism and separating government from Muslim religious control.

JANUARY 11, 1923 Demanding Germany keep up with its war payments [April 1921], French and Belgian **TROOPS OCCUPY GERMANY'S RUHR VALLEY**. The French threaten to seize the money directly from the coal and steel industries there if voluntary payments are not resumed. With the Weimar government encouraging resistance, workers in the Ruhr begin a general strike.

## Life in the Roaring Twenties

SEPTEMBER 15, 1924 **SAKS FIFTH AVENUE** opens today, offering an unprecedented selection of extremely expensive merchandise. Fronted by large display windows, this luxury store caters to the needs of newly rich Americans. Among Saks's offerings are three-thousand-dollar pigskin trunks and silver pocket flasks, which sell out the first day.

JANUARY 1, 1925 The **FIGHTING IRISH OF NOTRE DAME** upset Stanford in the Rose Bowl, capping an undefeated season. Coach Knute Rockne helped make his alma mater a football legend with such innovations as the forward pass, the backfield shift, and separate squads for offense and defense.

## Arts & Entertainment

AUGUST 5, 1924 Harold Gray's cartoon strip **"LITTLE ORPHAN ANNIE"** appears for the first time in the *New York Daily News*. The popular comic follows the adventures of the orphan Annie; her dog, Sandy; and her guardian, Daddy Warbucks. Most of Annie's troubles involve Communism, liberalism, and other movements that Gray believes threaten free enterprise and "the American way."

OCTOBER 1, 1924 Political comedian **WILL ROGERS** begins a six-month nationwide tour. Rogers, who is part-Cherokee, got his start performing rope tricks in Wild West shows, but he introduced folksy humor into his act in 1915. "My folks didn't come on the *Mayflower*," Rogers says, referring to the Pilgrims, "but they met the boat."

## Science & Technology

MARCH 16, 1926 Physicist Robert H. Goddard launches the first **LIQUID-FUELED ROCKET** at his Aunt Effie's farm in Auburn, Massachusetts. The experimental rocket reaches an altitude of only forty feet, but the fact that it flew at all convinces Goddard that one day humans will travel to the moon.

**ROBERT H. GODDARD • The press nicknamed Goddard "Moonie."**

APRIL 7, 1927 American Telephone and Telegraph president Walter Gifford hosts the first **PUBLIC DEMONSTRATION OF TELEVISION IN THE UNITED STATES** at Bell Laboratories in New York. The first images are those of Commerce Secretary Herbert Hoover delivering a speech in Washington. Hoover's voice is transmitted simultaneously over telephone wires.

HOOVER ELEMENTARY SCHOOL
INSTRUCTIONAL MATERIAL CENTER
COMMUNITY SCHOOL DISTRICT

AUGUST 3, 1923 President **HARDING DIES** in a San Francisco hotel room after collapsing during a tiring cross-country speaking tour. His vice president, Calvin Coolidge, becomes the thirtieth president. Observers suspect that the strain of the Teapot Dome scandal [April 7, 1922] weakened Harding's health and undermined his spirit.

SEPTEMBER 15, 1923 When the terrorist activities of the Ku Klux Klan [November 25, 1915] get out of hand, Governor J.C. Walton declares **MARTIAL LAW** in Oklahoma. Under the leadership of Imperial Wizard Hiram Evans, the Klan has recently expanded from its traditional base in the Southeast to become a powerful force in the Midwest as well.

SEPTEMBER 1923 As **INFLATION IN GERMANY** spins out of control, Germans begin using wheelbarrows to carry around the huge piles of money needed even for such small purchases as a loaf of bread. When inflation finally peaks, German currency is no longer worth the paper on which it is printed.

AUGUST 8, 1925 Forty thousand members of the **KU KLUX KLAN** march past the White House in full hooded costumes. The politically active Klan claims four million members. Attacking Catholics and Jews as well as blacks, the Klan has undeniably expanded its influence, which is now felt nationwide. Rain prevents the Klansmen from burning a cross beside the Washington Monument.

# Bootleggers and Gangsters

## Capone Rules Chicago

**During Prohibition, Capone's gang supplied up to ten thousand Chicago-area speakeasies with illegal liquor. Capone himself used bribes and threats to control many of Chicago's judges and politicians.**

THE BOOTLEGGING business flourished during Prohibition, and so did the criminals who ran it. Mobsters sold homemade liquor, or "bathtub gin," to illegal bars called "speakeasies," and gangs of them fought for control of major cities.

One of the most ruthless mobsters was Al Capone. Most Chicagoans knew him as "Scarface" because of the long knife scar that ran down his cheek. Capone was incredibly violent. He first came to Chicago in 1919. Yet within three years, he managed to build a seven-hundred-man private army that virtually took over the city. In 1929, after Capone ordered the St. Valentine's Day Massacre, Chicago newspapers used the killings to build public support for a crackdown on mob violence.

Capone never served jail time for any of the murders he committed or ordered. But in 1931 he was found guilty of income tax evasion because he never paid tax on the money he made illegally. Capone served eight years in several high-security federal prisons, including Alcatraz in San Francisco Bay, before winning parole for good behavior in 1939.

## Politics

**November 8–9, 1923** Hoping to take advantage of Germany's distress, Adolf Hitler's Nazis attempt to topple the Weimar government. Although the **BEER HALL PUTSCH** in Munich is put down, the Nazis prove that they have strong support. Hitler spends just nine months in jail, where he writes *Mein Kampf,* which outlines his biased theories about the dangers posed by Jews and Communists.

**January 21, 1924** Lenin dies at the age of fifty-three, setting off a **POWER STRUGGLE BETWEEN JOSEPH STALIN AND LEON TROTSKY** for control of the Soviet Communist party. Meanwhile, Petrograd is renamed Leningrad in the Soviet leader's honor, and his likeness appears in town squares across the Soviet Union.

**March 10, 1924** Zealous crime fighter **J. EDGAR HOOVER** becomes acting director of the Federal Bureau of Investigation. To clean up the FBI's image after the Harding administration scandals, Hoover raises the standards for FBI agents, all of whom must now be college graduates, and starts a national fingerprint file and crime laboratory.

## Life in the Roaring Twenties

**October 1925** Out-of-control **FLORIDA LAND SPECULATION** peaks when investors learn that the beachfront property they have purchased is actually swampland or even underwater. Among those who fueled the hysteria is the noted swindler Charles Ponzi, whose "Ponzi schemes" conned many investors in Boston out of their life savings.

**1925** The *Louisville Courier Journal* hosts the first **NATIONAL SPELLING BEE**. Spelling bees soon become a national craze in this decade of crazes, with scholarships usually awarded as prizes.

**March 1926** Harry Scherman starts the **BOOK-OF-THE-MONTH CLUB**. This new mail-order service provides thousands of American readers with less expensive editions of the best current books selected by a board of judges. Scherman's service is particularly useful to rural readers, who live far away from well-stocked libraries and bookstores.

**CHARLES A. LINDBERGH • The celebrated aviator beside *The Spirit of St. Louis.***

## Arts & Entertainment

**1925** Virtually every American youth is "doing it, doing it," as the **CHARLESTON CRAZE** sweeps the nation. Experts trace the fast, flailing step back to Charleston, South Carolina, but it never received much notice until it appeared in the all-black Broadway show *Running Wild* in 1923. Police blame the collapse of a Boston nightclub on the shaking caused by a Charleston dance party.

**August 23, 1926** The sudden death of movie star **RUDOLPH VALENTINO** leads to mass hysteria among his fans, mostly young women. Several commit suicide after learning the news. The dark, exotic Valentino charmed audiences in such silent films as *The Sheik* (1921) and *Blood and Sand* (1922). More than one hundred thousand people view his coffin at a New York City funeral parlor.

## Science & Technology

**May 21, 1927** Flying his single-engine monoplane, ***THE SPIRIT OF ST. LOUIS***, twenty-five-year-old Charles A. Lindbergh touches down at Le Bourget airfield outside Paris, completing the first solo transatlantic flight. The former stunt-show pilot took 33 1/3 hours to accomplish the feat, which wins him worldwide acclaim and sparks immense interest in the possibilities of commercial aviation.

**November 13, 1927** The **HOLLAND TUNNEL** underneath the Hudson River opens to traffic. The first underwater automobile tunnel, it links New York City with New Jersey. The most difficult aspect of the construction was the venting of the twin tunnel tubes. This was accomplished with a powerful system of fans and suction ducts.

1900 1910 1920  1930 1940

MAY 26, 1924 Congress passes the **JOHNSON-REED ACT**, which further restricts U.S. immigration [May 19, 1921]. The number of immigrants is cut back from 357,000 to 164,000 per year. The quotas for eastern and southern Europeans are reduced drastically, and Asian immigrants are barred completely. The Ku Klux Klan is among the most enthusiastic supporters of the legislation.

AUGUST 16, 1924 Chicago banker Charles G. Dawes convinces an international commission to agree on a plan to ease Germany's financial crisis [September 1923]. According to the **DAWES PLAN**, U.S. banks will loan money to Germany so it can resume making war payments to Britain and France. In return, the French and Belgian troops will leave the Ruhr Valley [January 11, 1923].

NOVEMBER 4, 1924 Despite revelations in the Teapot Dome scandal [April 7, 1922], Republican Calvin Coolidge wins the **1924 PRESIDENTIAL ELECTION** by a large majority. Two months later, the conservative Coolidge makes a speech to the Society of American Newspaper Editors, announcing that the "business of America is business."



JUNE 24, 1926 When evangelist and radio preacher **AIMEE SEMPLE McPHERSON** disappeared from a southern California beach on May 18, people believed she had drowned. But Sister Aimee reappears today, claiming she had been kidnapped. An investigation reveals that McPherson had actually run off for a romantic fling with an official of her $1.5-million church in Los Angeles.

# Margaret Mead

## Anthropology Comes of Age

IN 1928, MARGARET Mead published *Coming of Age in Samoa*, in which she described teenage life among islanders in the South Pacific. Mead had lived and worked among the Samoans and was able to describe their customs and culture as an insider. But Mead's ambition was much greater. In her book, the young anthropologist explained that studying Samoan culture had given her insights into all of human behavior.

According to Mead, her observations of Samoans proved that a person's behavior depends more on how that person is raised, or nurtured, than on natural laws. Mead's book provoked discussions in the United States about whether human beings are shaped by nature or by "nurture."

In 1928, most Americans still believed that women were naturally suited to the roles of mother and housewife and that any woman who wanted a career in business or politics was behaving unnaturally. Mead's ideas challenged that belief. *Coming of Age in Samoa* and Mead's other books demonstrated that women in other cultures behaved differently.

**Mead traveled to Samoa for the first time in 1925. It was then highly unusual for a young woman to undertake such an adventure by herself, but Mead refused to be limited by what other people thought was proper.**

## Politics

JANUARY 5, 1925 Nellie Tayloe Ross takes office as the governor of Wyoming, becoming the first **WOMAN GOVERNOR** in U.S. history. Ross succeeds her late husband, who died just before the 1924 election. Mrs. Ross loses a reelection bid in 1926, but she goes on to serve on the Democratic National Committee and in 1933 becomes the first female director of the U.S. Mint.

DECEMBER 25, 1926 With the death of Emperor Yoshito the day before, **HIROHITO BECOMES EMPEROR OF JAPAN**. Unlike his father, the younger and more active Hirohito will become intimately involved in Japan's political affairs. Under his influence, Japan's military strength will grow quickly, and the nation will become more aggressive in foreign affairs.

MARCH 1927 During his successful Northern Expedition to unite China under one government, **CHIANG KAI-SHEK CAPTURES SHANGHAI AND NANJING**, where his Kuomintang troops loot the businesses and homes of foreigners. When blame for the looting falls upon Communist members of the Kuomintang, Western business interests encourage Chiang to expel the Communists.

## Life in the Roaring Twenties

AUGUST 6, 1926 Despite very rough water, Gertrude Ederle of New York City becomes the **FIRST WOMAN TO SWIM THE ENGLISH CHANNEL**. A 1924 Olympic gold medalist, Ederle made the crossing in fourteen hours, thirty-one minutes, beating the previous record (set by a man) by more than two hours.

GERTRUDE EDERLE • The swimmer permanently damaged her hearing during her record-breaking swim.

SEPTEMBER 27, 1927 Babe **RUTH HITS HIS SIXTIETH HOME RUN** of the season, setting a record that will stand for thirty-four years. The New York Yankees slugger, nicknamed the Sultan of Swat, clears the fences against Washington Senators pitcher Tom Zachary. Ruth bats third in the Yankee's Murderer's Row lineup, which sweeps the World Series that year in four straight games.

## Arts & Entertainment

1926 Ernest Hemingway publishes his first novel, ***THE SUN ALSO RISES***, which he sets in Europe during the years after World War I. Its principal character, an American named Jake Barnes, drifts through Paris before attending the bull fights in Pamplona, Spain. Hemingway's simple, clear style establishes him as one of the most promising young writers of the Lost Generation.

1926 English author A.A. Milne publishes his first collection of stories about Piglet, Kanga, Roo, and a certain stuffed bear. Originally written for his son Christopher Robin, the stories in ***WINNIE-THE-POOH*** charm young readers all over the world. The characters usually run into trouble but always learn a valuable lesson along the way.

## Science & Technology

1927 Flying over the plains of southern Peru, a **PILOT DISCOVERS HUGE SHAPES** of animals drawn on the plains' surface. Visible only from the air because of their enormous size, these mysterious figures will be traced back to a pre-Inca civilization around 700 A.D. There will be much speculation about why and how these drawings were made.

1927 The fossilized remains of *Sinanthropus pekinsis*, or **PEKING MAN**, are discovered in a cave near China's capital. Beginning with the discovery of one tooth, Canadian archaeologist Davidson Black develops a complete profile of this primitive human who lived hundreds of thousands of years ago. Black's findings indicate that Peking man hunted, used tools, and cooked with fire.

1927 German physicist Werner Heisenberg formulates his famous **UNCERTAINTY PRINCIPLE**, which suggests that the universe is much more complicated than had been previously thought. Heisenberg's theory states that it is impossible to know precisely both the location and the speed of a subatomic particle at a given time because measuring subatomic objects inevitably changes their motion.

1900 1910 1920 1930 1940

MAY 10, 1927 President **COOLIDGE SENDS FIVE THOUSAND MARINES TO NICARAGUA**, where General Augusto César Sandino has taken up arms against the U.S.-backed government. Sandino flees to the mountains, where he and his men elude both the U.S. troops and the Nicaraguan National Guard. Sandino's stubborn guerrilla campaign wins him admirers throughout Latin America.

AUGUST 23, 1927 Despite international protests that their trial was unfair, **SACCO AND VANZETTI** are electrocuted in Massachusetts's Dedham Prison. A committee was appointed to review the trial [July 14, 1921], but it found no fault with Judge Webster Thayer's procedure. The governor did admit that Thayer had behaved badly during the trial, though he refused to stop the execution.

SEPTEMBER 19, 1927 After the Kuomintang army crushes Mao Zedong's **AUTUMN HARVEST UPRISING**, the Chinese Communist leader escapes with several hundred of his followers into the mountains of Hunan. During the Communists' twenty-two years "in the wilderness," Mao trains them in the techniques of guerrilla warfare.



1927 The Continental Baking Company introduces **WONDER BREAD**. Wonder becomes the nation's first sliced bread in 1930 when Continental begins selling it already cut up. Consumers initially greet the presliced bread with skepticism, but that changes quickly, and Chicago-based Continental builds more than one hundred plants nationwide to handle the demand.

# The Lost Generation

## WRITERS SHAPED BY WAR

DURING THE 1920s, MANY of the best American writers lived in Paris, where they gathered about fellow author Gertrude Stein. Paris had always been a favorite city for dissatisfied Americans, but during the Roaring Twenties it seemed to overflow with talent. Novelists such as Ernest Hemingway and F. Scott Fitzgerald lived there because their World War I experiences made it difficult for them to live at home. They found it hard to relate to Americans who were enjoying the new prosperity and seemed to have forgotten the war's brutality.

One day Stein told Hemingway: "You are all a lost generation." She meant that Hemingway and the other young Americans in Paris had no sense of purpose or direction. Somehow, the First World War had taken that away.

**Ernest Hemingway was a Red Cross ambulance driver during World War I. On July 8, 1918, he became the first American wounded in Italy when he was hit by shrapnel and machine-gun fire. His injuries left him with 227 scars.**

**One of the many young men killed in World War 1 trench warfare.**

The war did profoundly affect an entire generation of artists. Millions of people had died horrible deaths in the trenches of western Europe for no apparent reason. As a result, for the Lost Generation life seemed without purpose, and the moneymaking atmosphere of the Roaring Twenties seemed shallow to them.

The Lost Generation's novels, such as Fitzgerald's ***The Great Gatsby*** and Hemingway's ***The Sun Also Rises***, all reflect this sense of emptiness. But their struggles to find meaning in a changing world produced brilliant literature.

## Politics

JANUARY 1928 Winning the struggle for control of the Soviet Union [January 21, 1924], Joseph **STALIN EXILES LEON TROTSKY**, his chief rival. Stalin then moves to replace Lenin's New Economic Policy [March 1921] with his own plan to collectivize, or have the state take over, privately run peasant farms. In order to do this, Stalin executes millions of uncooperative peasants.

**DUKE ELLINGTON • By the time he was eighteen years old, Ellington had given up classical music for the new jazz. His band members often improvised parts within Ellington's written compositions.**

## Life in the Roaring Twenties

JUNE 10, 1928 The New York City Board of Health halts the Dance Derby of the Century in its 428th hour when health officials learn that a contestant has been hospitalized after vomiting up blood. Of the ninety-one couples who began the **DANCE MARATHON**, only nine remain. During the competition, as many as seven thousand people watched the exhausted dancers as they struggled to stay awake.

1928 Health departments blame 1,565 deaths on **BAD LIQUOR**, and many more people are blinded by "moonshine" whiskey. Meanwhile, tolerance of illegal speakeasies leads to a general atmosphere of lawlessness. As patience for Prohibition wanes, Democratic presidential candidate Al Smith takes up the "wet" cause.

## Arts & Entertainment

OCTOBER 6, 1927 The first major motion picture with sound, ***THE JAZZ SINGER***, opens to great acclaim. The film stars Al Jolson, whose first words are, "Wait, you ain't heard nothin' yet." Although *The Jazz Singer* features only a few brief moments of dialogue mixed in with Jolson's songs, the success of "talkies" revolutionizes the film industry.

DECEMBER 4, 1927 Jazz band leader **DUKE ELLINGTON** opens at Harlem's dapper Cotton Club. His "Black and Tan Fantasy" draws huge crowds. The music appeals to both blacks and whites and brings people together.

NOVEMBER 18, 1928 The first cartoon with sound, Walt Disney's *Steamboat Willie* opens in New York today, featuring **MICKEY MOUSE**. Disney designed the squeaky-voiced mouse to show off the new sound technology, but Mickey and his girlfriend, Minnie, soon become institutions. Disney himself finds great success developing other animal characters that behave like people.

## Science & Technology

1927 Belgian astrophysicist Georges Lemaître proposes his Cosmic Egg theory of the origin of the universe, which later becomes known as the **BIG BANG**. Starting from Edwin Hubble's premise that the universe may be expanding [1924], Lemaître suggests that the universe began with a massive explosion billions of years ago.

OCTOBER 1928 A young girl at Boston Children's Hospital becomes the first polio patient to be treated with an **IRON LUNG**. This device uses an airtight chamber and an electric motor to force air in and out of a patient's lungs. Polio has received much attention since a rising political star named Franklin Delano Roosevelt contracted the virus in 1921.

1928 Scottish bacteriologist Alexander Fleming discovers **PENICILLIN** when a particular bread mold accidentally kills some bacteria he has been growing. Fleming's work shows that penicillin's bacteria-fighting properties can dramatically improve the treatment of countless infectious diseases.

AUGUST 27, 1928 Fifteen nations sign the ambitious **KELLOGG-BRIAND PACT** in Paris. This international treaty, negotiated by Secretary of State Frank B. Kellogg and French Foreign Minister Aristide Briand, outlaws war as a means of achieving national ends. However, the lack of a way to enforce the treaty makes it useless.

NOVEMBER 6, 1928 Republican Herbert Hoover wins a landslide victory in the **1928 PRESIDENTIAL ELECTION**. Hoover's experience as a mining engineer appeals to voters who want a modern, scientific president. Hoover is also helped by voter prejudice against the Democratic candidate, New York governor Alfred E. Smith, who is Catholic.

AUGUST 1929 Tensions over Jewish use of the Wailing Wall lead to the first major **ARAB ATTACKS ON JEWS IN PALESTINE**. The situation is particularly bad in Jerusalem, where Judaism, Christianity, and Islam all have sacred sites. Great Britain, which currently controls Palestine, has already supported the idea of a Jewish homeland there, a position that has outraged Arab residents.

FEBRUARY 14, 1929 Chicago mobsters, most likely sent by mob boss Al Capone, kill seven members of the rival Bugs Moran gang in the brutal **ST. VALENTINE'S DAY MASSACRE**. Gang warfare for control of the illegal liquor trade has claimed more than 250 lives since Prohibition began on January 16, 1920.

# TALKIES

## HOLLYWOOD SPEAKS!

AFTER THE RELEASE OF *The Jazz Singer* in 1927, every movie studio in Hollywood rushed to convert from silent pictures to sound. The result was temporary chaos as writers, directors, and actors struggled to adapt.

Silent movies had not been entirely without sound. Even the smallest movie theater employed a piano player or a violinist to accompany the screen action. Occasionally, a few lines of written dialogue would appear on the screen in title cards. There was usually just enough dialogue so that the audiences could understand the plots, which were generally either exaggerated dramas or slapstick comedies. Slapstick comedians like Charlie Chaplin and Buster Keaton used physical and visual humor to get laughs. During one scene in *The Gold Rush* (1925), for example, Chaplin, playing a hungry prospector, eats his shoe as if it were a steak.

The introduction of "talkies" changed everything. Movie theater piano players lost their jobs, and so did squeaky-voiced silent film stars. The rest of the actors had to take voice lessons, and Hollywood studios began hiring Broadway actors, playwrights, and directors, who were experienced with dialogue. While many silent film stars moved easily into talkies, others—like Buster Keaton and Theda Bara—faded away.

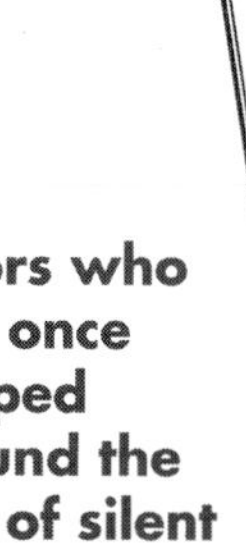

Actors who had once jumped around the sets of silent films now had to learn how to play to microphones that did not move with them. As a result, movies became less swashbuckling for a time, and the action on-screen became less dramatic and more like the real lives of the audience.

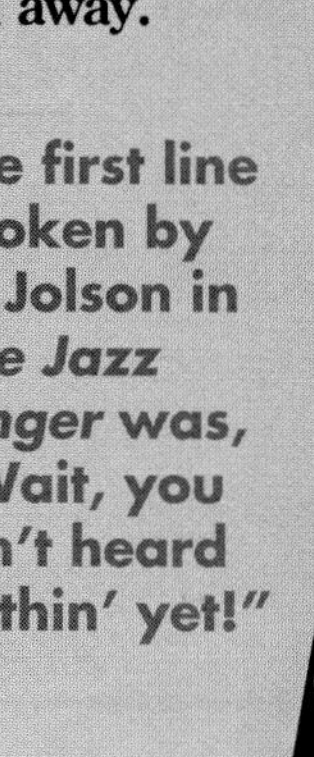

The first line spoken by Al Jolson in *The Jazz Singer* was, "Wait, you ain't heard nothin' yet!"

# The Great

AMERICANS THOUGHT THE Roaring Twenties would never end. The stock market kept going up and up. In fact, stocks seemed such a good investment that people often borrowed money to buy them. When the market finally crashed, its collapse nearly destroyed American society. Thousands of businesses closed, and millions of people were thrown out of work. Suddenly unable to feed their families, the unemployed looked to the government for help.

Herbert Hoover had been elected president because people thought his policies would keep the United States prosperous. But he had no idea how to deal with an economic crisis, and the country floundered until Franklin Roosevelt replaced Hoover in 1933. During his first hundred days in office, Roosevelt revolutionized the federal government. Whereas Hoover had tried to help businesses recover, Roosevelt's New Deal programs targeted the unemployed directly.

In the meantime, many Americans who believed that capitalism had failed them joined the Communist and Socialist parties. Others sought escape in movie theaters, where Shirley Temple and the Marx Brothers helped them forget their troubles.

★

# Depression

## Politics

1929 Soviet dictator Joseph Stalin begins the governmental takeover of Russian agriculture, which he calls **COLLECTIVIZATION**. When his policy provokes opposition from landowning peasants, called *kulaks*, Stalin responds by cutting off food shipments to the starving farmers. Three million die of famine alone, and many more are sent to labor camps or killed by the army.

MARCH 7, 1930 **"PROSPERITY IS JUST AROUND THE CORNER,"** an out-of-touch President Herbert Hoover announces. "All the evidences indicate that the worst effects of the crash will have passed within sixty days." The Great Depression continues to worsen, however, as the number of unemployed Americans tops four million.

## Life in the Great Depression

OCTOBER 29, 1929 On what will become known as **BLACK TUESDAY**, the stock market collapses. Prices plunge as the combined value of New York Stock Exchange listings drops about nine billion dollars in just one day. The panic is caused by frantic investors who have purchased stock using credit. Many order their brokers to sell at any price in a futile effort to save their fortunes.

**BLACK TUESDAY • Ambulances rushed to Wall Street after rumors spread that stockbrokers were committing suicide.**

1929 Donald F. Duncan markets the first **YO-YO**. Based on a sixteenth-century weapon used by hunters in the Philippines, Duncan's toy is an immediate success with American youth, who buy them as quickly as they can be made.

## Arts & Entertainment

1930 Author Sinclair Lewis, whose novels question the conservative values of midwestern small towns, becomes the **FIRST AMERICAN TO WIN THE NOBEL PRIZE FOR LITERATURE**. He has already refused the Pulitzer Prize for his 1925 novel *Arrowsmith,* which is critical of the medical profession.

1930 Grant Wood, who lives in Iowa, paints ***AMERICAN GOTHIC***, a somber portrait of the country's vanishing rural life-style. For models, Wood uses his sister and their dentist. The painting, bought by the Art Institute of Chicago for three hundred dollars, brings Wood overnight fame and creates a new popular interest in American regional painting.

1930 **EDWARD HOPPER** paints *Early Sunday Morning,* a street scene featuring a deserted row of stores including a barbershop. Many of Hopper's favorite subjects, such as vacant apartment buildings and diners at night, capture the loneliness of city life.

## Science & Technology

FEBRUARY 18, 1930 While comparing photographs taken on January 23 and 29, astronomer Clyde Tombaugh discovers the ninth planet, **PLUTO**. Tombaugh has been working at the observatory near Flagstaff, Arizona, built by Percival Lowell, who had predicted Pluto's existence in 1914. Tombaugh finds Pluto in approximately the same place that Lowell said the planet would be.

MAY 1, 1931 The 102-story **EMPIRE STATE BUILDING**, the world's tallest structure, opens in New York City. Constructed in just thirteen months, the 1,245-foot-tall skyscraper is supported by a steel skeleton that allows some swaying in high winds. The recent skyscraper boom is made possible by inexpensive steel and the development of efficient electric elevators.

OCTOBER 25, 1931 The Port Authority of New York completes construction of the **GEORGE WASHINGTON BRIDGE** across the Hudson River under budget and eight months ahead of schedule. The bridge connecting Manhattan and New Jersey more than doubles the longest span yet.

**March 12, 1930** Indian National Congress president Mohandas K. Gandhi announces a ***SATYAGRAHA***, or passive resistance campaign, to end the tax on salt and thereby weaken British colonial rule [April 13, 1919]. Gandhi's nonviolent crusade results in the arrest of sixty thousand of his followers but also produces an invitation to attend talks in London.

**June 17, 1930** Although a thousand economists ask him to veto the bill, President Hoover still signs the **SMOOT-HAWLEY TARIFF**, which imposes the highest tariff rates in U.S. history. Congress intends these taxes on imported goods to protect struggling U.S. businesses during the depression. Instead, as many predicted, these tariff increases spark an international trade war.

**September 1930** In nationwide elections for the Reichstag, or parliament, more than six million Germans vote for **ADOLF HITLER'S NATIONAL SOCIALIST PARTY**. The results transform the Nazis from an extremist fringe group into the country's second most powerful political party. The election results show how deeply the global depression has affected German politics.



**May 15, 1930** Ellen Church becomes the first **STEWARDESS** when she takes care of passengers during a United Airlines flight from San Francisco to Cheyenne, Wyoming. She is one of eight nurses hired by the airline to help passengers overcome their fear of flying. All of the flight attendants are attractive twenty-five-year-old women with pleasant personalities.

# HOOVERVILLES

## Homelessness During the Great Depression

A policeman evicts a homeless man from his shanty.

At the start of the Great Depression, many Americans wanted to believe that the hard times would be only temporary. They took comfort from President Herbert Hoover's claim that prosperity was "just around the corner." But that prosperity took a long time arriving. By 1932, one in four Americans was out of work. Unable to pay their rent or keep up with mortgage payments, many families lost their homes.

Many homeless people moved into shacks they built out of scrap sheet metal and wooden packing boxes. Small shantytowns soon sprang up on the outskirts of large cities. They were called Hoovervilles after the president, because he still refused to approve government aid for the poor.

Although Hoover certainly did not cause the Great Depression, many Americans felt that the president's policies made it worse. They also thought he was not sympathetic enough to the troubles faced by ordinary people. Hoover believed that state governments and private charities should help the poor and the starving. However, these groups were low on funds, just like everyone else, and could not afford the massive costs involved.

## Politics

SEPTEMBER 19, 1931 Confirming their government's policy of taking land by force, **JAPANESE TROOPS SEIZE THE PROVINCE OF MANCHURIA** in northern China. The League of Nations condemns the invasion, but member nations refuse to send troops on China's behalf. Instead, the invasion becomes an important symbol of Japan's intention to rule all of Asia.

DECEMBER 8, 1931 In his State of the Union address, President **HOOVER REFUSES TO SUPPORT AID TO THE UNEMPLOYED** A firm believer in American individualism, Hoover says that a "dole" would just produce more unemployed people. The president gives this speech one day after hungry marchers, requesting jobs at a minimum wage, were turned away from the White House.

JANUARY 22, 1932 President Hoover signs a bill creating the **RECONSTRUCTION FINANCE CORPORATION**, which will loan billions of dollars to failing businesses, especially banks and railroads. Federal officials hope the RFC will put an end to the epidemic of bank failure. But New York congressman Fiorello H. La Guardia criticizes the plan, calling it a "millionaire's dole."

## Life in the Great Depression

AUGUST 1930 The first **SUPERMARKET**, King Kullen, opens in Queens, New York. "Pile it high and sell it cheap" is the store's motto. Owner Harry Socoloff changes grocery shopping forever by presenting goods in a huge open space and allowing customers to choose what they want. Before the supermarket, people shopped mostly in small stores where clerks brought them what they needed.

1930 Unemployed engineer Charles Darrow invents the game **MONOPOLY**. The original sets, which he makes at home in Atlantic City, come with a circular board and houses cut from ceiling molding. Parker Brothers rejects the game at first because of its complex rules, but Monopoly's success at the Wanamaker's store in Philadelphia during the 1934 Christmas season changes the company's mind.

1930 Wallace Fard founds the **BLACK MUSLIM** movement in Detroit. He tells his followers that blacks were the superior race before "white devils" enslaved them. He also claims to be a messenger of the Islamic god Allah. When he disappears in 1934, control of the Nation of Islam passes to his closest disciple, Elijah Muhammad.

## Arts & Entertainment

1932 Songwriter E.Y. "Yip" Harburg pens **"BROTHER, CAN YOU SPARE A DIME?"** after he sees a bread line several blocks long. The song soon becomes identified with the Great Depression despite the current trend in popular music toward lighthearted tunes. Typical hit songs include "Life Is Just a Bowl of Cherries" and "Wrap Your Troubles in Dreams, and Dream Your Troubles Away."

1932 French artist Marcel Duchamp calls Alexander Calder's suspended wire sculptures **MOBILES** because their parts spin around. Calder's imaginative and playful sculptures are an important advance in kinetic art, or art that moves. Most of Calder's mobiles are so well balanced that a slight breeze can alter the arrangement of their elements.

**DUSTBOWL • Thick clouds of dust sweep over the town of Elkhart, Kansas.**

## Science & Technology

NOVEMBER 11–13, 1933 Erosion problems become the focus of concern when a dust storm carries South Dakota topsoil as far east as New York. The government begins funding soil conservation programs, but a drought makes the situation worse. In May 1936, clouds of dirt kicked up by a storm in the **DUST BOWL** of Texas and Oklahoma eclipse the sun as far east as the Appalachians.

1934 Adolf Hitler commissions engineer Ferdinand Porsche to design a low-cost "people's car" that can be easily maintained. The result is the **VOLKSWAGEN**. Although the first Volkswagen factory is not built until 1938, the company eventually sells more than eighteen million Volkswagen Beetles, surpassing the record set by Henry Ford's Model T.

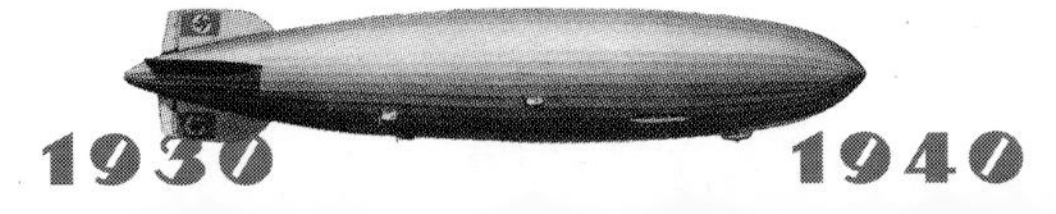

SEPTEMBER 1932 Already in prison for his acts of civil disobedience [March 12, 1930], **GANDHI ANNOUNCES THAT HE WILL FAST UNTIL HE DIES** unless the British agree to end segregation of the "untouchables," India's lowest social group. The Indian leader—known as Mahatma, or Wise Soul—ends his fast when the British agree six days later to improve the status of the untouchables.

NOVEMBER 8, 1932 Democratic candidate Franklin Delano Roosevelt wins the **1932 PRESIDENTIAL ELECTION**, defeating Republican incumbent Herbert Hoover by more than seven million votes. Hoover never had much of a chance, having become personally associated with the worsening depression. The key to Roosevelt's victory is his New Deal program to improve the economy.

FEBRUARY 27, 1933 German chancellor Adolf Hitler uses the **REICHSTAG FIRE**, which destroys the parliament building, to take emergency powers. Also using the mysterious fire as an excuse, Nazi storm troopers begin a campaign of political terror. In elections held on March 5, the Nazis win enough votes to force passage of the Enabling Act, creating a dictatorship they call the Third Reich.

APRIL 6, 1931 Nine black youths charged with raping two white women on a freight train go on trial in Scottsboro, Alabama. Although a doctor who examined the women testifies that he found no evidence of rape, the all-white jury still votes to convict the **SCOTTSBORO BOYS**. Eight are sentenced to death, and the ninth, who is just twelve years old, receives life imprisonment.

# Woody Guthrie

**IN 1935, A DUST STORM HIT THE town of Pampa, Texas, where twenty-three-year-old Woody Guthrie was living with his wife and family. The storm inspired Guthrie to write the song "Dusty Old Bowl," which later became famous as "So Long, It's Been Good to Know You." Guthrie had been writing songs since his teenage years in Oklahoma, where he learned to play music on a battered old guitar. Because his parents were too poor to afford lessons, Woody taught himself.**

**As the years passed, Guthrie remained poor. He left school at the age of thirteen, but he never made much money at the odd jobs he found. In 1936, when the Great Depression was at its peak, Guthrie decided to leave his family and take to the road.**

**Following other Dust Bowl farmers whose crops had been destroyed by drought, Guthrie made his way to California, where he wrote "Hard Travelin' " and "Deportee" about the terrible conditions faced by migrant workers. Although Guthrie's songs used traditional folk melodies, his lyrics were original and powerful. To earn some money, he performed them at rodeos, at dances, and in bars. In 1937, he was offered a spot on a radio show, which helped launch his career as a professional musician.**

**During the 1930s, before he became famous, Woody Guthrie lived as a hobo, traveling from town to town in freight cars and sleeping in flophouses. In February 1940, while staying at a dingy hotel in New York City, he wrote "This Land Is Your Land," which many people consider to be the greatest song ever written about the United States.**

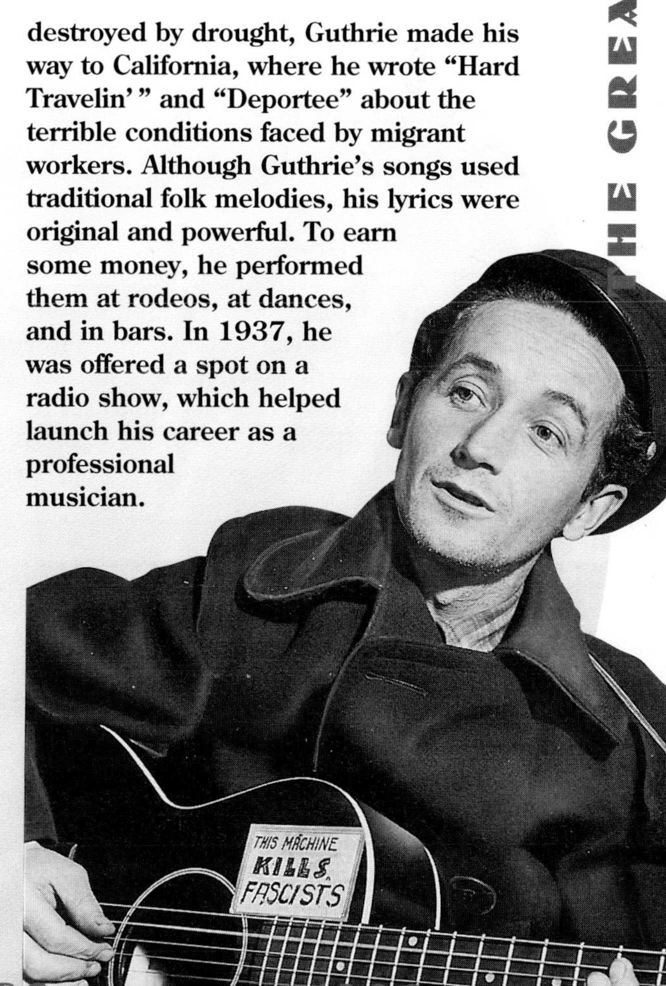

## Politics

MARCH 1, 1933 **SIX GOVERNORS TEMPORARILY CLOSE THE BANKS** in their states to prevent nervous depositors from withdrawing their savings. Depositors have reason to worry, because five thousand banks have failed since the 1929 stock market crash, wiping out nine million savings accounts. The governors believe a "run" of panicked withdrawals will collapse the banking system.

MARCH 4, 1933 The national banking crisis peaks on the morning of Franklin Roosevelt's inauguration when New York governor Herbert Lehman orders a bank holiday at 4:30 A.M. In his inaugural address, the new president blames the country's bankers and financiers. "First of all," he begins, "let me assert my firm belief that **THE ONLY THING WE HAVE TO FEAR IS FEAR ITSELF**."

MARCH 4, 1933 In his inaugural address, President Roosevelt outlines his **GOOD NEIGHBOR POLICY**. Since the Monroe Doctrine of 1823, the United States had intervened in Latin America at will. But Roosevelt adopts a friendlier attitude. He withdraws troops from Nicaragua [May 10, 1927] and has Congress void the Platt Amendment [March 2, 1901].

## Life in the Great Depression

OCTOBER 17, 1931 Bootlegger, racketeer, and murderer **AL CAPONE** receives an eleven-year sentence for not paying taxes on his illegal income. Capone's imprisonment ends his control of organized crime in Chicago. During his twelve years there, Capone had reportedly ordered more than three hundred murders, including the St. Valentine's Day Massacre [February 14, 1929].

KING KONG • Although the ferocious gorilla looked gigantic on the screen, he was actually an eighteen-inch model.

1931 Journalism professor George Gallup develops the first techniques for conducting market surveys of magazine readers. Working with the Young and Rubicam ad agency, he conducts the first **GALLUP POLLS**, in which he asks people their opinions on various subjects. Gallup later uses his polling methods to predict correctly the outcome of the 1936 presidential election.

## Arts & Entertainment

1932 **THOMAS HART BENTON** paints the mural *Arts of the West*. Benton, who was once a cartoonist, uses bright, vivid colors to present scenes of American farm life. Rejecting the influence of French painters, he champions art that draws its inspiration from daily life in the rural Midwest.

1933 The legendary ape **KING KONG** appears on movie screens for the first time, swatting airplanes as if they were mosquitoes. The savage primate stars opposite Fay Wray and the Empire State Building [May 1, 1931], completed just two years earlier. *King Kong*'s special effects, created by Willis O'Brien, take advantage of important recent advances in filmmaking technology.

## Science & Technology

MAY 24, 1935 Twenty-five thousand fans watch the Philadelphia Phillies defeat the Cincinnati Reds in the major leagues' **FIRST NIGHT BASEBALL GAME**. In Washington, D.C., President Franklin Roosevelt uses a remote hookup to turn on the new thousand-kilowatt floodlights at Cincinnati's Crosley Field.

1935 Charles Richter, a seismologist at the California Institute of Technology, creates the **RICHTER SCALE** to measure the intensity of earthquakes. The scale is logarithmic, which means that with each step from one to ten, the power of the earthquake increases tenfold.

MARCH 4, 1933 President Roosevelt appoints as his secretary of labor Frances Perkins, who becomes the **FIRST WOMAN TO HOLD A CABINET POST**. Perkins had served as a state industrial commissioner from 1929 to 1933 while Roosevelt was governor of New York. She is one of the many committed reformers Roosevelt brings with him to Washington.

MARCH 6, 1933 President Roosevelt orders a national bank holiday, closing all the banks that remain open, and calls Congress into special session. On March 9, the House and Senate pass the **EMERGENCY BANKING ACT**, which keeps the banks closed until federal auditors can examine their books. It also sets up procedures for reopening those banks found to be financially sound.

MARCH 10, 1933 In the town of Dachau outside Munich, the Germans establish their first **CONCENTRATION CAMP** on the grounds of an old ammunition factory. The officers in charge of the camp are members of the elite *Schutzstaffel* unit, commonly known as the SS. More than two hundred thousand people are imprisoned there before Allied troops liberate Dachau in 1945.

MARCH 1, 1932 The infant son of Charles Lindbergh disappears from his New Jersey home. The Lindberghs pay a fifty-thousand-dollar ransom, but the kidnappers fail to return the child. Despite intense news coverage and the efforts of five thousand federal agents, the fate of the **LINDBERGH BABY** remains a mystery until May 12, when a truck driver finds his body in a shallow grave.

# Shirley Temple

SIX-YEAR-OLD Shirley Temple made her motion-picture debut in 1934, when she charmed audiences with a brief song-and-dance number in *Stand Up and Cheer*. Her performance quickly led to starring roles in a string of box-office hits, including *Little Miss Marker* (1934) and *The Little Princess* (1939). Suddenly, the dimpled, curly-haired child became a major national phenomenon.

During some of the worst years of the Great Depression, Shirley Temple's cheerfulness helped lift the country's sagging spirits. Even President Roosevelt acknowledged her contribution. "It is a splendid thing," he said, "that an American can go to a movie and look at the smiling face of a baby and forget his troubles." Temple's films created a magical universe in which criminals turned honest, orphans found their parents, and poor people became millionaires. There was always singing, tap dancing, and a happy ending.

Young children clamored for Shirley Temple clothing, books, and other merchandise. Despite the hard times, parents found the money to buy more than six million Shirley Temple dolls. Temple's career began to fade, however, as she grew up, and she retired in 1941 at the age of thirteen.

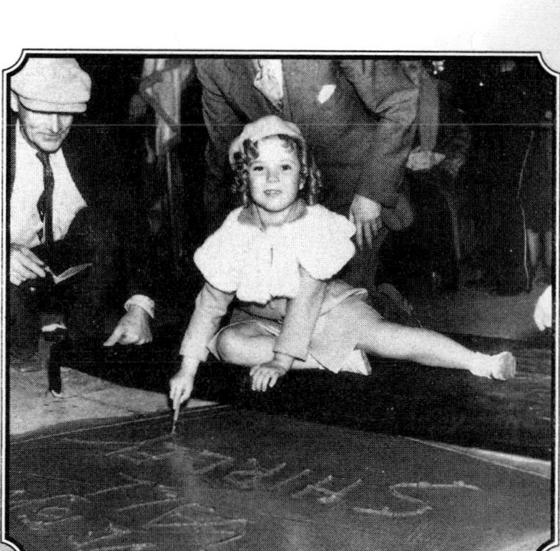


**Shirley Temple's films did so well at the box office that they kept several studios out of bankruptcy.**

## Politics

MARCH 31, 1933 The Reforestation Unemployment Act creates the **CIVILIAN CONSERVATION CORPS**, whose tree-planting and road projects will provide jobs for nearly three million young men between the ages of eighteen and twenty-five. Most CCC workers live together in wilderness camps. Of the thirty dollars they earn each month, twenty-two is sent home to help their families.

BONUS ARMY • Unemployed veterans camp out on the lawn of the Capitol.

MAY 12, 1933 The **AGRICULTURAL ADJUSTMENT ACT**, passed today, sets a new farm policy for the nation. The law tries to solve the problem of crop surpluses, which push down farm prices, by having farmers paid to limit the amount of crops they grow. Critics, however, attack the notion that farmers should be paid to reduce the food supply while poor city people are starving.

## Life in the Great Depression

MAY 29, 1932 Nine thousand World War I veterans participate in the **BONUS MARCH** on Washington, D.C. They want Congress to move up payment of bonuses that were voted to them in 1924. Congress had originally awarded the bonuses in the form of insurance that could be redeemed for cash in 1945. But the veterans argue that, because of the depression, they might not live until 1945.

JULY 28, 1932 A frustrated and impatient President Hoover personally orders federal troops under General Douglas MacArthur to remove the **BONUS ARMY** from the nation's capital. Army troops, supported by cavalry and tanks, brutally throw out the veterans who had been camping near the Capitol. Hundreds are injured and at least two people are killed.

## Arts & Entertainment

1933 Gertrude Stein, an American living in Paris, writes the ***AUTOBIOGRAPHY OF ALICE B. TOKLAS***. Supposedly written about her companion, Toklas, the book actually chronicles Stein's own life. Stein is best known as a critic who can make or break an artist's or a writer's reputation with even an offhand remark.

1933 Mexican artist **DIEGO RIVERA** paints the mural *Man at the Crossroads* for Rockefeller Center in New York City. Rivera's work inspires protests, however, because one of the figures resembles Soviet revolutionary leader Vladimir Lenin. When Rivera refuses to change the mural, John D. Rockefeller, Jr., dismisses him from the project and orders the mural chipped off the wall.

AUGUST 21, 1935 Clarinetist Benny Goodman opens at the Palomar Ballroom in Los Angeles. After playing two sets of standard dance music, his band devotes its third set to a new jazz style called **SWING**. When the crowd goes wild, a popular music craze is born. A year later, Goodman forms the first integrated jazz quartet when he teams up with black musicians Teddy Wilson and Lionel Hampton.

## Science & Technology

OCTOBER 1936 Workers complete the 726-foot-high **BOULDER DAM**, later renamed for Herbert Hoover. Among the new construction techniques that make the dam possible are cooling tubes that harden cement quickly. If older methods had been used, the cement would have taken a century to set. In addition to providing cheap hydroelectric power, the dam creates Lake Mead in Nevada.

MAY 6, 1937 The airship ***HINDENBURG*** explodes while landing at Lakehurst, New Jersey, killing thirty-five passengers and a member of the ground crew. Coincidentally, Herbert Morrison is there to cover the German airship's arrival for the nation's first coast-to-coast radio broadcast. The hydrogen-filled *Hindenburg* had begun making regular transatlantic flights in May 1936.

MAY 27, 1937 More than two hundred thousand people celebrate the opening of the **GOLDEN GATE BRIDGE** with fireworks, music, and other festivities. The longest suspension bridge in the world, it links San Francisco and the Marin peninsula in northern California.

MAY 18, 1933 Congress establishes the **TENNESSEE VALLEY AUTHORITY**, whose mission is to modernize one of the nation's poorest regions. One of the TVA's many accomplishments is building a series of hydroelectric dams that control Tennessee River flooding and bring inexpensive power to poor farmers who have never before used electricity.

JUNE 16, 1933 Congressional passage of the National Industrial Recovery Act sets up the **NATIONAL RECOVERY ADMINISTRATION**. This key New Deal agency encourages business owners and labor unions to work together in regulating prices, production, and wages. The NRA itself works with these groups to establish a series of voluntary "codes of fair competition."

JUNE 16, 1933 The Glass-Steagall Act sets up the **FEDERAL DEPOSIT INSURANCE CORPORATION**, which will insure bank deposits up to five thousand dollars. The purpose of these federal guarantees is to make another banking crisis [March 1, 1933] much less likely. The new law also makes it illegal for banks to use depositors' money to invest in the stock market.

NOVEMBER 7, 1932 The Supreme Court reverses the conviction of the **SCOTTSBORO BOYS** [April 6, 1931] because they were not assigned lawyers until the first day of their trial. This left the attorneys little time to prepare a defense. The Scottsboro Boys are tried and convicted again, but the Court overturns this conviction also, on the grounds that blacks were intentionally kept off the jury.

# The Rise of Radio

## America Tunes In

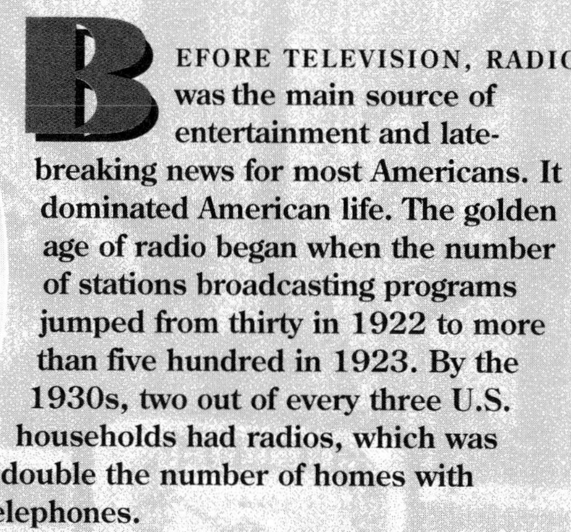

"The Lone Ranger"

BEFORE TELEVISION, RADIO was the main source of entertainment and late-breaking news for most Americans. It dominated American life. The golden age of radio began when the number of stations broadcasting programs jumped from thirty in 1922 to more than five hundred in 1923. By the 1930s, two out of every three U.S. households had radios, which was double the number of homes with telephones.

The clever sound effects helped listeners with active imaginations create a magical world. During the Great Depression, popular dramatic shows, including "Amos 'n' Andy" and "The Lone Ranger," helped many people all over the country forget their troubles.

President Roosevelt made particularly effective use of the radio. His regular radio speeches, known as Fireside Chats, explained his policies and reassured Americans that the country would indeed survive the hardships of the depression.

## Politics

DECEMBER 5, 1933 Utah's ratification of the Twenty-first Amendment makes it the law of the land, ending fourteen years of Prohibition in the United States [October 28, 1919]. The legalization of alcohol brought about by the **REPEAL OF PROHIBITION** destroys the illegal liquor trade, known as bootlegging. As a result, criminal empires built on bootlegging collapse overnight.

BESSIE SMITH • Born into poverty in 1898, the Empress of the Blues later sang with musical legends Louis Armstrong and Benny Goodman.

JUNE 6, 1934 President Roosevelt signs a new law creating the **SECURITIES AND EXCHANGE COMMISSION**. In doing so, he keeps his campaign promise to reform financial practices such as buying stocks using credit. Many economists believed that the use of too much credit caused the 1929 stock market crash [October 29, 1929].

## Life in the Great Depression

DECEMBER 1932 Newspaper editor Carl Magee files the first patent for a **PARKING METER**. The first meters are installed in Magee's hometown of Oklahoma City in July 1935. Police officers spend the next few months explaining to the public that the coin-operated devices are not slot machines and do not pay jackpots.

1932 As the Great Depression grows worse than most people imagined possible, a number of well-known **INTELLECTUALS BEGIN TO ENDORSE THE COMMUNIST PARTY**, including authors Theodore Dreiser and John Dos Passos. The terrible realities of unemployment and poverty make radical ideas more appealing to the average American.

## Arts & Entertainment

OCTOBER 10, 1935 George Gershwin's masterpiece, ***PORGY AND BESS***, about a poor black couple in the South, opens at New York's Alvin Theater. Long a successful composer of popular music, Gershwin challenged himself to write a serious modern opera. The result—which he composed with his brother, Ira—features an innovative blend of jazz, pop, and operatic technique.

SEPTEMBER 26, 1937 African-American blues singer **BESSIE SMITH** dies from injuries received in an auto accident. She might have lived, however, had she not been refused treatment at a segregated hospital in Memphis, Tennessee. Known as the Empress of the Blues for her powerful and moving performances, Smith often sang about poverty, defeat, and the cruelty of the world.

DECEMBER 1937 Walt Disney's ***SNOW WHITE AND THE SEVEN DWARFS***, the first full-length animated movie, opens in Hollywood. The film's $1.5-million cost has pushed Disney close to bankruptcy, but its instant box-office success leads to first-year ticket sales of $8.5 million. The fact that Disney personally auditioned 149 singers for the voice of Snow White reflects the care he put into the project.

## Science & Technology

JULY 2, 1937 Pilot **AMELIA EARHART** disappears during a flight from New Guinea to tiny Howland Island in the middle of the South Pacific. Earhart and her navigator, Fred Noonan, were attempting to fly around the world. For the next sixteen days, a naval search party hunts for the plane but finds no trace of the Lockheed Electra or its crew.

1937 Du Pont chemist Wallace H. Carothers patents **NYLON**, the first manufactured fiber. The first nylon product is a toothbrush with nylon bristles sold by Du Pont in 1938. Nylon stockings are introduced at the New York World's Fair a year later. Both products become scarce, however, when Du Pont turns over its production lines to parachute-making during World War II.

1937 British mathematician **ALAN TURING** demonstrates that complicated math problems can be solved mechanically as long as they are broken down into simple tasks that a machine can perform. Although just a doctoral student at Princeton University in New Jersey, Turing gains notoriety with his claim that machines can eventually be taught to think.

1900 1910 1920 1930 1940

**OCTOBER 15, 1934** Having just signed a truce with Japan [September 19, 1931], Chinese Nationalist leader Chiang Kai-shek returns to the task of eliminating his Communist enemies. Chiang's troops close in on the forces of Mao Zedong, but Mao breaks out and leads one hundred thousand followers westward on the year-long, six-thousand-mile **LONG MARCH**. Only eight thousand survive.

**MAY 6, 1935** Congress reorganizes all of its New Deal relief programs under a single federal agency: the **WORKS PROGRESS ADMINISTRATION**. According to director Harry Hopkins, the WPA will employ one-third of the eleven million people still looking for work. Among those hired will be writers, actors, and painters because, Hopkins says, artists have "got to eat just like other people."

**MAY 27, 1935** In the case of ***SCHECHTER POULTRY V. U.S.***, the Supreme Court strikes down the National Industrial Recovery Act [June 16, 1933]. The Court's highly conservative opinion states that Congress went too far in regulating interstate business. Seven months later, the Court frustrates Roosevelt again when it overturns the Agricultural Adjustment Act [May 12, 1933].



**1932** Cosmetics salesman Charles Revson borrows money to found **REVLON NAIL ENAMEL**. Giving his nail polishes exotic names like Tropic Sky (orange) and Fish Belly White (gray), Revson finds a market for his products at beauty salons. His extreme sales tactics, which include pushing competitors' displays off counters, lead to nearly complete control of the beauty salon market by 1941.

**BY 1930, CHARLES LINDBERGH HAD already crossed the Atlantic Ocean safely, but most Americans continued to believe that flying was an extremely dangerous enterprise. Heroic pilots still played a crucial role in helping people feel more comfortable about air travel. With her sporty appearance and personal charm, Amelia Earhart quickly emerged as one of the most popular aviation pioneers.**

**Earhart first fell in love with flying while attending an airplane stunt show. Soon afterward, she learned how to fly in her own small plane. In 1928, the year after Lindbergh's flight, New York publisher George Palmer Putnam suggested that she become the first woman to cross the Atlantic Ocean by plane. The flight was indeed historic, but Earhart traveled only as a passenger. Four years later, she flew the Atlantic solo in a record time of fifteen hours.**

**In the meantime, Earhart promoted women's rights as much as she did the cause of aviation. In 1931, she agreed to marry George Putnam, yet her views on marriage, like her career, were quite unconventional. Unlike other brides of the time, Earhart kept her own name and made no plans to have children. She even asked Putnam to sign an agreement promising not to interfere with her flying career.**

Earhart standing on her twin-engined Lockheed Electra.

**Politics**

JULY 5, 1935 In the aftermath of the Schechter Poultry case, Congress passes the **NATIONAL LABOR RELATIONS ACT**. Also known as the Wagner Act, it reinstates many of the protections granted labor unions under the National Industrial Recovery Act. The Wagner Act also sets up the National Labor Relations Board to investigate and punish unfair labor practices.

AUGUST 14, 1935 President Roosevelt signs the **SOCIAL SECURITY ACT**, establishing a federal pension system for elderly Americans. Beginning in 1942, Americans sixty-five years and older receive monthly checks paid for by payroll deductions and matching employer contributions. Social Security will also provide benefits to the unemployed and the disabled.

SEPTEMBER 15, 1935 The Nazi government of Germany enacts the **NUREMBERG LAWS**, which take away the citizenship rights of German Jews. Soon-to-be-released guidelines define as a Jew anyone with at least one Jewish grandparent. The new laws also forbid intermarriage between Jews and Aryan Germans because the Nazis believe that marriages to Jews will cause "racial pollution."

**Life in the Great Depression**

MARCH 12, 1933 President Roosevelt begins a series of informal radio speeches called **FIRESIDE CHATS**. The president's goal is to reduce the level of fear in the country by explaining his New Deal policies directly to the people. His confident, reassuring voice calms Americans listening in their living rooms even more than his explanations do.

**FIRESIDE CHATS • President Roosevelt speaks to the nation during one of his weekly broadcasts.**

SEPTEMBER 1933 Despite the economic innovations of Roosevelt's first hundred days in office, the depression continues to pound local governments. As the school year begins, **TWO THOUSAND RURAL SCHOOLS LACK THE FUNDS TO OPEN**. Fifteen hundred private schools and colleges also close their doors, forcing nearly two million school-age children to stay at home.

**Arts & Entertainment**

1937 **ZORA NEALE HURSTON** writes *Their Eyes Were Watching God*, based on her experiences growing up in Eatonville, Florida, a town founded by freed slaves. Much of Hurston's work concerns the adaptation of African-American folklore to urban settings. Tragically, Hurston's novels are neglected for years, forcing her to earn her living as a maid.

1937 **"WHAT'S UP, DOC?"** says wise-guy rabbit Bugs Bunny for the first time in the Warner Brothers cartoon *Porky's Hare Hunt*. Providing the voice of Bugs, Porky Pig, and nearly all the Warner Brothers characters is Mel Blanc. Bugs's quick-witted comic sense soon wins over the many animation fans who have become bored with squeaky-clean Mickey, Walt Disney's moralistic mouse.

**Science & Technology**

OCTOBER 22, 1938 After four years of experiments, Chester Carlson produces the first photocopy. Carlson's **XEROXING** process uses wax paper, a coated zinc plate, and flashlight powder. Carlson names the process *xerography*, after the Greek word *xeros*, which means "dry."

1938 Hungarian journalist Laszlo Biro develops the first practical **BALLPOINT PEN**, which he patents after fleeing to Argentina to escape the Nazis. His design uses a rotating steel ball and quick-drying ink. Called "biros," the pens first become popular in England, where Royal Air Force tests show that they write even at high altitudes.

OCTOBER 3, 1935 The **ITALIAN ARMY INVADES ETHIOPIA** as part of dictator Benito Mussolini's plan to create an Italian colonial empire in East Africa. "It is us today. It will be you tomorrow," the Ethiopian emperor tells the League of Nations, which condemns the invasion but does little more. Ethiopia falls to Italy the following year.

JULY 17, 1936 The **SPANISH CIVIL WAR** begins when General Francisco Franco mutinies against the recently elected socialist government. Quickly, Spanish democrats form a Loyalist army to oppose him. Although Franco receives military aid from fellow fascists in Germany and Italy, the Western democracies do little to help the Loyalists because of isolationist pressures at home.

AUGUST 1936 Soviet leader Joseph Stalin orders the first in a long series of **MOSCOW SHOW TRIALS** designed to remove his opponents within the Communist party. Stalin uses as an excuse the 1934 assassination of Leningrad party boss Sergei Kirov. Historians have since proved that Stalin himself ordered the murder because he believed Kirov was becoming too powerful.

JULY 22, 1934 FBI agents gun down bank robber **JOHN DILLINGER** outside the Biograph Theater in Chicago. The fashionably dressed Dillinger was the first criminal named Public Enemy No. 1 by FBI director J. Edgar Hoover. During his fourteen-month run of successful holdups, Dillinger became known as a modern-day Robin Hood, stealing from banks that were themselves stealing from the poor.

# Dorothea Lange & Walker Evans

## PORTRAITS OF HARD TIMES

**One of the photographs of migrant workers Lange took for the FSA.**

**During the Great Depression, Lange spent most of her time traveling in the Far West.**

THE FARM SECURITY Administration was one of the many New Deal agencies created by President Franklin Roosevelt to help farmers survive the Great Depression. As part of its work, the FSA hired photographers to document the terrible living conditions endured by these people. The photographs were then exhibited around the country so that city people could see what was happening to farmers in the countryside.

Dorothea Lange was one of the first photographers hired by the FSA. Before the 1929 stock market crash, she had made a living taking portraits of wealthy people in San Francisco. For the FSA, however, Lange took stark black-and-white photographs of poor migrant farm workers, who crisscrossed the country looking for seasonal work. Her images were so powerful that they generated a movement to improve conditions in the migrant camps.

Walker Evans also took many famous photographs while employed by the FSA. His scenes of daily life revealed the pride that still persisted in many poor farming families. In 1940, on leave from the FSA, Evans documented the lives of sharecroppers in Alabama. His photos were later published, with text by James Agee, in a celebrated book entitled *Let Us Now Praise Famous Men*.

## Politics

OCTOBER 25, 1936 Following German recognition of Italy's new Ethiopian empire, Mussolini announces that he and Hitler have agreed to form the **ROME-BERLIN AXIS**, an alliance between Italy and Germany. A month later, Germany negotiates the Anti-Comintern Pact with Japan, which Italy also signs. This agreement leads to a more wide-ranging alliance among the three countries.

FEBRUARY 5, 1937 Frustrated by the Supreme Court's opposition to his New Deal [May 27, 1935], President Roosevelt proposes that an additional justice be appointed for each current justice seventy years of age or older. Roosevelt claims that the older justices need help with their workloads, but his intention is clearly to **PACK THE SUPREME COURT** with justices favorable to his policies.

MAY 1, 1937 To stop the arms trade with Spain, Congress extends the **NEUTRALITY ACT** to include civil wars. The act, first passed in 1935, already made it illegal to sell weapons to warring nations. The new law reflects isolationist sentiment in the United States among people who believe that arms dealers are "merchants of death" who conspire to begin wars and then profit from them.

## Life in the Great Depression

SEPTEMBER 8, 1935 Senator **HUEY LONG** of Louisiana is assassinated at the state capitol in Baton Rouge by the son-in-law of a politician whose career he had ruined. As governor of Louisiana, Long had used public works projects and welfare reform to win the votes of the state's poorest citizens. As a senator, he pursued the same populist approach with his Share the Wealth program.

APRIL 3, 1936 Illegal German immigrant Bruno Hauptmann is electrocuted for the kidnapping of the **LINDBERGH BABY** [March 1, 1932]. Hauptmann maintained his innocence throughout the trial, and the prosecutor could produce no witnesses to the crime. But the discovery of the ransom money in Hauptmann's house provided the jury with enough circumstantial evidence to convict him.

MARCH 12, 1937 The **FLINT SIT-DOWN STRIKE** ends when the United Auto Workers union reaches agreement with General Motors on a new contract. Workers took over the GM plant in Flint, Michigan, on December 20, 1936, when they found equipment being shipped to nonunion plants. Supporters on the outside supplied the strikers inside with food and first-aid supplies.

## Arts & Entertainment

JUNE 1938 Faster than a speeding bullet and more powerful than a locomotive, **SUPERMAN** debuts in Action Comics No. 1. The Man of Steel's creators are two high school buddies, writer Jerry Siegel and illustrator Joe Shuster. They each make fifteen dollars per week for their efforts.

**GONE WITH THE WIND • *Vivien Leigh starred as Scarlett O'Hara and Clark Gable played Rhett Butler in Oscar-nominated performances.***

DECEMBER 15, 1939 Producer David O. Selznick creates an unprecedented flurry of publicity for the world premiere in Atlanta of his new film, ***GONE WITH THE WIND***, starring Vivien Leigh and Clark Gable. Selznick's movie is based on the Pulitzer Prize–winning novel by Margaret Mitchell, which broke every sales record following its publication in 1936.

## Science & Technology

AUGUST 2, 1939 Albert Einstein writes a letter to President Roosevelt warning him of the "danger threatening all humanity" should the Nazis build an **ATOMIC BOMB**. Einstein alerts the president to rumors that the Germans may already be working on such a weapon. Roosevelt soon creates the Advisory Committee on Uranium to investigate the possibility of developing an American bomb.

1939 Swiss chemist Paul Müller develops **DDT**, the first modern chemical pesticide. He creates DDT to fight an insect currently threatening Switzerland's potato crop. Müller wins a Nobel Prize in 1948 for his work, which is initially hailed as an inexpensive and effective tool for farmers.

OCTOBER 5, 1937 In his **QUARANTINE SPEECH** condemning renewed Japanese attacks against China, President Roosevelt asks that the world's peace-loving nations work together to control aggressor nations as though they were diseases. "We are determined to keep out of war," Roosevelt says, but the world's interdependence "makes it impossible for any nation to completely isolate itself."

DECEMBER 13, 1937 Japanese forces capture the Chinese city of Nanjing, where they massacre an estimated two hundred thousand civilians in what becomes known as the **RAPE OF NANJING**. Although Communist and Nationalist forces temporarily halt their civil war [October 15, 1934] and join together to resist the invasion, the Japanese swiftly occupy China's major southern ports.

MARCH 12, 1938 The night before Austrian voters are scheduled to vote on a proposed union with Germany, Nazi troops cross the border without opposition and force the ***ANSCHLUSS***, or annexation, without a vote. When the vote finally takes place on April 10, 99.7% of those participating cast ballots in favor of Hitler's action.

JUNE 22, 1937 **JOE LOUIS** begins his twelve-year reign as world heavyweight boxing champion when he knocks out James J. Braddock. Louis's one loss came in 1936 to Max Schmeling, whom Adolf Hitler congratulated for proving the superiority of the white race. In 1938, in a much-publicized rematch, Louis knocks out Hitler's German superman in the first round.

# Jesse Owens

## Triumph at the Berlin Olympics

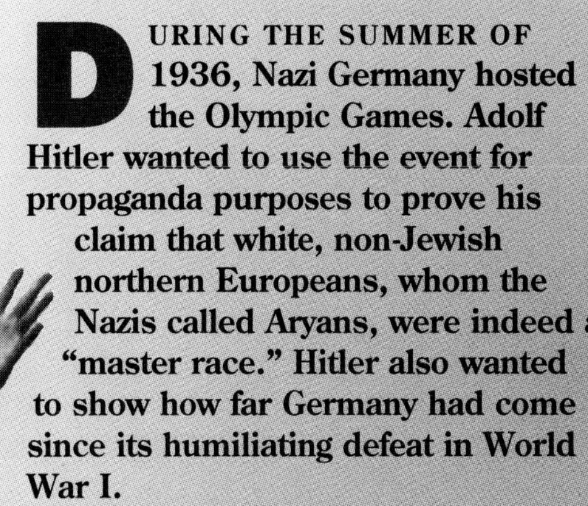

**DURING THE SUMMER OF 1936, Nazi Germany hosted the Olympic Games. Adolf Hitler wanted to use the event for propaganda purposes to prove his claim that white, non-Jewish northern Europeans, whom the Nazis called Aryans, were indeed a "master race." Hitler also wanted to show how far Germany had come since its humiliating defeat in World War I.**

**Hitler believed that German athletic success would impress the rest of the world, and the Nazis did win the most gold medals at the Berlin Olympics. But a young African-American sprinter on the U.S. track team confounded Hitler's racist theories. Twenty-two-year-old Jesse Owens won four gold medals, proving that he was the fastest man in the world. Owens tied an Olympic record in the one-hundred-meter dash and set new world records in the two hundred meters, the long jump, and the four-hundred-meter relay.**

## Politics

JUNE 25, 1938 President Roosevelt signs the **FAIR LABOR STANDARDS ACT**, the last major piece of New Deal legislation. The new law creates a minimum wage that will gradually rise to forty cents an hour. It also shrinks the work week to a maximum of forty hours. As a result, 750,000 workers get instant raises, while 1,500,000 benefit from shorter work hours.

SEPTEMBER 30, 1938 Meeting in Munich, the leaders of Great Britain, France, and Italy agree to allow a German takeover of the Czech Sudetenland. Hitler had demanded the right to "protect" three million Germans living there. Afterward, British prime minister Neville Chamberlain declares "Peace in our time." But the real reason for his **APPEASEMENT** of Hitler is fear of war with Nazi Germany.

NOVEMBER 9–10, 1938 After a Jew kills a Nazi official in Paris, propaganda chief Joseph Goebbels unleashes ***KRISTALLNACHT***, or the Night of Broken Glass. During the rioting, 7,500 Jewish businesses, synagogues, and homes are looted and burned, and the streets are filled with glass from broken windows. Afterward, the Nazis arrest thirty thousand Jews and ship them to concentration camps.

## Life in the Great Depression

OCTOBER 30, 1938 A Halloween radio broadcast of **"THE WAR OF THE WORLDS,"** based on H.G. Wells's science-fiction masterpiece, sparks a nationwide panic when listeners come to believe that Martians are actually landing in New Jersey. Performed by Orson Welles's Mercury Theater of the Air, the realistic drama makes the twenty-three-year-old Welles an instant celebrity.

APRIL 9, 1939 **MARIAN ANDERSON** performs a free Easter morning concert at the Lincoln Memorial in Washington, D.C. The Daughters of the American Revolution had earlier denied her permission to sing at Constitution Hall because she is black. When First Lady Eleanor Roosevelt heard about the incident, she resigned from the organization and used her influence to arrange another site.

## Arts & Entertainment

1939 John Steinbeck's ***THE GRAPES OF WRATH*** calls attention to the plight of migrant families who have left the Dust Bowl for the promise of a better life in California. Steinbeck based his novel on experiences he had while traveling with Okies just like the fictional Joad clan. In California, however, instead of "pastures of plenty," Steinbeck found poverty, violence, and despair.

1939 **GRANDMA MOSES** becomes a household name after the Museum of Modern Art in New York City exhibits her primitive paintings of simple country life. Previously unknown, the seventy-nine-year-old Anna Mary Robertson Moses started painting only three years ago, when her arthritis no longer permitted her to practice her favorite hobby, embroidery.

## Science & Technology

1939 Radio pioneer Edwin Armstrong spends more than three hundred thousand dollars of his own money constructing the world's first **FM RADIO STATION**. Armstrong's new system uses frequency modulation (FM) instead of amplitude modification (AM), thereby reducing static and providing a clearer sound.

**"THE WAR OF THE WORLDS" • To make the terror of a Martian landing seem real, Orson Welles divided his radio play into four segments, interrupting the CBS radio network's regular music programming.**

MARCH 28, 1939 The fall of Madrid to Franco's troops ends the bloody **SPANISH CIVIL WAR** [July 17, 1936], which has taken an estimated half a million lives. In the months that follow, Franco's fascist Falangist party establishes tyrannical rule over the exhausted country.

MAY 22, 1939 Hitler and Mussolini agree to the **PACT OF STEEL**, which strengthens the alliance between Nazi Germany and fascist Italy. The two countries commit themselves to mutual defense—or offense, as the case may be. "He's quite mad," Mussolini comments after his first face-to-face meeting with Hitler, "[but he] might do good business cheaply."

AUGUST 23, 1939 Foreign ministers Joachim von Ribbentrop and V.M. Molotov stun the world when they announce the signing of a **GERMAN-SOVIET NONAGGRESSION PACT**. They keep secret, however, the section that outlines how Poland will be divided after a German invasion. The pact relieves Hitler of the need to fight the western Europeans and the Soviets at the same time.

1939 Pocket Books begins publishing **PAPERBACKS** in the United States, offering inexpensive editions of classic literature for as little as twenty-five cents each. Paperbacks first appeared in Britain in 1936, where they were published by Penguin Books and sold in F.W. Woolworth's five-and-dime stores [1912].

# DAVID DUBINSKY

## The Rise of the ILGWU

**In 1936, the ILGWU purchased a New York CIty theater, where it began to put on productions featuring union members. The most popular of these Labor Stage productions was *Pins and Needles*, which became so successful that the cast was invited to perform at the White House.**

IN 1908, THE GOVERNMENT of Tsar Nicholas II banished sixteen-year-old David Dubinsky to Siberia because of his work organizing labor unions in Russia. Three years later, Dubinsky escaped to the United States, where he took a job as a garment cutter in New York City. It was not long before Dubinsky found himself once again fighting for workers' rights.

Dubinsky's career as a labor organizer entered its most productive period in 1932 when he became president of the International Ladies Garment Workers Union. Soon after taking office, Dubinsky led a series of strikes that paralyzed the clothing industry. Seventy thousand workers walked off their jobs, but their efforts won better wages, improved working conditions, and shorter working hours. Under Dubinsky's leadership, the ILGWU grew from a small, debt-ridden group of forty-five thousand into a powerful international union representing nearly half a million people.

Dubinsky also believed that unions should do more than fight for better wages. Under his direction, the ILGWU became one of the first trade unions to establish a pension fund, health centers, and education programs for its members.

DURING THE GREAT DEPRESSION, few Americans cared much about foreign affairs. People focused on the crisis at home and paid little attention to events around the world. Even as economic conditions improved, many people remained isolationist. Some thought economic problems in Europe had "infected" the U.S. economy and caused its collapse. Others just did not like foreigners.

Their opinion was not shared by President Franklin Roosevelt, who grew increasingly concerned during the 1930s with the rise of fascism in Germany, Italy, and Japan. At first, he refrained from publicly challenging the isolationists. But once war broke out in Europe in 1939, he moved the nation firmly behind Great Britain and the other Allies.

When the United States entered the war itself after the Japanese attack on Pearl Harbor in Hawaii, the country mobilized fully for war. Women joined the work force as never before to fill jobs traditionally held by men, who were now serving in the armed forces. Meanwhile, the government rationed both food and many vital raw materials.

★

# World War II

## Politics

SEPTEMBER 1, 1939 World War II begins when **GERMANY INVADES POLAND**. More than a million German soldiers overrun western Poland in a *Blitzkrieg*, or "lightning war." Honoring a mutual defense treaty, Britain and France declare war on Germany on September 3. Two weeks later, in keeping with the German-Soviet pact [August 23, 1939], Soviet troops invade Poland from the east.

MAY 10, 1940 Following up the April 9 occupation of Denmark and Norway, the Germans begin their long-awaited **OFFENSIVE AGAINST FRANCE**. Rather than attack across the heavily defended Maginot Line, which the French built along their German border after World War I, German tanks invade from the north through Belgium and the Netherlands.

MAY 26–JUNE 4, 1940 Unable to stop the German advance, the British stage an emergency evacuation from the French port of **DUNKIRK**. When German bombing cuts off the harbor, the British navy calls on fishing boats, yachts, and other small craft to ferry troops from the beaches. The operation rescues 338,000 soldiers, but vast amounts of badly needed supplies are left behind.

## Life during World War II

OCTOBER 29, 1940 Secretary of War Henry Stimson randomly draws number 158, beginning the first **PEACETIME DRAFT** in U.S. history. A bill passed by Congress on September 16 had required young men between the ages of twenty-one and thirty-six to register with the Selective Service System. Nearly one million draftees are called up this year for military service.

1940 The promotion of Benjamin O. Davis to brigadier general makes him the **FIRST AFRICAN-AMERICAN GENERAL**. Davis began his long military career in 1899, when he dropped out of Howard University to enlist in the army.

## Arts & Entertainment

1940 Novelist Ernest Hemingway's ***FOR WHOM THE BELL TOLLS*** tells the timely story of an idealistic young American fighting on the Loyalist side during the Spanish Civil War [July 17, 1936]. Based on his own experiences with the Loyalists, Hemingway's best-selling book appeals to Americans concerned with the events unfolding in Europe.

1940 Thirty-two-year-old Richard Wright publishes his first novel, ***NATIVE SON***. Its success makes him a leading spokesman for the African-American community. The novel's main character, Bigger Thomas, is a young black man who accidentally kills his white employer. The shocking story of Bigger's escape, capture, and murder presents a rarely shown view of black life in America.

**ADOLF HITLER IN PARIS • The German dictator visits occupied Paris.**

## Science & Technology

MAY 15, 1940 Igor Sikorsky makes the first successful **HELICOPTER** flight in the United States. The Russian-born inventor flies the VS-300, an experimental machine designed by Sikorsky and manufactured by the Vought-Sikorsky Corporation. An improved version of the VS-300, the R-4, joins the war effort in 1942, when it goes into mass production.

APRIL 5, 1941 The Germans test the first **JET FIGHTER PLANE** just one month ahead of the British. Built by German engineer Ernst Heinkel, the He 280 edges out the British Gloster E28/29 designed by Frank Whittle. Jet fighters remain experimental until 1944, when the Gloster Meteor and the Messerschmitt Me 262 begin active service.

APRIL 1941 Workers at Henry J. Kaiser's California shipyard lay the first keel for a **LIBERTY SHIP**. Already famous for completing the Boulder Dam two years ahead of schedule [October 1936], Kaiser turns to shipbuilding to help the war effort. His pre-fabrication and assembly-line techniques cut the construction time for a cargo ship from twenty-seven to about four and a half days.

JUNE 14, 1940 Victorious **GERMAN TROOPS ENTER PARIS** and march down the Champs-Elysées. They intentionally mimic a November 1918 parade that celebrated the French victory over Germany in World War I. Two days later, after the resignation of French premier Paul Reynaud, World War I hero Philippe Pétain forms a new government and settles for peace on German terms.

JUNE 28, 1940 Passage of the Alien Registration Act, also known as the **SMITH ACT**, requires all foreigners living in the United States to register with the government and be fingerprinted. The Smith Act also makes it illegal for any person to encourage the overthrow of the U.S. government.

SEPTEMBER 7–NOVEMBER 2, 1940 German planes bomb London for fifty-seven consecutive nights, marking the peak of the **BATTLE OF BRITAIN**. The Luftwaffe's daily raids against both military and civilian targets are supposed to lower British morale and weaken resistance to a planned German invasion.

1940 Forrest Mars and Bruce Murrie of the Mars company develop **M&M CANDIES** for the U.S. Army. These candy-coated chocolates that "melt in your mouth, not in your hands" are perfect for soldiers in the field, who cannot afford to let their hands or weapons become sticky.

# Jitterbugging

## THE NEW DANCE CRAZE

Dancers showed off wild airborne steps, which included the man swinging his partner over his head and between his legs.

DURING THE 1940s, THE jitterbug was all the rage, and young Americans poured into dance halls to show off their fancy footwork. This energetic, athletic dance first became popular in black nightclubs during the Roaring Twenties, but it took ten years for the craze to penetrate the white teenage culture.

Typical jitterbuggers of the World War II years were young girls called "bobby-soxers." They wore white socks that came up just above their ankles, saddle shoes, and heavy makeup to look older. They danced the jitterbug in ballrooms and canteens where soldiers home on leave often went for entertainment.

In 1936, when Benny Goodman's band performed at the Paramount Theater in New York City, youngsters jitterbugged in the aisles. They created such a commotion that the fire department was called in. The excitement made newspaper headlines across the country.

Many older people disapproved of the new dance because they thought it was too physical and uninhibited. But they could do little to stop it, and the craze soon became an international phenomenon when U.S servicemen began dancing the jitterbug in England and Europe.

## Politics

SEPTEMBER 27, 1940 In Berlin, representatives of the Axis nations—Germany, Italy, and Japan—sign the **TRIPARTITE PACT**, which joins them in a ten-year military alliance. The agreement is primarily designed to keep the United States neutral and out of the war.

NOVEMBER 5, 1940 Democrat Franklin Roosevelt defeats Indiana Republican Wendell Willkie in the **1940 PRESIDENTIAL ELECTION**. This victory wins Roosevelt a third term in the White House. Until now, no president had served more than two terms. The approach of war hindered Willkie's campaign, as well as the fact that he agreed with the president on most major issues.

NOVEMBER 26, 1940 Describing the move as a health measure, German troops begin enclosing the Jewish neighborhood in Warsaw, Poland. When Jews from surrounding areas are moved there, the population of the **WARSAW GHETTO** swells to more than half a million. Soon the Germans begin shipping Jews every day to Treblinka, where 312,000 people die in the camp's gas chambers during 1942 alone.

## Life during World War II

JUNE 25, 1941 With black union organizer A. Philip Randolph threatening a march on Washington, D.C., President Roosevelt issues Executive Order 8802 **BANNING DISCRIMINATION AGAINST WORKERS** in defense industries because of their race or religion. Three weeks later, Roosevelt establishes the Fair Employment Practices Commission to carry out the policy.

JULY 17, 1941 Cleveland Indians pitchers Al Smith and Jim Bagby combine to end **JOE DIMAGGIO'S FIFTY-SIX-GAME HITTING STREAK**. During the record streak, the Yankees' Hall-of-Fame centerfielder hit .408. Just a year later, however, DiMaggio and many other major leaguers leave professional baseball for military service.

DECEMBER 27, 1941 After the Japanese navy cuts off rubber imports from Asia, the federal government announces the beginning of **RUBBER RATIONING**. This action limits the use of rubber in civilian life. The hastily organized Office of Price Administration later organizes programs for rationing gasoline, coffee, sugar, and shoes as well.

## Arts & Entertainment

1940 Walt Disney follows up the success of *Snow White and the Seven Dwarfs* [December 1937] with an even more ambitious animated film. Disney's ***FANTASIA*** combines cartoon visuals with classical music conducted by Leopold Stokowski. Screenings of the film feature the innovative (and hugely expensive) Fantasound multispeaker system, which plays the first crude examples of stereo recording.

1940 The Museum of Modern Art in New York City becomes the first major art museum to establish a separate department for **PHOTOGRAPHY**. The diverse images in the collection, which the museum began in 1935, include the work of journalists and amateurs as well as artists. By devoting a department to the medium, the museum speeds photography's acceptance as a new art form.

## Science & Technology

JUNE 28, 1941 Following Albert Einstein's advice [August 2, 1939], President Roosevelt creates the Office of Scientific Research and Development to supervise U.S. weapons research. Chief among its programs is the top-secret **MANHATTAN PROJECT**, which Roosevelt charges with developing an atomic bomb.

**ALBERT EINSTEIN • He called the potential of a Nazi bomb a "danger threatening all of humanity."**

1941 Lyle Goodhue and W.N. Sullivan develop the first disposable **AEROSOL CANS**, which they use to spray insecticide. The cans hold both the insect-killing liquid and a pressurized propellant. Decades later, scientists discover that these propellants, called chlorofluorocarbons, may be the cause of dangerous holes in the ozone layer of the earth's atmosphere.

DECEMBER 29, 1940 Speaking about the war during a Fireside Chat [March 12, 1933], President Roosevelt warns that "all our present efforts are not enough." Instead, "we must be the great **ARSENAL OF DEMOCRACY**." Although remaining formally neutral, Roosevelt commits the country to the Allied cause. He calls his policy "nonbelligerence" because it stops short of sending troops.

MARCH 11, 1941 President Roosevelt signs the **LEND-LEASE ACT**, which authorizes the transfer of war supplies to U.S. allies overseas. The new law gives Roosevelt the power to arm Britain, China, and later the Soviet Union in exchange for payments that can be put off until the end of the war. Altogether, Lend-Lease aid during the war tops fifty billion dollars.

JUNE 22, 1941 Hitler orders the **GERMAN INVASION OF THE SOVIET UNION** less than two years after agreeing not to attack [August 23, 1939]. The Nazis had originally scheduled Operation Barbarossa for 1943, but Hitler moves it up to intimidate Britain and discourage U.S. intervention in the war. Hitler expects Soviet defenses to fall within a few weeks.

FEBRUARY 10, 1942 The last new car rolls off the assembly line at Ford as automobile makers shift over to the exclusive production of **JEEPS, TANKS, AND OTHER WAR-RELATED VEHICLES**. Nationwide, the federal Office of Production Management begins to regulate the manufacture of items it considers nonessential to the war effort.

# PEARL HARBOR

## *The United States Enters the War*

**AT 7:58 A.M. ON DECEMBER 7, 1941, navy radios in Hawaii received this emergency message: "ENEMY AIR RAID. PEARL HARBOR. THIS IS NOT A DRILL." Three minutes earlier, Japanese warplanes had begun dive-bombing the U.S. Pacific fleet moored in Pearl Harbor. At nearby Hickam Field, Japanese bombers wiped out more than half the U.S. fighter planes while they were still on the ground.**

**Relations between the two countries had been steadily worsening since 1937, when Japan invaded southern China. In July 1941, two days after Japan seized French Indochina, the United States froze all Japanese assets in this country. On December 6, the U.S. ambassador delivered a personal note from President Roosevelt to Emperor Hirohito, but the plea for peace was too late.**

**On Monday, December 8, Roosevelt asked Congress for a declaration of war. Meanwhile, the Japanese were already attacking U.S. bases in the Philippines. Emperor Hirohito and his generals believed that the Pearl Harbor raid had so crippled the U.S. fleet that it could no longer challenge Japan's conquest of Asia.**

**The surprise attack on Pearl Harbor, which lasted less than two hours, destroyed six battleships and killed more than two thousand soldiers and sailors.**

## Politics

AUGUST 14, 1941 After a secret five-day meeting at sea off Newfoundland, President Franklin Roosevelt and British prime minister Winston Churchill issue the **ATLANTIC CHARTER**. This eight-point document outlines common war goals and the principles upon which peace should be based. These principles will later be incorporated into the charter for the United Nations.

JANUARY 20, 1942 Top-level Nazi bureaucrats meet in the quiet Berlin suburb of Wannsee to discuss the details of Hitler's **FINAL SOLUTION** to the "Jewish problem." The group works out such practical issues as where death camps should be located, how Jews will be transported there, and what extermination methods are the most efficient.

MARCH 11, 1942 **"I SHALL RETURN,"** General Douglas MacArthur vows as he leaves the Philippines for Australia. Following the landing of Japanese troops on December 10, MacArthur led the U.S. retreat from Manila to the islands of Bataan and Corregidor outside Manila Bay. Although MacArthur has been ordered to leave, the U.S. troops on Bataan and Corregidor continue to hold out.

## Life during World War II

FEBRUARY 20, 1942 The hysteria caused by the Japanese attack on Pearl Harbor provokes President Roosevelt to order the **INTERNMENT OF JAPANESE AMERICANS** living along the strategic California coastline. Executive Order 9066 authorizes the removal of some 110,000 people of Japanese ancestry to detention camps, even though two-thirds of them were born in this country.

MAY 14, 1942 Congress establishes the Women's Auxiliary Army Corps, which enlists women to perform noncombat duties at home and overseas. On July 30, another act of Congress establishes the Women Accepted for Voluntary Emergency Services. **WAACS AND WAVES** become the first women to serve officially in the U.S. military.

**WAACS AND WAVES • Over 350,000 women served in the U.S. armed forces during World War II.**

## Arts & Entertainment

NOVEMBER 1, 1941 Eight months after sculptor Gutzon Borglum's death, workers finish the last of the drilling on **MOUNT RUSHMORE** in the Black Hills of South Dakota. After Borglum's death, the sculptor's son, Lincoln, supervised the completion of the project. It took sixteen years to carve four presidential portraits into the mountain's face.

1941 Propelled by the success of his "War of the Worlds" broadcast [October 30, 1938], Orson Welles writes, directs, and stars in his feature-film debut, which features members of his Mercury Players. Loosely based on the life of publisher William Randolph Hearst, ***CITIZEN KANE*** tells the story of a newspaper magnate corrupted by power.

## Science & Technology

1941 For the first time, major U.S. drug companies begin to produce the "miracle drug" **PENICILLIN** in large quantities. The scientists responsible for developing penicillin [1928] are nearly all British, but wartime conditions in England make it impossible to manufacture the drug there.

DECEMBER 2, 1942 Manhattan Project scientists [June 28, 1941] under Italian-born physicist Enrico Fermi produce the first controlled, self-sustaining **NUCLEAR CHAIN REACTION** in a secret laboratory under the University of Chicago football stadium. Fermi's work proves the atom is indeed a potentially limitless source of power.

1942 Howard Hughes and Henry J. Kaiser form a partnership to build huge flying boats. These "flying box cars," holding up to 750 passengers, would resemble airborne versions of Kaiser's Liberty ships [April 1941]. Hughes and Kaiser spend twenty million dollars to build a single prototype, the ***SPRUCE GOOSE***, which Hughes flies once in November 1947 to prove that it works.

APRIL 9, 1942 Despite a heroic effort, the U.S. and Filipino forces on Bataan finally surrender. The following morning, Japanese soldiers force their prisoners to walk sixty-three miles to a prisoner-of-war camp. The infamous **BATAAN DEATH MARCH** kills as many as ten thousand of the seventy thousand captives. Later, many more die of starvation and disease in the camps.

APRIL 18, 1942 Colonel James H. Doolittle leads a squadron of B-25s in a bombing mission over Tokyo. The raid surprises the Japanese almost as much as their attack on Pearl Harbor surprised the Americans. Performing a feat that Japanese admirals thought impossible, **DOOLITTLE'S RAIDERS** take off from the deck of the aircraft carrier *Hornet*, landing nearly two thousand miles later in China.

JUNE 3–6, 1942 The pivotal battle of **MIDWAY** begins when U.S. dive bombers sweep down on a huge Japanese fleet near Midway Island in the North Pacific. During three days of intensive fighting, the Japanese fleet suffers heavy damage, including the loss of its four aircraft carriers and most of its best fighter pilots.

JUNE 13–17, 1942 German submarines, known as U-boats, set eight **SABOTEURS** ashore off New York and Florida beaches. After the FBI captures them easily, a military court tries and convicts them as spies. Six are executed on August 8.

# THE HOME FRONT

**FOR CIVILIANS WHO REMAINED on the Home Front, World War II was a time of great shortages. Food was often hard to come by, and so were many of the materials used to make common consumer goods. Rubber, tin, and aluminum, for example, were among the raw materials controlled by the government. All available supplies were set aside for military uses, including the construction of new planes and tanks. When rubber companies stopped making automobile tires, people had to patch and repatch their old ones. As the war went on, many more items were added to the list of controlled goods.**

**On May 14, 1942, Americans received their first War Ration Books, which limited each of them to one pound of sugar every two weeks. Families soon needed coupons to buy butter, coffee, and meat as well. To ease these food shortages, the government encouraged people to plant vegetable gardens in their backyards and even on city rooftops. By the end of the war, twenty million "victory gardens" produced about forty percent of the country's vegetables.**

**Not all Americans served in the armed forces during World War II, but every citizen was asked to contribute to the war effort. Rubber drives made up for supplies that used to come from Asia. VIctory gardens grew food that made up for rations sent overseas.**

## Politics

SEPTEMBER 1942 Two German armies join together for an assault on the Soviet stronghold of **STALINGRAD**. At one point, the Germans raise a swastika over the city's Communist party headquarters, but determined Soviet defenders push them back. The brutal five-month fight for Stalingrad costs the Germans four hundred thousand men and, soon enough, the war in eastern Europe.

NOVEMBER 7–8, 1942 Allied troops under the command of U.S. general Dwight D. Eisenhower land in North Africa as part of **OPERATION TORCH**, the Allies' first joint offensive of the war. More than one hundred thousand British and U.S. soldiers splash ashore near Casablanca, Oran, and Algiers before heading east to engage German general Erwin Rommel's Afrika Corps.

APRIL 19–MAY 16, 1943 In the Warsaw Ghetto [November 26, 1940], Polish Jews, armed with just a dozen pistols, begin resisting deportation to the Treblinka death camp. The **WARSAW GHETTO UPRISING** at first surprises the Germans, but overwhelming reinforcements quickly crush the rebellion, killing at least seven thousand Jews and sending fifty thousand more to Treblinka.

## Life during World War II

JUNE 17, 1942 The phrase ***G.I. JOE*** appears for the first time in the debut issue of the army newspaper *Yank* in a cartoon by Lieutenant Dave Gerger. The name is supposed to refer to the average infantry soldier, or grunt. The initials stand for *government issue*, two words that were often stenciled onto crates of army supplies.

**GLENN MILLER • A plane carrying the bandleader from England to France in December 1944 disappeared in bad weather. No trace was ever found.**

## Arts & Entertainment

1941 H.H. Rey and his wife, Margaret, publish ***CURIOUS GEORGE*** one year after fleeing their native France. The Reys, who escaped from Paris by bicycle just before the city fell to the Germans, eventually made their way to the United States. Their work becomes so popular that the misadventures of the curious monkey named George and the man in the yellow hat continue in six sequels.

FEBRUARY 10, 1942 To commemorate sales of more than one million copies of "Chattanooga Choo-Choo," RCA-Victor gives band leader **GLENN MILLER** the first "gold record," a gold-plated copy of the disk. Miller soon disbands his own orchestra and forms an army band that will broadcast to Allied troops worldwide.

DECEMBER 31, 1942 Twenty-seven-year-old singer **FRANK SINATRA** makes his solo debut at the Paramount Theater in New York. Sinatra's fans, particularly the young women in the audience, become so excited that they almost cause a riot. Many faint at the sight of the handsome blue-eyed crooner.

## Science & Technology

JANUARY 15, 1943 Completion of the **PENTAGON**, the largest office building in the world, brings the entire War Department together under a single roof. Located on thirty-four acres in a Virginia suburb of Washington, D.C., the five-sided building is so huge that messengers have to use motorized golf carts to travel its seventeen miles of corridors.

1943 In collaboration with engineer Emile Gagnan, French naval officer Jacques Yves Cousteau invents the **AQUALUNG**. Cousteau's device allows divers to swim underwater without being connected to air tanks on the surface. Cousteau and Gagnan's major technological breakthrough is the demand valve, which supplies compressed air as needed through the aqualung's mouthpiece.

1944 Oswald Avery and his colleagues at the Rockefeller Institute Hospital in New York City show that the genetic material of all living things is made up of deoxyribonucleic acid, or **DNA**.

**JUNE 22, 1944** President Roosevelt signs the Servicemen's Readjustment Act, commonly known as the **G.I. BILL OF RIGHTS**. This new law, designed to ease their transition into civilian life, provides millions of returning veterans with low-interest housing loans and generous college scholarships.

**JULY 20, 1944** As part of a **PLOT TO KILL HITLER**, German colonel Claus von Stauffenberg plants a bomb at Hitler's headquarters in Rastenburg. After surviving the blast, Hitler orders the death of five thousand alleged conspirators, including Erwin Rommel. Because of his status as Germany's greatest war hero, Rommel is spared a firing squad and allowed to commit suicide on October 14.

**OCTOBER 20, 1944** With film crews rolling, General Douglas **MACARTHUR RETURNS TO THE PHILIPPINES**, as he promised he would [March 11, 1942]. MacArthur arrives at the start of the battle for Leyte Gulf, during which the Japanese begin to use kamikaze, or suicide, pilots. Kamikazes crash their aircraft into U.S. ships, hoping to sink them.

**JUNE 22, 1942** A transport plane carries the first Victory mail, or **V-MAIL**, from New York to London. V-mail drastically reduces bulky mail shipments by microfilming individual letters and then shipping the microfilm. The letters are then reprinted for delivery. V-mail quickly becomes a part of daily life for U.S. personnel overseas.

# THE D-DAY INVASION

ON JUNE 6, 1944, ALLIED TROOPS began the D-Day invasion of German-occupied France. During the night, five thousand troop ships carried more than 150,000 U.S., British, and Canadian soldiers across the English Channel. As dawn approached, the first landing craft reached the heavily fortified beaches of Normandy.

The invasion, which was the largest ever mounted, actually began about one in the morning when transport planes dropped two divisions of U.S. paratroopers behind enemy lines. High winds scattered the units, but their presence in France, more than their fighting ability, confused the German troops.

View from a landing craft approaching the Normandy coast.

Allied commander-in-chief Dwight Eisenhower had used false intelligence reports and phony troop movements to convince Hitler that the Allies would attack north at Calais. When the massive attack came at Normandy instead, the Germans were not as prepared as they might have been.

Allied casualties were heaviest at Omaha Beach, where more than two thousand Americans died on D-Day. In fact, the invasion troops might have been pushed back into the sea had the Germans on the bluff above the beach been reinforced. Instead, all five beachheads were secured by the end of the first day, giving the Allies their crucial foothold in Europe.

U.S. soldiers storming the beach to carry out the D-Day invasion

## Politics

DECEMBER 16, 1944 As Allied forces regroup before advancing into Germany, Hitler orders a last-gasp counterattack that becomes known as the **BATTLE OF THE BULGE**. The tank offensive through the Ardennes forest in Belgium surprises the Allies and punches a bulge in their lines. The battle ends when General George Patton's Third Army stops the German advance and forces a retreat.

FEBRUARY 4–11, 1945 Now that Germany's defeat seems close, the Big Three meet at the Soviet resort of **YALTA** to debate the future of Europe. Although Roosevelt and Churchill want to hold free elections in Poland, Stalin insists on setting up a postwar government that he can control. Critics later charge that Roosevelt, obviously in poor health, gave in too much to Stalin.

FEBRUARY 23, 1945 Joe Rosenthal of the Associated Press snaps a picture of six Marines raising the U.S. flag over Mount Suribachi on the Pacific island of **IWO JIMA**. The Pulitzer Prize–winning image actually shows a reenactment of the flag raising. The battle for Iwo Jima is not yet over, however, and three of the men pictured die later in the fighting.

## Life during World War II

1942 The Wrigley Company begins making **K RATIONS** for the army. These emergency food supplies become notorious for their awful taste. Each package contains biscuits, canned meat, sugar pills, four cigarettes, and a stick of Wrigley's chewing gum. The breakfast ration includes water-soluble coffee that General Foods later introduces to the public as Maxwell House Instant Coffee.

JUNE 14, 1943 The Supreme Court rules that **SCHOOLCHILDREN CANNOT BE FORCED TO SALUTE THE U.S. FLAG** if such a salute conflicts with their religious beliefs. The decision comes in the case of *West Virginia Board of Education v. Barnette*, which involves a member of the Jehovah's Witnesses.

JUNE 20–22, 1943 **RACE RIOTS ERUPT IN DETROIT**, where three hundred thousand black and white Southerners have moved to compete for jobs in defense plants. Thirty-five people are killed and more than six hundred wounded before federal troops restore order. Racial tensions also boil over this summer in Los Angeles and New York City.

## Arts & Entertainment

MARCH 31, 1943 The Richard Rodgers–Oscar Hammerstein musical ***OKLAHOMA!*** opens at the St. James Theater on Broadway in New York City and easily becomes the most popular show of the year. *Oklahoma!* breaks new ground in the musical theater by incorporating lyrics into the plot as though they were spoken lines.

**OKLAHOMA • The hit musical's carefree innocence appealed to many war-weary audiences.**

1943 Hip urban young men begin wearing oversize suits with trousers that narrow down to tight cuffs around the ankles. The baggy **ZOOT SUITS** are particularly useful for dancing the jitterbug and other popular dances that involve jumping and spinning. Some sociologists claim zoot suits got their start when teenagers began wearing clothing left behind by older family members gone to war.

## Science & Technology

1944 Harvard University mathematician Howard Aiken designs the first digital computer. Built with a five-hundred-million-dollar grant from IBM, the thirty-five-ton **MARK I COMPUTER** can find the product of two eleven-digit numbers in just three seconds.

1944 Hungarian-born mathematician John von Neumann and German-born economist Oskar Morgenstern publish *Theory of Games and Economic Behavior*. This ground-breaking work explains how mathematical equations can be used to model decision-making processes and turn them into games. **GAME THEORY** quickly becomes essential in the development of advanced computers.

**April 12, 1945** Only four months into his fourth term, **FRANKLIN ROOSEVELT DIES** of a brain hemorrhage in Warm Springs, Georgia. Vice President Harry Truman succeeds him. Roosevelt has kept Truman ignorant of important military secrets, including the atomic bomb. When Truman asks Eleanor Roosevelt if there is anything he can do for her, she says, "You're the one in trouble now."

**April 15, 1945** British soldiers liberating the Bergen-Belsen concentration camp in northern Germany find the first graphic evidence of the **HOLOCAUST**. In addition to the surviving inmates, whom one soldier describes as "walking skeletons," the British find thirty-five thousand corpses.

**April 25–June 26, 1945** Delegates from fifty nations meet in San Francisco to work out the details of the **UNITED NATIONS CHARTER**. The new international organization includes a General Assembly in which every nation has a vote and an eleven-member Security Council with the United States, the Soviet Union, Britain, France, and China as permanent members.



**November 1943** Japanese radio puts the silken-voiced **TOKYO ROSE** on the air. Her English-language broadcasts are intended to discourage U.S. servicemen on duty in the Pacific. Rose often suggests, for example, that their wives are forgetting about them. Some people believe Tokyo Rose is missing aviator Amelia Earhart [July 2, 1937], but she is actually American-born Iva Toguri d'Aquino.

# Rosie the Riveter

## *Women Join the Work Force*

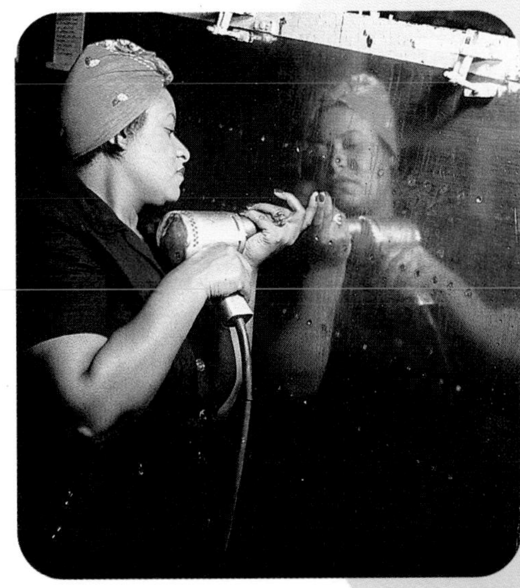

Factory jobs provided women with more money than they had ever earned before and the satisfaction of knowing that they could perform these jobs as well as men.

**Before World War II, less than one-third of American women had jobs outside the home. Those who did were usually poorly paid, working primarily as teachers, nurses, secretaries, and maids. After Pearl Harbor, however, the situation changed dramatically. With the U.S. entry into World War II, millions of working men left their jobs for the armed forces, causing a serious labor shortage. To keep the factories running, five million women joined the labor force. Many of them took jobs in defense industries, where they built airplanes, ships, and other military equipment.**

**To recruit more women for this important work, the federal government created posters that appealed to women's patriotism and their sense of duty. The star of these advertising campaigns was a character named Rosie the Riveter, who worked in a defense factory attaching airplane parts with metal fasteners called rivets.**

**When the war ended and the men returned home, many working women quit their jobs so they could become housewives. Those who did not quit were often fired to make their jobs available for the returning soldiers.**

Politics

APRIL 30, 1945 As Soviet soldiers raise their flag above the Reichstag in Berlin, Adolf Hitler finishes lunch at his bunker beneath the Chancellery and kills himself. His longtime mistress, Eva Braun, whom he had married two days earlier, also commits suicide. The bodies of **HITLER AND BRAUN** are then taken above ground and cremated.

**BEBOP • Jazz trumpeter Dizzy Gillespie explains his new style of improvisational jazz.**

MAY 7, 1945 On Victory-in-Europe Day, the Germans surrender unconditionally to General Dwight D. Eisenhower in Reims, France. Soviet, French, and British officers witness the signing of the surrender papers, which formally end the war in Europe at midnight on May 8. Within a week after **V-E DAY**, U.S. forces in Europe transfer half their planes to the Pacific, where the fighting continues.

Life during World War II

JULY 28, 1945 Early on a foggy Saturday morning, a bomber returning from Europe accidentally flies into the Empire State Building in New York City. The **B-25 CRASH** kills the three men aboard the plane as well as ten people on the streets below. The plane itself becomes lodged between the seventy-eighth and seventy-ninth floors of the skyscraper.

JULY 1945 At the Potsdam conference [July 17–August 2, 1945], Soviet leader Joseph Stalin finds the phrase **"KILROY WAS HERE"** scribbled in a men's washroom. U.S. soldiers have been scrawling Kilroy's name all over the world, including the Arc de Triomphe in Paris, the Marco Polo Bridge in Peking, and wherever G.I.s happen to find themselves with little to do.

Arts & Entertainment

1943 Former presidential candidate Wendell Willkie [November 5, 1940] publishes ***ONE WORLD***, based on his 1942 trips to the Middle East, China, and the Soviet Union as President Roosevelt's personal representative. Willkie's book, which sells one million copies in just two months, argues for the establishment of a postwar peacekeeping organization similar to the United Nations.

1944 The word ***BEBOP*** first comes into the language. It refers to a new style of improvisational jazz music developed by Charlie "Bird" Parker, Dizzy Gillespie, and Thelonius Monk while playing together at Harlem nightclubs in New York City. At first, jazz purists scoff at bebop's unconventional rhythms, but the style quickly gains popularity.

1944 Composer **AARON COPLAND** completes the score for his ballet *Appalachian Spring*, which wins him a Pulitzer Prize. Copland becomes famous for expressing popular American themes, including jazz and folk tunes, in a modern classical style.

Science & Technology

JULY 16, 1945 The Manhattan Project team [June 28, 1941], working under scientific director J. Robert Oppenheimer, tests the first **ATOMIC BOMB** in the New Mexican desert near Alamogordo. The successful experiment lights up the sky for 180 miles around and fuses the sand beneath the tower into glass.

1945 After dental researchers discover that small amounts of fluoride can dramatically reduce tooth decay in children, Grand Rapids, Michigan, begins **FLUORIDATION** of its water supply. The country's first such program sparks controversy when highly conservative citizens charge that the health measure is actually a Communist plot to soften American minds.

FEBRUARY 14, 1946 J. Presper Eckert and John W. Mauchly display **ENIAC**, the first electronic digital computer. ENIAC stands for *E*lectronic *N*umerical *I*ntegrator *a*nd *C*omputer. Filling a thirty- by sixty-foot room with more than nineteen thousand vacuum tubes, ENIAC can perform in just two hours calculations that it would take one hundred engineers a full year to complete.

**July 17–August 2, 1945** Three months into his presidency, Harry Truman meets with Stalin and Churchill in **POTSDAM**, a suburb of Berlin, to plan the occupation of Germany. During one meeting, Truman tells Stalin that the United States has developed an atomic bomb [July 16, 1945]. The conference ends with a joint ultimatum to Japan that it surrender or face "prompt and utter destruction."

**August 6, 1945** When Japan fails to respond to the Potsdam ultimatum, the B-29 bomber *Enola Gay* drops the uranium bomb code-named Little Boy on the Japanese city of **HIROSHIMA**. The explosion kills eighty thousand people and levels four square miles of the city. Three days later, the plutonium bomb code-named Fat Man is dropped on Nagasaki. On August 10, Japan agrees to surrender.

**October 18, 1945** The International Military Tribunal holds its first sessions in Nuremberg, Germany. This multinational court hears the cases of Nazis accused of crimes against humanity. All but three of the original twenty-four defendants in the **NUREMBERG TRIALS** are convicted. Half are sentenced to death by hanging.

**January 1946** "A Major U.S. Problem: Labor" reads the cover of *Life* magazine as **WORKERS AROUND THE NATION GO ON STRIKE** now that the war is over. Two hundred thousand people strike Chicago meat-packing plants. More than eight hundred thousand steel workers walk out in Pittsburgh. Altogether, more than four million workers strike in 1946, the most since 1919.

# Anne Frank

## *A Diary from the Holocaust*

**On her thirteenth birthday, Anne Frank received a diary as a gift from her parents. The date was June 12, 1942. Anne's family was living in the Netherlands, which the Nazis had occupied following the start of World War II. Just two weeks after Anne's birthday, the Germans announced that all Dutch Jews, including the Franks, would be sent to concentration camps.**

**Rather than face almost certain death in the camps, the Franks went into hiding. They made a home for themselves in a secret room at the back of an office building, where friends brought them supplies. For the next two years, the Franks never left the single cramped room.**

**On August 4, 1944, police found their hiding place and deported the Franks to different concentration camps. Only Anne's father survived. After the war, a Dutch friend who had found Anne's diary returned it to her father. The diary, which was published in the United States in 1953, tells the vivid tale of the family's life in hiding. It remains full of hope, humor, and the belief that "people are good at heart" despite the evil things that they do.**

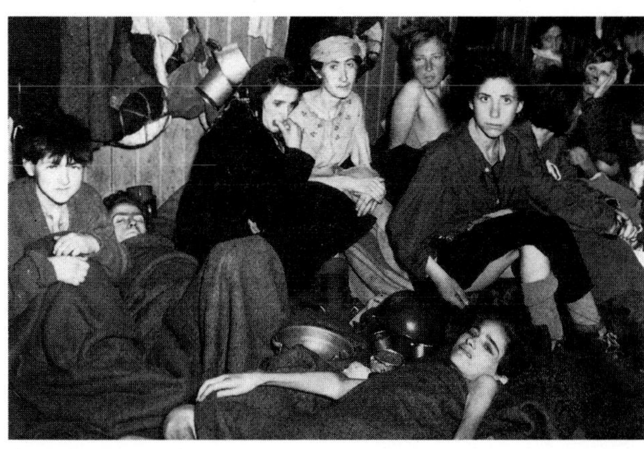

**This photograph was taken at Bergen-Belsen concentration camp in Germany, where Anne died during the spring of 1945, shortly after the death of both her mother and her sister. She was fifteen years old.**

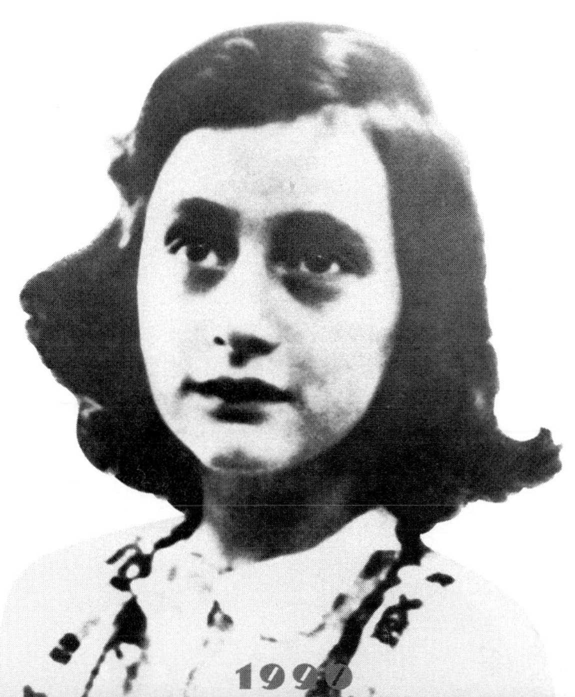

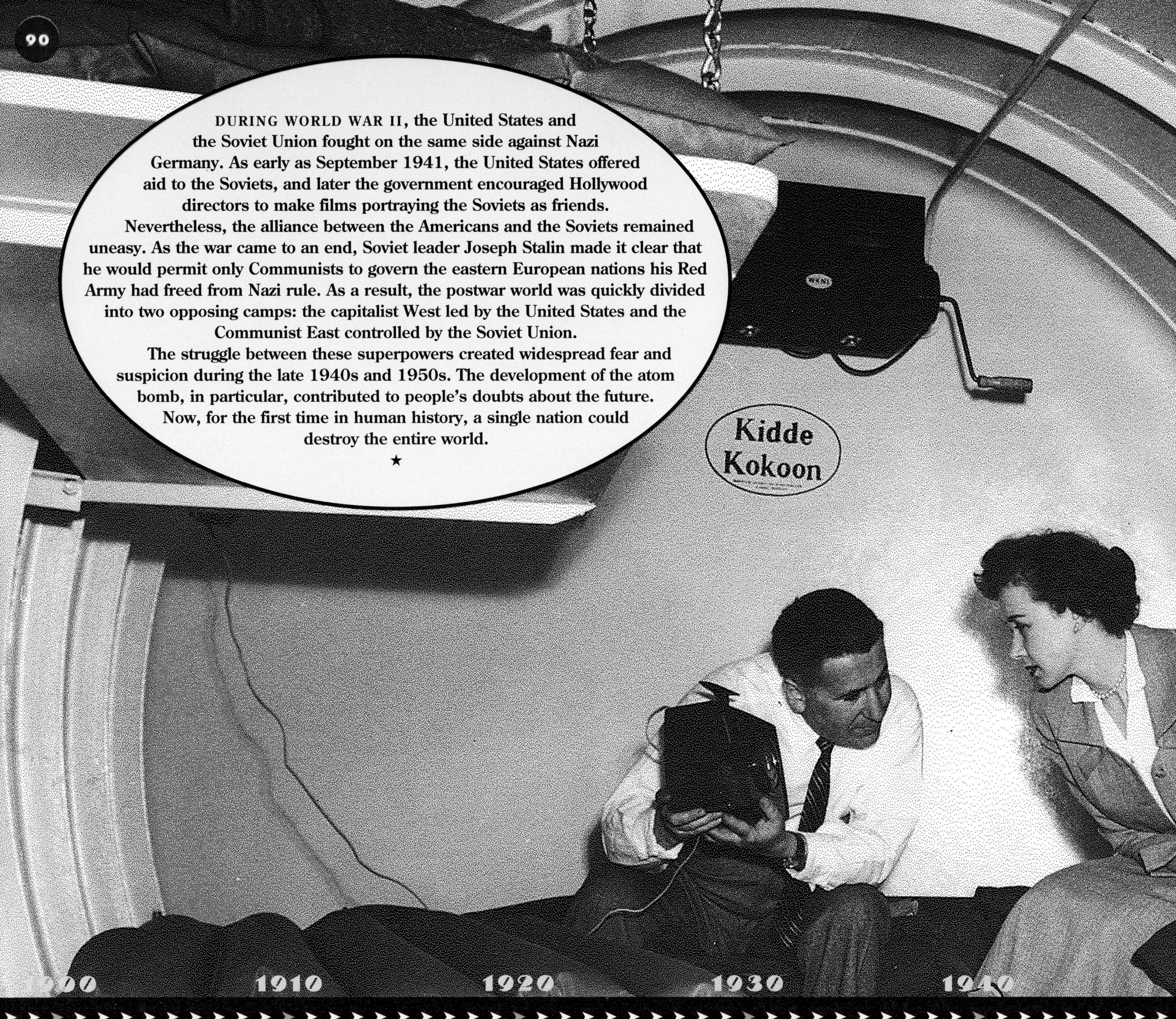


DURING WORLD WAR II, the United States and the Soviet Union fought on the same side against Nazi Germany. As early as September 1941, the United States offered aid to the Soviets, and later the government encouraged Hollywood directors to make films portraying the Soviets as friends.

Nevertheless, the alliance between the Americans and the Soviets remained uneasy. As the war came to an end, Soviet leader Joseph Stalin made it clear that he would permit only Communists to govern the eastern European nations his Red Army had freed from Nazi rule. As a result, the postwar world was quickly divided into two opposing camps: the capitalist West led by the United States and the Communist East controlled by the Soviet Union.

The struggle between these superpowers created widespread fear and suspicion during the late 1940s and 1950s. The development of the atom bomb, in particular, contributed to people's doubts about the future. Now, for the first time in human history, a single nation could destroy the entire world.

★

# The Cold War

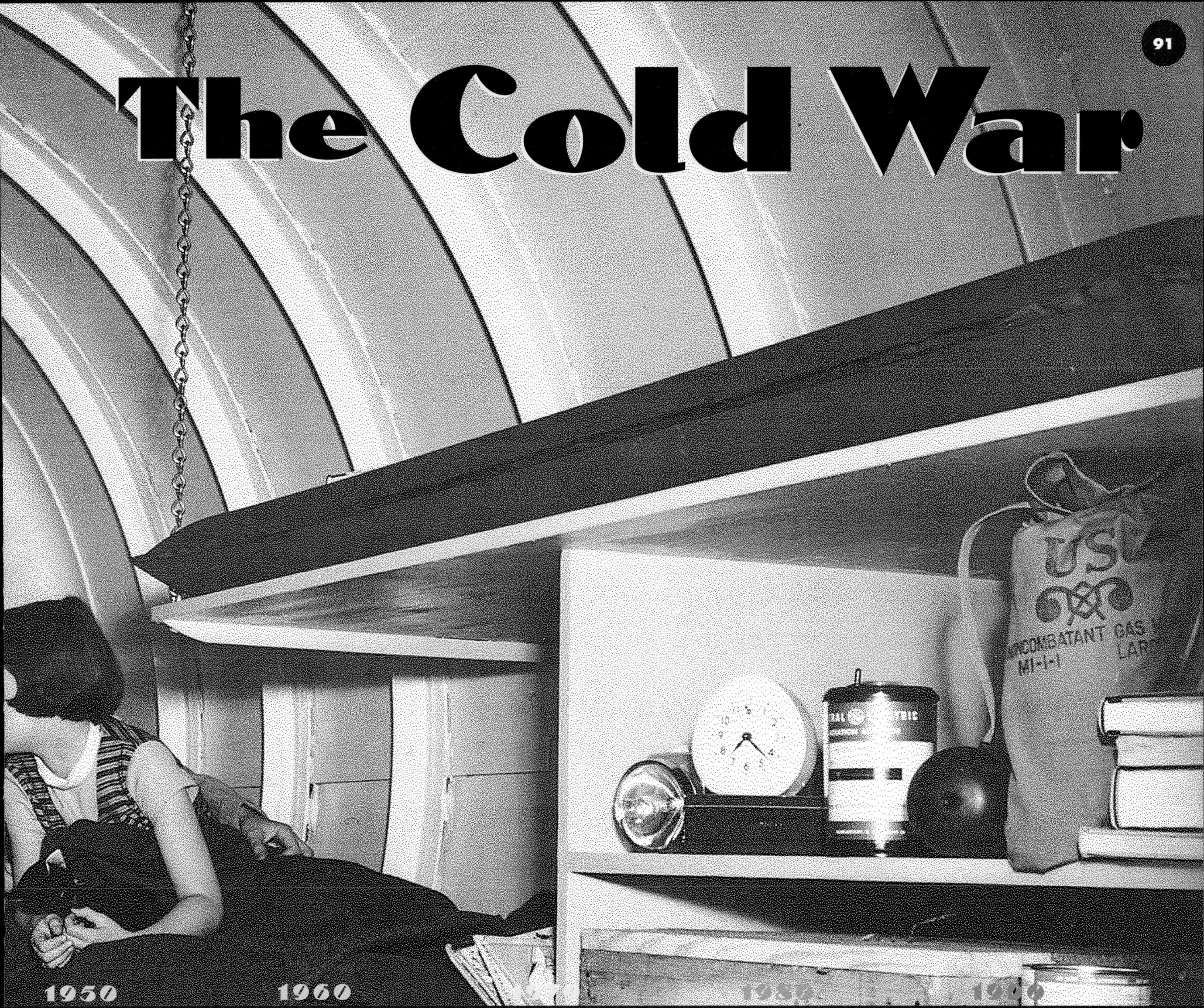

1950 1960 1970 1980 1990

## Politics

MARCH 5, 1946 At a speech in Fulton, Missouri, former British prime minister Winston Churchill calls on Britain and the United States to resist Soviet expansion in eastern Europe. "An iron curtain has descended across the Continent," he declares. Churchill's ***IRON CURTAIN*** phrase soon comes to describe the barrier between the Communist East and the democratic West.

MARCH 12, 1947 President Truman asks Congress to provide four hundred million dollars in aid to Greece and Turkey. Although the governments of both countries treat their people poorly, Truman's main concern is the Communist threat they face. His policy of aiding countries that are threatened by Communist rebellion comes to be known as the **TRUMAN DOCTRINE**.

APRIL 16, 1947 Financier and statesman Bernard Baruch coins the phrase ***COLD WAR*** in a speech before the South Carolina state legislature. "Let us not be deceived," he says in his address on U.S.-Soviet relations. "We are in the midst of a cold war." The phrase comes to mean a clash between nations that remains just below the "hot" stage of actual fighting.

## Life during the Cold War

1947 During World War II, fabric shortages and women's need for work clothes made casual pants and low-heeled shoes fashionable. Now that the war is over, French designer Christian Dior introduces his feminine **NEW LOOK**, which brings back full skirts over crinolines and nipped-in waists.

HIROSHIMA • When the atomic bomb exploded over Hiroshima, many of that city's buildings were instantly destroyed.

JULY 26, 1948 By executive order, President Truman bans racial discrimination in federal hiring and ends **SEGREGATION IN THE ARMED FORCES**. Nearly one million African Americans served during World War II in blacks-only units, which were often given the worst duties, quarters, and supplies.

## Arts & Entertainment

AUGUST 31, 1946 *The New Yorker* magazine devotes an entire issue to John Hersey's report on the Japanese city of Hiroshima one year after the United States dropped an atomic bomb there [August 6, 1945]. Hersey bases his article, later published as the book ***HIROSHIMA***, on extensive interviews with six survivors of the gruesome explosion.

OCTOBER 18, 1947 Congress's House Un-American Activities Committee begins investigating whether Communists have infiltrated Hollywood. When ten witnesses refuse to answer questions about their politics, they are charged with contempt. The movie industry then blacklists the **HOLLYWOOD TEN**, refusing to let them work because of their suspected Communist sympathies.

## Science & Technology

OCTOBER 14, 1947 Flying a top-secret Bell X-1 rocket plane, test pilot Chuck Yeager becomes the first human to break the **SOUND BARRIER**. The twenty-four-year-old air force captain reaches a top speed of seven hundred miles per hour, or sixty miles faster than the speed of sound.

1947 Norwegian anthropologist Thor Heyerdahl sails five thousand miles from Peru to Tahiti aboard the ***KON-TIKI***, a primitive raft he made from balsa wood and rope. Heyerdahl undertakes the difficult 101-day voyage to prove his theory that the South Pacific islands could have been settled by ancient South Americans.

1947 Shepherd boys exploring caves near the Dead Sea discover a jar containing ancient scrolls written around the time of Jesus. These and other **DEAD SEA SCROLLS** found later help scholars date the compilation of the Old Testament, or Hebrew Bible. The authors of the manuscripts were a sect of Jews called Essenes, who were massacred by the Romans in the year A.D. 68.

MAY 3, 1947 A new **JAPANESE CONSTITUTION** takes effect. It eliminates the political power of the emperor, prohibits the use of military force, and gives women the vote. Much credit for these reforms goes to General Douglas MacArthur, commander of the army that has occupied Japan since the end of World War II. MacArthur successfully resisted pressure to create a military government.

JUNE 23, 1947 The Republican-controlled Congress overrides President Truman's veto to pass the **TAFT-HARTLEY ACT**. This bill takes away many of the gains made by labor unions under the New Deal. Responding to a rash of strikes [January 1946], the Taft-Hartley Act makes it more difficult for unions to organize and bans the closed shop, which is a business that hires only union members.

JULY 26, 1947 Congress passes the **NATIONAL SECURITY ACT**, which unifies the armed forces under the Department of Defense and creates the Central Intelligence Agency. Modeled on the wartime Office of Strategic Services, the CIA will coordinate the gathering of intelligence on foreign countries. Although the CIA can spy on other countries, only the FBI can spy legally on Americans.

MAY 31, 1949 Former State Department official **ALGER HISS** goes on trial for lying to a federal grand jury. The grand jury had been investigating Hiss's activities as an alleged Communist spy during the late 1930s. Hiss was indicted after Whittaker Chambers, a confessed Soviet agent, helped investigators retrieve stolen State Department documents said to belong to Hiss.

# The Marshall Plan

## *Rebuilding Europe*

THE RELENTLESS ALLIED bombing of Europe during World War II left the continent in ruins. Apartment buildings and factories where people had lived and worked were now piles of rubble. There was also little food to be had, especially in West Germany, where many people died of starvation. Secretary of State George Marshall worried about Europe's slow recovery from the war. He feared that, without economic aid, all of Europe might fall to Communism.

On June 5, 1947, the former army chief of staff outlined a plan for the rebuilding of Europe. Under the Marshall Plan, the United States would provide nearly fourteen billion dollars' worth of aid during the next four years.

The most controversial part of the plan was the offer of aid to West Germany. France was particularly concerned that a rebuilt Germany might again threaten world peace. In addition, many Americans objected to tax dollars being spent on their defeated enemy. Marshall argued strongly, however, that a weakened West Germany would be vulnerable to the Soviets. In the end, he won the argument.

Economically, the Marshall Plan was a huge success. Between 1947 and 1951, U.S. aid boosted Europe's industrial production by more than forty percent.

Children in London drink orange juice provided by the United States under the Marshall Plan.

Marshall Plan aid was also offered to the Soviet Union and the rest of eastern Europe. The Soviets and their allies declined, however, because they felt that accepting U.S. money meant accepting U.S. influence as well.

## Politics

**AUGUST 15, 1947** The pacifist resistance movement led by Mohandas K. Gandhi [March 12, 1930] finally convinces the British to grant **INDEPENDENCE TO INDIA** after two hundred years of colonial rule. With independence, however, fighting breaks out between religious groups. The country is soon divided into the Hindu state of India and the Muslim state of Pakistan.

**NOVEMBER 29, 1947** The United Nations calls for the partition of British-controlled **PALESTINE** into Jewish and Arab states. Jerusalem would remain an international city shared by both. When neither side gives up its demand for complete control of the territory, violent clashes between Palestinian Arabs and Jews become more frequent.

**JANUARY 27, 1948** Congress votes to fund the **VOICE OF AMERICA** radio network. This government-run service will broadcast U.S. propaganda to Soviet-dominated countries behind the Iron Curtain [March 5, 1946]. Although the Soviets try to control the information available to their citizens, they cannot jam the Voice of America, which broadcasts both news and music.

## Life during the Cold War

**DECEMBER 28, 1949** An air force report dismisses recent **UFO SIGHTINGS** as hallucinations, hoaxes, and naturally occurring events. However, the air force does continue to investigate new reports of unidentified flying objects as they come in. It calls the effort Project Blue Book.

**1949** French feminist Simone de Beauvoir publishes ***THE SECOND SEX***. This landmark work attacks the traditional view that women are inferior to men and foreshadows much of the Women's Movement that emerges in the United States during the 1960s.

**1949** Arthur Koestler publishes ***THE GOD THAT FAILED***, in which he writes of his disillusionment with Communism. Like many U.S. intellectuals during the 1930s [1932], Koestler was first attracted to Communism by its idealism. *The God That Failed* marks a decline among intellectuals in their sympathy for the Communist cause.

## Arts & Entertainment

**1947** **JACKSON POLLOCK** develops his drip style of painting, which is later hailed as a turning point in modern art. Pollock creates his abstract paintings by pouring cans of house paint directly onto the canvas. *Time* magazine soon dubs him "Jack the Dripper."

**1948** Leo Fender begins marketing the Broadcaster, the first mass-produced solid-body **ELECTRIC GUITAR**. Fender's guitars, including the Telecaster and Stratocaster models that follow, are the tools that will make rock'n'roll bands possible.

**1948** Twenty-five-year-old Norman Mailer publishes ***THE NAKED AND THE DEAD***, his antiwar novel about a battle between U.S. and Japanese soldiers on a Pacific island. Based on Mailer's experiences during World War II, *The Naked and the Dead* shocks readers with its graphic descriptions of sex and coarse language.

## Science & Technology

**1947** Freethinking engineer Buckminster Fuller builds his first **GEODESIC DOME**. Its geometric design has two main virtues: It encloses the most space using a given amount of material, and it distributes the weight of the structure evenly. In 1952, the air force makes use of Fuller's design to build shelters for radar stations in the Arctic.

**GEODESIC DOME •** Designer Buckminster Fuller believed that one day cities could be covered with huge geodesic domes to keep out bad weather.

JANUARY 30, 1948 A Hindu fanatic, enraged at Gandhi's agreement to the creation of a Muslim state in Pakistan [August 15, 1947], kills the Indian pacifist leader. Remarkably, the widespread shock caused by **GANDHI'S ASSASSINATION** greatly reduces the religious violence that has rocked India since the country became independent.

MAY 10, 1948 The United Nations Temporary Commission supervises **KOREAN ELECTIONS** held in the U.S.-occupied south but not in the Soviet-controlled north. The Korean peninsula has been divided since August 1945, when the United States ordered Japanese troops to surrender to U.S. officers south of the thirty-eighth parallel and to Soviet officers north of that line.

MAY 14, 1948 At midnight, with Britain about to withdraw its troops, Jews in Palestine disregard competing Arab claims and announce the creation of **ISRAEL**. With hopes for a peaceful partition gone, President Truman waits just eleven minutes before formally recognizing the new Jewish state and pledging U.S. support.

JANUARY 17, 1950 In Boston, seven men wearing Halloween masks rob the headquarters of the Brink's Express armored car company. The **BRINK'S ROBBERY**, which nets nearly three million dollars, is easily the biggest hold-up in U.S. history. FBI director J. Edgar Hoover claims that the thieves are part of a Communist conspiracy.

# The Baby Boom

**VETERANS RETURNING HOME FROM World War II were usually eager to get on with their lives. For most, that meant starting a family. Between 1946 and 1960, sixty-three million babies were born in the United States, up twenty-two million from the fifteen-year period before that. This steep jump in the birth rate came to be known as the Baby Boom.**

**Before the war, American children were raised very strictly. They were often told to be "seen and not heard." After the war, however, young parents raised their children according to different ideas. Dr. Benjamin Spock's *Common Sense Book of Baby and Child Care*, published in 1946, emphasized flexibility in child rearing. Spock's best-selling manual encouraged parents to listen to their children and respond to their wishes.**

**Critics who believed that the old ways of raising children were best accused Spock of being too permissive. They thought his ideas would spoil children. But Spock opposed harsh discipline because he thought there was "no such thing as a bad boy." By this he meant that, although a child's behavior may be bad, the "boy" himself is not. Millions of Baby Boom parents were influenced by Spock's advice, which revolutionized the way children were raised.**

New parents quickly made Dr. Spock's book the best-selling book in U.S. publishing history. By 1952, sales had reached four million copies, and they continued at the rate of one million copies per year for the next eighteen years.

Politics

**MAY 26, 1948** South Africa's Nationalist party wins a narrow victory in parliamentary elections. Once in power, the new government extends that country's segregation of the races [May 31, 1910], launching **APARTHEID**. This policy keeps political and economic power completely in the hands of the white minority.

**JUNE 26, 1948** In response to a **SOVIET BLOCKADE OF WEST BERLIN**, the United States and Britain begin airlifting supplies into the former German capital located deep within Soviet-controlled East Germany. Like the rest of the country, Berlin is divided into an eastern zone controlled by the Soviets and a western zone controlled jointly by the United States, Britain, and France.

**AUGUST 15, 1948** In a divided **KOREA**, the new government in the south [May 10, 1948] establishes the Republic of Korea with Syngman Rhee as its first president. Meanwhile, on September 9, North Koreans announce the formation of the Democratic People's Republic under Communist leader Kim Il Sung. Both governments claim authority over all of Korea.

Life during the Cold War

**JANUARY 21, 1950** Although **ALGER HISS** continues to maintain his innocence, a federal jury convicts him of lying about his Communist past [May 31, 1949]. Hiss's chief adversary has been Representative Richard M. Nixon of California. Nixon was the first to bring the Hiss case to national attention, and since then he has made a name for himself as a fierce opponent of Communism.

**BERLIN AIRLIFT • Allied planes delivered 2,500 tons of food per day to keep the citizens of West Berlin from starving. At peak hours, they landed at the rate of one per minute.**

Arts & Entertainment

**FEBRUARY 10, 1949** Arthur Miller's ***DEATH OF A SALESMAN*** opens on Broadway in New York City. The play focuses on Willy Loman, an aging traveling salesman who has never experienced his dream of success. Critics praise the Pulitzer Prize–winning drama for pointing out the emptiness of many American ideals.

**1949** Jazz trumpeter Miles Davis releases his *Birth of the Cool* album, which introduces the innovative and hugely influential "cool" style of jazz. Davis had previously played with Charlie Parker, one of those credited with developing lively bebop jazz [1944]. **COOL JAZZ** is a mellower style, characterized by thoughtful instrumental solos.

Science & Technology

**JULY 1948** Columbia Records introduces the first **LP**, or long-playing phonograph record. Columbia employee Peter Goldmark invented the LP using techniques for making training records first developed by the British during World War II. The LP, which holds six times as much music as previous records, helps create the modern recording industry.

**JULY 1948** Three Bell Laboratories physicists display their invention, the **TRANSISTOR**, which will revolutionize the field of electronics. Transistors regulate the flow of electric current in the same way that vacuum tubes do, but they are much smaller, cheaper, sturdier, and faster.

**NOVEMBER 1948** Edwin Land introduces the **POLAROID LAND CAMERA**, the first camera to produce finished prints almost instantly. Land's Polaroid Corporation had previously specialized in sunglasses and other polarizing filters that reduce glare.

**November 2, 1948** Benefiting from the biggest electoral upset in U.S. history, Democratic incumbent Harry Truman beats Republican challenger Thomas E. Dewey in the **1948 PRESIDENTIAL ELECTION**. Even on Election Day, political experts were so sure of a Dewey victory that the *Chicago Tribune* headlined its early edition, "Dewey Defeats Truman."

**April 4, 1949** The United States, Canada, and ten western European nations create the **NORTH ATLANTIC TREATY ORGANIZATION**. NATO's members agree that an attack upon one will be considered an attack upon them all. The primary purpose of NATO is to discourage the spread of Communism in general and Soviet expansion in particular.

**May 12, 1949** The Soviet Union ends its blockade of West Berlin [June 26, 1948], giving up its attempt to force the Western democracies out of the city. The **BERLIN AIRLIFT**, nicknamed Operation Vittles, continues until September 30, however. In fifteen months, the airlift delivered more than two million tons of food, fuel, and other supplies at a cost of $224 million.

**February 1950** Businessman Frank MacNamara and his friend Ralph Schneider introduce the Diners Club card. This **CREDIT CARD**, the first in history, allows members to charge food and drink at twenty-eight participating restaurants in New York City. MacNamara developed the idea for the card when he realized, in the middle of an important lunch, that he had no cash with him.

# *Jackie Robinson* Breaking the Color Barrier

With Robinson's help, the Brooklyn Dodgers won the National League pennant in 1947 but lost to their crosstown rivals, the New York Yankees, in the World Series.

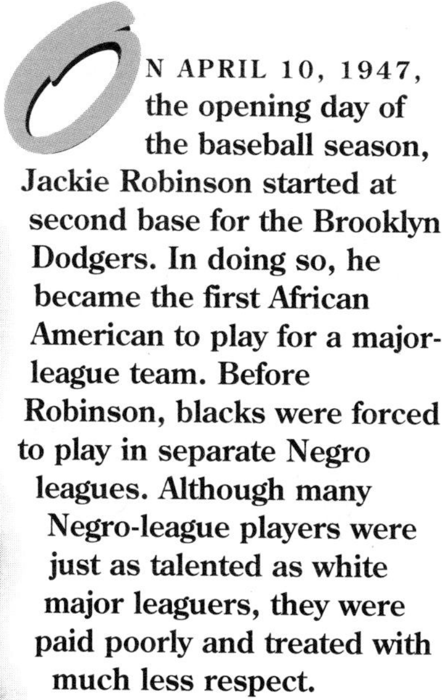

On April 10, 1947, the opening day of the baseball season, Jackie Robinson started at second base for the Brooklyn Dodgers. In doing so, he became the first African American to play for a major-league team. Before Robinson, blacks were forced to play in separate Negro leagues. Although many Negro-league players were just as talented as white major leaguers, they were paid poorly and treated with much less respect.

In 1945, Dodgers general manager Branch Rickey decided that it was time for a change. He knew that black players could help the Dodgers, so he decided to sign Robinson to a contract. He picked the twenty-six-year-old Kansas City Monarch star because he believed Robinson could take the abuse that would surely come his way.

At first, the pressure of being the only black player hurt Robinson's performance. He and his family were threatened by racist fans, and many of his own teammates refused to accept him. But Robinson persevered. Meanwhile, his hitting improved enough to win him the 1947 Rookie of the Year award. By the time Robinson won the National League's Most Valuable Player award in 1949, every team in the majors had at least one black player.

## Politics

**May 23, 1949** German state legislatures in the occupation zones controlled by Britain, France, and the United States form the Federal Republic of Germany, also known as West Germany. On October 7, 1949, in the Soviet zone, East German Communists establish the Soviet-controlled German Democratic Republic. As a result, the **POSTWAR DIVISION OF GERMANY** becomes formalized.

**October 1, 1949** Having defeated Chiang Kai-shek's Nationalist army in the Chinese civil war, Communist party chief Mao Zedong creates the **PEOPLE'S REPUBLIC OF CHINA**. The remnants of Chiang's army flee to the island of Taiwan. In the United States, where fear of Communism has become an obsession, the nation asks, "Who lost China?"

**February 9, 1950** At a speech in West Virginia, Senator **JOSEPH MCCARTHY** claims to have "here in my hand" a list of 205 Communists working in the State Department. Although McCarthy never produces any evidence to support this outrageous charge, the junior senator from Wisconsin plays so well on the public's fear of Communism that the Senate launches a formal investigation.

**PEOPLE'S REPUBLIC OF CHINA • The triumph of the People's Army in the Chinese civil war ended fifteen years of guerrilla fighting. As leader of the victorious Communists, Mao Zedong ruled China for the next twenty-seven years until his death in 1976.**

## Life during the Cold War

**1950** Sociologist David Riesman publishes ***THE LONELY CROWD***, his study of the difficulties people have despite their prosperity. Riesman argues that modern pressures to conform make people "other-directed." That is, people now live according to social standards, rather than personal ones. As a result, they have trouble maintaining a sense of themselves and often feel alone.

## Arts & Entertainment

**1949** George Orwell sets his novel ***1984*** in a grim future that is distant yet recognizable. In this fictional world, filled with two-way television screens, the government's motto is "Big Brother Is Watching You." Orwell intends the novel as a warning. He worries that governments may grow more and more powerful until individual freedoms disappear completely.

**October 15, 1951** ***"I LOVE LUCY"*** premieres on CBS television. Starring husband-and-wife team Desi Arnaz and Lucille Ball, the Monday-night show is an immediate hit. During its six years on the air, the half-hour situation comedy never falls below third in the network popularity ratings. President Eisenhower even delays a televised speech in order to avoid competing with the show.

**1951** J.D. Salinger captures the frustration and gloominess of modern American teenagers in his best-selling first novel, ***THE CATCHER IN THE RYE***. The book's narrator, sixteen-year-old Holden Caulfield, rejects the adult world because it is full of "phonies." Salinger uses the money he earns from sales of the novel to buy a house in Vermont, where he lives in isolation and refuses to give interviews.

## Science & Technology

**1948** Harvard psychologist B.F. Skinner publishes a novel, ***WALDEN TWO***, in which he describes a society planned according to his psychological ideas. Skinner's theories suggest that scientific methods can be used to predict and control human behavior. In the world of *Walden Two*, there are no problems because people are rewarded for being good and punished for being bad.

**1948** In "The Origin of Chemical Elements," George Gamow and Ralph Alpher propose the **BIG BANG** theory of the creation of the universe [1927]. Gamow and Alpher suggest that the universe began as an incredibly hot and dense ball of energy whose explosion formed the universe. They base their theory on evidence that the universe is still expanding.

**September 23, 1949** President Truman announces that the Soviets have successfully tested an atomic bomb. The news shocks the American public as well as many experts who had believed a working Soviet bomb was years away. The **SOVIET BOMB** dramatically shifts the global balance of power, ending the U.S. monopoly on atomic weapons.

FEBRUARY 14, 1950 China and the Soviet Union sign the **SINO-SOVIET PACT**, naming the United States and Japan as mutual enemies. The Soviets also agree to give the Chinese economic aid. Although the Western democracies fear an alliance between these two Communist powers, the Sino-Soviet relationship will remain unstable, and cooperation between the two countries will be limited.

MAY 1, 1950 President Truman approves aid for France in its failing war against Communist rebels in **VIETNAM**. Since World War II, the French colonial government has faced opposition from the nationalist Viet Minh, who demand independence for Vietnam. Soon, the United States will be paying for eighty percent of France's war costs.

JUNE 25, 1950 Crossing the thirty-eighth parallel, North Korean troops launch a surprise **INVASION OF SOUTH KOREA**. Using Soviet-made tanks, the raiders quickly overwhelm the South Korean defenders. Within forty-eight hours, President Truman orders U.S. naval and air units to aid the South Koreans. Even these reinforcements, however, do not stop the North Korean advance.

1952 After a summer trip, during which his family has difficulty finding decent places to stay, Kemmons Wilson founds the **HOLIDAY INN** hotel chain. Wilson's Holiday Inns have enormous appeal to traveling families, who appreciate the clean, comfortable, and affordable rooms. Highway construction and increased automobile traffic will soon create a huge demand for dependable lodgings.

**On December 2, 1954, the Senate condemned McCarthy by a vote of 67-22 for his "habitual contempt" of people. According to one colleague, news of the Wisconsin senator would now be "buried back with the classified ads."**

# McCarthyism

DURING THE MOST DIFFICULT years of the Cold War, many Americans began to imagine Communist conspiracies all around them. As these self-proclaimed patriots became obsessed with worries about Communist subversion, or sabotage, they began to accuse people, often unjustly, of being traitors to their country.

The most famous source of these "Red scares" was Senator Joseph McCarthy. His common practice of accusing people without any evidence came to be known as McCarthyism. The senator built and maintained his power by creating a climate of fear. If people attacked him for his methods, he simply accused them of being Communists, too.

McCarthy's principal targets were Americans who had joined Communist-led organizations during the Great Depression of the 1930s. At special Senate hearings, McCarthy forced these people to testify about others who might have attended the same meetings. Witnesses who refused to "name names" were often blacklisted, which meant that many companies refused to hire them. Many famous writers, actors, and directors were illegally denied the opportunity to work because studios did not want to appear unpatriotic.

Politics

SEPTEMBER 15, 1950 With South Korean and United Nations forces trapped near Pusan, UN commander Douglas MacArthur stages a daring amphibious landing behind enemy lines at **INCHON**. MacArthur's brilliant move catches the North Koreans off guard and quickly shifts the momentum of the Korean War. Within two weeks, retreating North Koreans recross the thirty-eighth parallel.

OCTOBER 9, 1950 **UN FORCES CROSS THE THIRTY-EIGHTH PARALLEL** into North Korea. Although their original war goal was the restoration of South Korea, Truman and MacArthur have recently agreed to reunite the two Koreas. MacArthur disregards China's warning that it will not "sit back with folded hands and let the Americans come to the [Chinese-North Korean] border."

NOVEMBER 26, 1950 Six days after UN forces reach the Yalu River border between China and North Korea, the **CHINESE ENTER THE KOREAN WAR**. With a huge advantage in numbers, the Red Army inflicts heavy casualties on UN troops, forcing them back across the thirty-eighth parallel. Declaring that "there is no substitute for victory," MacArthur urges attacks upon China itself.

Life during the Cold War

MAY 29, 1953 New Zealand mountaineer Edmund Hillary and Nepalese guide Tenzing Norgay reach the summit of **MOUNT EVEREST**. Located in the Himalayas on the border between Nepal and Tibet, Mount Everest is the tallest mountain in the world.

Seven teams had failed in the climb before Hillary's group becomes the first to reach the 29,028-foot peak.

**3-D MOVIES • In *Bwana Devil*, spears appeared to fly out of the screen at theater audiences. To see this effect, audience members had to wear special 3-D glasses. Despite the popular gimmick, most critics still panned the film.**

Arts & Entertainment

NOVEMBER 26, 1952 *Bwana Devil*, the first **3-D MOVIE**, premieres in Los Angeles. To appreciate the new special effect, viewers must wear specially tinted goggles. *Bwana Devil*'s advertising slogan is "A lion in your lap," because the three-dimensional effect is so lifelike. The movie sparks a short-lived craze for 3-D horror movies, such as *The Creature from the Black Lagoon*.

NOVEMBER 1952 The first issue of *MAD Comics* goes on sale. Created by publisher William Gaines and editor Harvey Kurtzman, ***MAD*** is the first humor comic to make fun of all aspects of American popular culture. Its zany spirit is symbolized by *MAD* mascot Alfred E. Newman, a grinning fool whose motto is "What, me worry?"

Science & Technology

1949 Physicist Harold Lyons builds the first **ATOMIC CLOCK** for the National Bureau of Standards. Based on the regular vibrations of ammonia molecules, which pulsate twenty-four billion times a second, the clock is accurate to within a few seconds over fifty years, making very precise scientific measurements possible.

JUNE 14, 1951 The Remington Rand Company introduces **UNIVAC**, the first electronic digital computer to be sold commercially. The first customer is the Census Bureau, which uses a UNIVAC machine to analyze the recent 1950 census results. UNIVAC incorporates a number of advances made by designers J. Presper Eckert and John W. Mauchly since their ENIAC project [February 15, 1946].

DECEMBER 20, 1951 An Atomic Energy Commission reactor in Idaho Falls, Idaho, produces the first electricity generated by nuclear fission. **NUCLEAR POWER PLANTS** use the heat of fission reactions to convert water into steam. The steam is then used to drive a generator, which produces electricity.

APRIL 11, 1951 A furious President **TRUMAN RELIEVES MACARTHUR** of command following the general's public criticism of the way Truman has been conducting the Korean war. Eight days later, MacArthur makes a nationally televised farewell speech before a joint session of Congress. "Old soldiers never die," he says. "They just fade away."

JULY 8, 1951 As U.S. casualties alone reach twenty thousand, **KOREAN WAR PEACE TALKS** begin between UN and North Korean negotiators in the border city of Panmunjom. Nearly five months later, on November 27, the two sides finally agree to a cease-fire. But two crucial issues remain unresolved: the enforcement of the truce and the exchange of prisoners of war.

APRIL 8, 1952 When a United Steelworkers strike threatens to shut down steel production all over the country, President Truman orders a **FEDERAL TAKEOVER OF THE STEEL MILLS**. Truman claims he has the necessary authority because steel is vital to the Korean War effort. The Supreme Court disagrees, however, and overrules him on June 2, restoring private control of the mills.

DECEMBER 21, 1953 The federal government informs **J. ROBERT OPPENHEIMER** of a military security report that accuses him of befriending Communists during the 1930s. A hearing clears the "father of the atom bomb" [July 16, 1945] of treason but takes away his security clearance, which had given him access to top-secret government information.

# LEVITTOWN

## BUILDING THE FUTURE

People camped out overnight for the chance to buy the four-room homes, which sold for $7,990 and included an outdoor barbecue, a washing machine, and a built-in television.

**AFTER WORLD WAR II, the federal government provided servicemen returning home with special housing loans as part of the G.I. Bill. In turn, these inexpensive, guaranteed loans created a huge demand for affordable homes.**

**During the war, the New York construction firm of Levitt & Sons had developed mass-production techniques for the navy. William Levitt soon adapted these techniques to home construction. In 1949, on a Long Island potato field, he built Levittown, the first mass-produced suburban community. Using prefabricated sections, a twenty-seven-step construction process, and non-union crews, Levitt & Sons built identical, inexpensive houses at the remarkable rate of thirty a day.**

**To encourage community spirit, the Levitts planted trees and built neighborhood pools and playgrounds. However, critics charged that the lookalike houses encouraged people living in them to act alike as well. Others attacked the racism of Levittown's whites-only policy. Nevertheless, suburban developments such as Levittown met the needs of many young veterans and their families. Levitt's blueprint was soon copied by developers all over the country.**

## Politics

**September 23, 1952** Accused of keeping a campaign fund for personal use, Republican vice-presidential candidate Richard Nixon goes on television to deny the charges. In his **CHECKERS SPEECH**, Nixon insists he did not profit financially. He says he accepted only one gift, a dog named Checkers. The speech evokes public sympathy and saves Nixon's place on the ticket with Dwight D. Eisenhower.

**October 20, 1952** The British colonial government in Kenya declares a state of emergency because of the **MAU MAU UPRISING**. The Mau Mau, a warlike faction of native East African tribesmen, want to end British rule in Kenya, but the British fight back. During the next four years, the British kill eleven thousand rebels and place twenty thousand more in detention camps.

## Life during the Cold War

**1953** C.A. Swanson & Sons introduces the first **TV DINNER** designed to be eaten in front of the television set. Selling for ninety-eight cents each, the frozen meals are served in aluminum trays that can be reheated in the oven. They consist of turkey with gravy, cornbread stuffing, peas, and whipped potatoes.

**ELVIS PRESLEY • The singer's career took a major step forward when Sun Records sold his contract to RCA in November 1955 for $35,000, plus a $5,000 bonus for Presley.**

## Arts & Entertainment

**1953** Former British naval intelligence officer Ian Fleming publishes *Casino Royale*, the first of his twelve **JAMES BOND** novels. Secret service agent 007's thrilling adventures, which sell more than eighteen million copies worldwide, underscore the constant Cold War struggle between the democratic West and the Communist East.

**July 6, 1954** Nineteen-year-old truck driver **ELVIS PRESLEY** makes his first record, "That's All Right, Mama," for Sam Phillips's Sun Records in Memphis, Tennessee. Phillips has always said that he could make a million dollars if he could only find a white singer who "sang black." Now he has found one who combines the "rock" of black rhythm-and-blues with the "roll" of white country music.

**1954** In ***THE WILD ONE***, Marlon Brando stars as the leader of a motorcycle gang that terrorizes a small town. Brando's memorable character, Johnny, is moody and tense. He also has difficulty expressing himself. These qualities appeal strongly to teenage audiences. "What are you rebelling against, Johnny?" one character asks Brando, who replies, "Whaddya got?"

## Science & Technology

**November 1, 1952** At Eniwetok in the South Pacific, the United States explodes the first **HYDROGEN BOMB**. The H-bomb is five hundred times more powerful than the bombs dropped on Hiroshima and Nagasaki [August 6, 1945]. Unlike those bombs, which split atoms, the hydrogen bomb forces atoms together in a process called fusion. The Soviets test their own H-bomb on August 12, 1953.

**1952** Japan's Sony Corporation licenses the transistor from Bell Laboratories [July 1948] for $25,000. Two years later, the company introduces the first **TRANSISTOR RADIO** using a technology that U.S. engineers had thought was impractical.

**April 1953** Working in Cambridge, England, U.S. biochemist James Watson and British physicist Francis Crick develop the first accepted model for the **STRUCTURE OF DNA**, which contains the genetic information for all living things [1944]. According to Watson and Crick, DNA takes the shape of a double helix, which looks something like a miniature spiral staircase.

**NOVEMBER 29, 1952** Republican president-elect Dwight D. Eisenhower fulfills a campaign promise when he flies to Korea for a three-day visit. **"I WILL GO TO KOREA,"** Eisenhower said before his November 5 election victory over Democrat Adlai Stevenson. While in Korea, the former general attempts to revive the stalled peace talks.

**JUNE 17, 1953** Soviet troops and tanks in **EAST BERLIN** fire on crowds of striking workers, killing several hundred. The workers were demonstrating against high building quotas imposed by the Soviet-dominated East German government. The speed and brutality of the response demonstrates that the Soviets will not tolerate any dissent behind the Iron Curtain [March 5, 1946].

**JULY 27, 1953** Concluding the peace talks at Panmunjom [July 8, 1951], United Nations and North Korean officials sign an **ARMISTICE ENDING THE KOREAN WAR**. In the three years of fighting, more than one million Chinese and Korean soldiers have died, as well as 55,000 Americans. Korea remains divided at the thirty-eighth parallel, just as it was before the war began [June 25, 1950].

**1953** After the Justice Department informs **CHARLIE CHAPLIN** in Switzerland that it will challenge his return to the United States, he surrenders his reentry permit. Because the British-born actor never became a U.S. citizen, he can be denied a visa if the government thinks he is sympathetic to Communism. Chaplin's troubles illustrate the growing American panic regarding potential "subversives."

# THE ROSENBERGS
## *Communism on Trial*

**IN THE SPRING OF 1950, A COUPLE of months after the arrest of nuclear physicist Klaus Fuchs, the FBI picked up Philadelphia chemist Harry Gold. The two men, both members of the Communist party, were charged with espionage, because Fuchs had been passing atomic secrets to the Soviet Union through Gold. From Gold, the FBI learned that Sergeant David Greenglass, a machinist stationed at the Los Alamos atomic laboratory, had also been spying for the Soviets. After his arrest, Greenglass told the FBI that the leaders of his spy ring were Julius and Ethel Rosenberg, his sister and brother-in-law. At the Rosenbergs' trial, Greenglass testified as the government's chief witness. The Rosenberg case soon became one of the most controversial in U.S. history. Because the Rosenbergs provided a focus for Cold War fears, they were prosecuted with zeal. Judge Irving Kaufman even blamed them for the war in Korea and the fifty thousand American lives lost there. Greenglass got fifteen years in prison, but Julius and Ethel Rosenberg were sentenced to the electric chair. On June 19, 1953, they became the first, and only, U.S. civilians put to death for spying.**

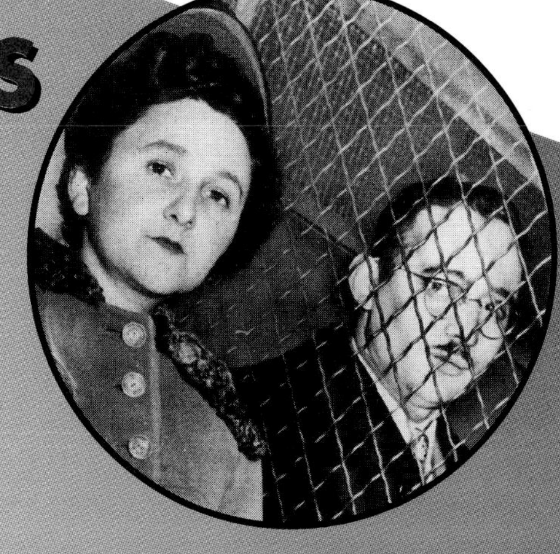

Ethel and Julius Rosenberg

**Thousands of Americans, especially those opposed to the Communist "witch hunts" being conducted by Senator Joseph McCarthy, wrote letters to President Eisenhower pleading for mercy for the Rosenbergs. But Eisenhower refused to reduce their sentences to life imprisonment, even though they would be leaving two young sons behind.**

1950 1960 1970 1980 1990

## Politics

SEPTEMBER 30, 1953 President Eisenhower appoints California governor **EARL WARREN** to succeed the late Frederick Vinson as chief justice of the Supreme Court. Eisenhower expects Warren, a lifelong Republican, to uphold the party's conservative policies, but the opposite occurs. Instead, the Warren court legislates the most progressive civil rights laws since Reconstruction.

EARL WARREN • The chief justice on his first day at the Supreme Court.

APRIL 7, 1954 Speaking about Vietnam [May 1, 1950], President Eisenhower presents his **DOMINO THEORY**. Comparing the nations of Southeast Asia to a row of dominoes, he says, "You knock over the first one, and what will happen to the last one is the certainty that it will go over very quickly." Vietnam's fall might therefore lead to the collapse of Cambodia, Thailand, and even Japan.

## Life during the Cold War

MARCH 1, 1954 Four **PUERTO RICAN NATIONALISTS** open fire from the visitor's gallery of the House of Representatives, wounding five congressmen. The attack follows a recent vote in which Puerto Ricans rejected independence from the United States. Four years earlier, two Puerto Rican terrorists had tried to kill President Truman.

JULY 12, 1954 The Eisenhower administration proposes a network of multilane highways to link major U.S. cities and make it easier for goods to reach market. Congress approves a federal gasoline tax in 1956 to pay for the plan. The forty-two-thousand-mile **INTERSTATE HIGHWAY SYSTEM** will make it possible for Americans to drive coast to coast without stopping for a single traffic light.

## Arts & Entertainment

JULY 9, 1955 **"ROCK AROUND THE CLOCK,"** the first rock'n'roll song to reach Number One, tops the pop music charts. The record by Bill Haley and His Comets at first went nowhere after its release in 1954. But the song caught on after appearing on the soundtrack for *Blackboard Jungle*. Haley's energetic music and the film's juvenile-delinquent plot sparked rioting in some theaters.

SEPTEMBER 30, 1955 Teen idol **JAMES DEAN** dies in an automobile crash. The twenty-four-year-old actor often played misunderstood characters with a remarkable combination of toughness and sensitivity. He will be best remembered for his role in *Rebel Without a Cause*, scheduled for release next month.

1955 University of Maryland freshman Jim Henson creates the first of his **MUPPETS** for a local television show. He makes his marionette-puppets special by giving them lifelike expressions and personalities. In 1957, the Muppets make their first national appearance on Steve Allen's "Tonight" show, during which Kermit the Frog performs "I've Grown Accustomed to Your Face."

## Science & Technology

DECEMBER 8, 1953 In a speech to the UN General Assembly, President Eisenhower unveils his **ATOMS FOR PEACE** program. He proposes that atomic materials be managed by a single international agency. The International Atomic Energy Agency is created in October 1956 to monitor the spread of nuclear technology and to research peaceful applications of atomic energy.

JANUARY 21, 1954 The U.S. Navy launches the first **ATOMIC SUBMARINE**, the *Nautilus*. Built at a cost of fifty-five million dollars, the *Nautilus* gets its power from an on-board nuclear reactor. The reactor gives the ship the ability to sail around the world while remaining underwater. In 1958, the *Nautilus* becomes the first submarine to pass under the North Pole.

OCTOBER 4, 1957 In a surprise move that shocks the world, the Soviet Union launches **SPUTNIK**, the first manmade satellite, into orbit. In Russian, *sputnik* means "fellow traveler." The spherical satellite, which weighs about thirty-eight pounds, contains a radio transmitter, a battery, and four whip aerials. The success of Sputnik dramatically weakens U.S. technological superiority.

APRIL 22–JUNE 17, 1954 The Senate's **ARMY-MCCARTHY HEARINGS** look into charges by Joseph McCarthy [February 9, 1950] that army secretary Robert Stevens has been protecting Communists within his service. Meanwhile, Stevens counters that McCarthy aide Roy Cohn has used the senator's influence to help recently drafted friend David Schine obtain easy army assignments.

MAY 7, 1954 After a two-month siege, French troops at the stronghold of **DIEN BIEN PHU** in Vietnam surrender to the Viet Minh [May 1, 1950]. France had pleaded for U.S. troops, but President Eisenhower refused to get actively involved. The fall of Dien Bien Phu convinces the French to give up the fight that has cost them ninety-five thousand soldiers and eleven billion dollars since 1946.

JUNE 9, 1954 The Army-McCarthy hearings reach their climax when army lawyer Joseph Welch takes on McCarthy personally. After McCarthy attacks a young Welch assistant, the distinguished Boston lawyer says, "Until this moment, Senator, I think I never really gauged your cruelty or your recklessness. . . . **HAVE YOU NO DECENCY, SIR, AT LONG LAST?** Have you left no sense of decency?"

OCTOBER 1954 In response to published claims by a New York psychiatrist that horror comics are harmful to children, comic book publishers form the Comics Code Authority to regulate the amount of violence in comic books. Soon afterward, *MAD Comics* [November 1952] begins calling itself a magazine in order to avoid the censorship of the **COMICS CODE**.

# BROWN v. BOARD OF EDUCATION

## *Intregrating the Schools*

ON MAY 17, 1954, IN THE case of ***Brown v. Board of Education***, the Supreme Court unanimously outlawed segregation by race in public schools. The case had been brought by Oliver Brown, who sued the Board of Education in Topeka, Kansas. The school system there had refused to let his nine-year-old daughter attend a school in her own neighborhood because that school was for whites only and the Browns were black.

The arguments in the case focused on a key 1896 Supreme Court decision in the case of ***Plessy v. Ferguson***. In that case, the Court had ruled that blacks could be kept apart from whites as long as equal facilities were provided for both races. As a result of this decision, laws were passed throughout the South and in other states to keep blacks separate from whites.

**The chief lawyer for Oliver Brown was Thurgood Marshall, head of the NAACP Legal Defense Fund. Marshall (center) had been arguing segregation cases before the Supreme Court for more than a decade. Each of these small victories pecked away at the "separate but equal" doctrine until it was finally overturned in the Brown case.**

**Many of the whites who opposed school integration believed that blacks were inferior to them. They feared that exposure to blacks would corrupt their children.**

However, the schools, trains, and buses provided for them were far from equal.

Psychologist Kenneth Clark provided important evidence that helped overturn the Plessy decision. He showed that segregation itself made black children feel inferior. In psychological tests, Clark allowed black students to play with two dolls: one black and one white. Then he asked them to pick the nasty doll. Almost always, the children picked the black one.

Politics

JULY 21, 1954 In Geneva, Switzerland, **FRENCH AND VIET MINH OFFICIALS AGREE TO A CEASE-FIRE**. The two sides also agree to divide the country along the seventeenth parallel until reunification elections are held within two years. In the meantime, the Viet Minh occupy North Vietnam, while the United States offers military aid to the South Vietnamese government of Ngo Dinh Diem.

MAY 14, 1955 The Soviet Union and the countries it dominates in eastern Europe sign the **WARSAW PACT**, which creates a military alliance similar to NATO [April 4, 1949]. The Warsaw pact nations agree to coordinate their military efforts in the event any of them are attacked by the West.

OCTOBER 26, 1955 After rigging the October 23 election with help from the Central Intelligence Agency, Ngo Dinh Diem declares himself the first president of the new republic in **SOUTH VIETNAM**. Although Diem claims to have won ninety-eight percent of the vote, returns from certain precincts show that the new president has received more votes than there are registered voters.

Life during the Cold War

1954 RCA begins mass production of the first **COLOR TELEVISION** sets, which cost more than a thousand dollars each. The color is not very reliable, however, and most shows are still broadcast only in black and white. Because of the high cost of changing over, most television stations will not broadcast in color for another ten years.

DISNEYLAND • Over twenty-eight thousand people visited Disneyland on its opening day.

JULY 17, 1955 Walt Disney opens **DISNEYLAND** on one hundred acres in Anaheim, California. Unlike amusement parks of the past, the seventeen-million-dollar theme park rejects freak shows and Tunnels of Love in favor of wholesome family entertainment. Disney's plan includes a maze of underground passageways so that visitors never see any delivery vans in the Magic Kingdom.

Arts & Entertainment

SEPTEMBER 9, 1956 **ELVIS PRESLEY'S APPEARANCE ON THE ED SULLIVAN TELEVISION SHOW** attracts a record audience of fifty-four million viewers. Sullivan, who once called the hip-swinging Presley's music "unfit for a family audience," orders his cameraman to show "Elvis the Pelvis" only from the waist up.

1956 Allen Ginsberg becomes an instant celebrity once City Lights Books publishes his *Howl and Other Poems* in its Pocket Poets series. **"HOWL"** describes the wildness hiding beneath the calm surface of 1950s America. Ginsberg and other writers of his generation soon come to be known as "beatniks" because of the rhythmic jazz music they adore.

Science & Technology

NOVEMBER 3, 1957 The Soviet Union confirms its lead in the new "space race" with the launch of **SPUTNIK 2**. A larger version of the first satellite, Sputnik 2 contains the first passenger, a dog named Laika. Soviet scientists use a series of instruments connected to Laika to learn whether living things can survive in space. Laika fares well until her oxygen runs out a week later.

DECEMBER 6, 1957 A navy Vanguard rocket that was supposed to carry the first U.S. satellite into orbit blows up on the launch pad at Florida's Cape Canaveral. Many scientists blame the failure on political pressure to match the success of the Soviets' Sputnik program. The press calls the fiasco **"FLOPNIK"** and "kaputnik."

JANUARY 16, 1956 In an article in *Life* magazine, Secretary of State John Foster Dulles reveals that the United States has been on the brink of war three times during the past three years. "If you try to run away from it, if you are scared to go to the brink, you are lost," he writes of the confrontational tactics that come to be known as **BRINKMANSHIP**.

FEBRUARY 25, 1956 At the Twentieth Congress of the Communist Party in Moscow, Soviet leader Nikita **KHRUSHCHEV DENOUNCES THE LATE JOSEPH STALIN**. He describes the ruthless tactics used by Stalin to maintain personal power, then follows up his speech by temporarily relaxing censorship and reducing the power of the Soviet secret police.

JULY 19, 1956 Citing Egypt's growing friendliness with the Soviet Union, Secretary of State John Foster Dulles withdraws his offer of aid for the **ASWAN HIGH DAM** project. The planned dam would control flooding along the river Nile. Britain also refuses aid to the Egyptians for the same reason, infuriating Egyptian president Gamal Abdel Nasser.

AUGUST 28, 1955 Visiting relatives in Mississippi, **EMMETT TILL** says, "Bye, baby" to a white woman. Three days later, two men come for the black teenager in the middle of the night. His beaten body is later found at the bottom of a river. Because Till's brutal death is widely reported, the acquittal of his killers awakens Northerners to the violence faced by blacks in the South.

# THE POLIO VACCINE

## Dr. Salk Finds a Cure

Dr. Jonas Salk displays his new vaccine.

**ON APRIL 12, 1954, DR. JONAS Salk of the University of Pittsburgh announced the results of the first large-scale tests of his new polio vaccine. The tests proved that Salk's vaccine helped children develop a resistance to the disease. Poliomyelitis, also known as infantile paralysis, had long been one of the most feared childhood diseases. Polio killed thousands of Americans every year and left many more paralyzed. In 1952 alone, more than twenty thousand Americans contracted the crippling disease. Many who survived needed mechanical "iron lungs" to help them breathe. The best-known victim of polio was President Franklin Roosevelt, who contracted the disease in 1921. He remained confined to a wheelchair for the rest of his life. Salk made his vaccine from the polio virus itself. He showed that injecting the dead virus into a patient's bloodstream helped build up resistance to the live virus. After first testing the vaccine on himself and his family, Salk arranged a number of more elaborate tests. As soon as the government licensed Salk's vaccine in 1954, schools began organizing vaccination programs for their students. Soon polio faded as a public health problem in the United States.**

The polio virus as seen through a powerful microscope.

**About the same time that Salk was developing his dead-virus vaccine, Albert Sabin was experimenting with a live-virus vaccine. Sabin's syrupy serum, which could be swallowed, had the potential to last longer than Salk's. Sabin found little financial support in the United States, however, and instead conducted his research in the Soviet Union, where he proved that his vaccine was indeed more effective.**

## Politics

JULY 20, 1956 Fearing that Communist leader Ho Chi Minh would easily win a nationwide vote, South Vietnamese president Ngo Dinh **DIEM REFUSES TO HOLD REUNIFICATION ELECTIONS** before the deadline agreed to in Geneva [July 21, 1954]. Diem bases his decision on U.S. assurances that hundreds of millions of dollars in aid will continue to flow into South Vietnam.

JULY 26, 1956 Egyptian president Gamal Abdel **NASSER NATIONALIZES THE SUEZ CANAL** between the Mediterranean and Red Seas. Nasser plans to use canal tolls to pay for the Aswan Dam [July 19, 1956]. He also wants to reduce the European presence in his country. But seizing the canal, which is owned mostly by British and French stockholders, sets off an international crisis.

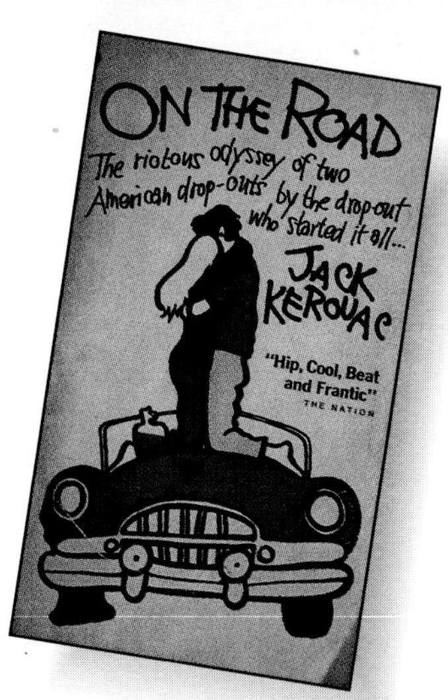


***ON THE ROAD* • Kerouac wrote the novel in 1951, but it took him six years to find an editor willing to publish it.**

## Life during the Cold War

1956 Procter & Gamble introduces **CREST**, the first fluoride toothpaste. The role of fluoride in preventing tooth decay first came to the public's attention when cities began fluoridating their water supplies [1945]. Crest quickly becomes the best-selling toothpaste in the country, displacing Colgate Dental Cream, which had held the top spot for some eighty years.

AUGUST 20, 1957 Owner Horace Stoneham announces that he will move his **NEW YORK GIANTS BASEBALL TEAM TO SAN FRANCISCO** at the end of the current season. On October 8, the Brooklyn Dodgers reveal their plans for a move to Los Angeles. Both teams cite the opportunity to build larger stadiums and earn more money in the booming state of California.

## Arts & Entertainment

SEPTEMBER 26, 1957 The premiere of Leonard Bernstein's ***WEST SIDE STORY*** dazzles audiences with its originality and spirit. A modern version of *Romeo and Juliet* set in a poor New York City neighborhood, the story pits two gangs against each other: the white Jets and the Puerto Rican Sharks. The show's remarkable social awareness breaks new ground in the musical theater.

1957 Jack Kerouac publishes ***ON THE ROAD***, the novel that comes to define the Beat Generation. A onetime football star, Kerouac attended Columbia University with poet Allen Ginsberg [1956] before dropping out to travel around the country and write. *On the Road* fictionalizes many of the experiences he had along the way.

1957 Theodor Seuss Geisel, writing under the name **DR. SEUSS**, publishes *The Cat in the Hat*. The picture book becomes one of his most popular stories for beginning readers. Using just 223 different words to accompany his goofy drawings, Seuss tells the story of a mischievous and messy cat who entertains two bored children on a rainy day.

## Science & Technology

JANUARY 31, 1958 Less than two months after Wernher von Braun takes over the U.S. rocket program, the former Nazi scientist supervises the first successful launch of a U.S. satellite. Boosted into orbit by a four-stage Juno rocket, **EXPLORER 1** carries a Geiger counter, which detects layers of radiation above Earth later named the Van Allen Belts.

SEPTEMBER 12, 1958 Engineer Jack Kilby shows colleagues at Texas Instruments the result of some recent tinkering. What Kilby has assembled using a few transistors [July 1948] and some other electronic parts is the first integrated circuit, or **MICROCHIP**. Kilby's invention permits the development of tiny electronic circuits capable of carrying out very complex tasks.

1958 Arthur Shawlow and Charles Townes of Bell Laboratories apply for the first patent on a **LASER**, which stands for *L*ight *a*mplification by *s*timulated *e*mission of *r*adiation. Two years later, Theodore H. Maiman builds the first successful laser at the Hughes Research Laboratory in California. Lasers are very concentrated and powerful beams of light capable of cutting through metal.

**October 23, 1956** Soon after Khrushchev's attack on Joseph Stalin [February 25, 1956], **STUDENTS IN BUDAPEST STAGE A HUGE DEMONSTRATION** to protest Soviet domination of Hungary. After police fire into the crowd, the Hungarian army joins the revolutionaries. Former premier Imre Nagy, ousted by the Soviets in 1955, returns to power and orders Soviet troops to leave the country.

**October 29, 1956** After making a secret deal with Britain and France, **ISRAEL INVADES EGYPT**. Its troops rout the Egyptian army and advance on the Suez Canal [July 26, 1956]. Using the Israeli action as an excuse, Britain and France land troops on November 5 and 6, supposedly to enforce a UN-ordered cease-fire but actually to take back the canal.

**November 4, 1956** Three days after Imre Nagy announces Hungary's withdrawal from the Warsaw Pact [May 4, 1955], **SOVIET TANKS ENTER BUDAPEST** at four in the morning to crush the Hungarian revolt [October 23, 1956]. The United States protests the Soviet action but does nothing more to stop it.

**September 4, 1957** Governor Orval Faubus calls out the Arkansas National Guard to prevent the enrollment of nine black students at Little Rock's Central High School. Faubus's action violates a federal court order to integrate Central High. After another court order removes the Guard, the **LITTLE ROCK NINE** travel to Central again, this time to face a violent mob threatening to lynch them.

**During the boycott, blacks in Montgomery walked, hitchhiked, arranged car pools, and even rode horses rather than take the bus. Many white housewives, unwilling to do housework themselves, unintentionally helped the boycott by using their cars to pick up black maids.**

# THE MONTGOMERY BUS BOYCOTT

**A policeman fingerprints Rosa Parks.**

**On December 1, 1955, Rosa Parks took her usual bus ride home from her job as a seamstress in a Montgomery, Alabama, department store. Local law divided the buses in Montgomery into two sections: one for blacks and one for whites. However, if the white section at the front of the bus became filled, the bus driver could expand it, forcing blacks to give up their seats. When a white man boarded Parks's crowded bus, the driver told her to stand. When she refused, he called the police, who arrested her. Montgomery's black community organized a boycott in support of Parks. The remarkably eloquent speeches of twenty-six-year-old Baptist minister Martin Luther King, Jr., helped persuade people to stay off the buses to protest the segregation law. The boycott, which began on December 5, was originally supposed to last just one day. But it was so successful that the organizers decided to extend it until the buses were completely integrated.**

**Angry whites bombed King's house, and the department store where Parks worked fired her, but the boycott continued. It lasted for more than a year until the Supreme Court ruled in December 1956 that segregation on public buses was unconstitutional.**

## Politics

**December 22, 1956** Britain and France withdraw their troops from Egypt [October 29, 1956], ending the **SUEZ CRISIS**. Control of the canal returns to Egyptian president Nasser, who lost the military battles but won the diplomatic war. The troop withdrawal follows repeated Soviet threats to enter the war on Egypt's side and President Eisenhower's refusal to support the British and French.

**March 6, 1957** Taking the name **GHANA**, the Gold Coast declares its independence from Great Britain, the first British colony in Africa to do so. Although Africa has been dominated by European colonial powers since the eighteenth century, many African nations follow Ghana's example, achieving independence for themselves within the next five years.

**March 25, 1957** France, Belgium, West Germany, the Netherlands, Luxembourg, and Italy sign the Treaty of Rome, which creates a new European Economic Community, or **COMMON MARKET**. Its purpose is to promote economic growth by making trade easier among member nations. Membership in the EEC will eventually include nearly all of western Europe.

## Life during the Cold War

**September 24–25, 1957** President Eisenhower sends **ARMY TROOPS TO LITTLE ROCK** to enforce the court-ordered integration of Central High School. Although Eisenhower prefers to work quietly behind the scenes in civil rights matters, he feels he cannot allow mob rule to undermine the authority of the federal courts.

**December 9, 1958** Retired candy maker Robert H.W. Welch founds the **JOHN BIRCH SOCIETY**, an ultraconservative organization dedicated to fighting Communism. Welch names his group after Baptist missionary and U.S. intelligence officer John Birch, who was killed by Chinese Communists on August 25, 1945. Welch considers Birch to be the first casualty of the Cold War.

**1958** California's Wham-O Manufacturing Company, which introduced the Frisbee in 1957, launches a new craze with the **HULA-HOOP**. Wham-O sells twenty million plastic toys in the first six months. The fad's creators, Arthur Melin and Richard Knerr, got the idea for the Hula-Hoop from rings of bamboo that Australian children would twirl about their waists in gym class.

## Arts & Entertainment

**1958** Eugene Burdick and William J. Lederer publish ***THE UGLY AMERICAN***, a novel about U.S. diplomacy in Southeast Asia. The book describes the futile efforts of one U.S. ambassador to generate goodwill in a country where none of his staff can even speak the language. Americans concerned with recent Communist advances in Southeast Asia find the book quite disturbing.

**1958** **LEONARD BERNSTEIN**, who wrote the music for *West Side Story* [September 26, 1957], becomes musical director of the New York Philharmonic. As the first American to conduct this prestigious orchestra, Bernstein calls attention to the works of living American composers, such as Aaron Copland [1944] and Randall Thompson.

**February 3, 1959** A plane crash kills rock'n'roll pioneer **BUDDY HOLLY**, who had played a show in Clear Lake, Iowa, earlier that night. The twenty-two-year-old Holly had been touring the Midwest with singers Ritchie Valens and the Big Bopper, who also die in the crash.

## Science & Technology

**January 2, 1959** The Soviet Union launches Lunik 1, the first **LUNAR PROBE**. Although Lunik 1 is supposed to strike the lunar surface, it actually misses the moon by about three thousand miles. However, Lunik 1 does have the distinction of being the first manmade object to leave Earth's orbit. Lunik 2, launched on September 12, crashes into the moon as planned two days later.

**LEONARD BERNSTEIN •** **The composer and conductor was also an accomplished pianist. He even performed occasionally as a soloist, leading his orchestra from the piano bench.**

**August 30, 1957** Senator Strom Thurmond of South Carolina sets a record for filibustering, or delaying, a piece of legislation when he speaks for twenty-four straight hours to hold up passage of the **CIVIL RIGHTS ACT OF 1957**. Although the exceptionally weak bill is finally passed by the Senate, Thurmond makes it clear that the South will strongly resist equal rights for African Americans.

**May 1958** Chinese Communist leader Mao Zedong announces new government policies called the **GREAT LEAP FORWARD** that are designed to increase China's economic production. Mao organizes farmers into large communes and encourages peasants to make steel in backyard furnaces. Despite these efforts, the Great Leap Forward becomes an economic disaster.

**August 23, 1958** After Sputnik [October 4, 1957] causes a panic, Congress responds to fears of a "missile gap" with the **NATIONAL DEFENSE AND EDUCATION ACT**. Americans are worried that their scientists are falling dangerously behind the Soviet Union's in missile technology. The new law provides $887 million in funding to improve science education in both high school and college.

**January 25, 1959** Shortly after his coronation, Pope John XXIII boldly announces plans for a second Vatican Council to consider controversial changes in the Roman Catholic Church. **VATICAN II** will be the first such conference since 1870. Pope John hopes the council can agree on changes that will modernize the Catholic Church and attract new believers.

# Television

## The New American Pastime

During the 1950s, television replaced radio as the most popular form of home entertainment. Television sets became more affordable, viewing screens got bigger, and reception also improved.

The first TV shows were much like those on the air today: sporting events, news programs, and game shows. The most popular situation comedy was "I Love Lucy," which starred Desi Arnaz as bandleader Ricky Ricardo and Lucille Ball as his zany wife. The weekly program became such a sensation that some department stores installed public TV sets so that customers could watch while they shopped.

"The Adventures of Ozzie and Harriet" featured former radio stars Ozzie and Harriet Nelson and their well-behaved teenage sons, David and Ricky. Like "I Love Lucy," "Ozzie and Harriet" supposedly based its scripts on the daily life of a typical American family. Of course, the Ricardos and the Nelsons were far from typical. Most of the idealized scenes in "Ozzie and Harriet," for instance, were set on weekends so that the boys would not appear to be missing school.

"I Love Lucy" was one of many family comedies that used the established radio formula of a wacky wife causing problems for her devoted but constantly annoyed husband.

Politics

JANUARY 1, 1959 Fidel Castro and his small band of rebels march into the Cuban capital of Havana. Completing a five-year struggle, they seize control from corrupt president Fulgencio Batista, who flees the country. Batista was so despised that few people oppose **CASTRO'S REVOLUTION**. However, when Castro nationalizes foreign property, the United States reconsiders its support for him.

JULY 8, 1959 During a Viet Cong raid on the U.S. base at Bien Hoa, military advisors Major Dale Buis and Sergeant Chester Ovnand become the **FIRST U.S. SOLDIERS KILLED IN VIETNAM**. Their mission had been to help the South Vietnamese crush the Communist Viet Cong, or VC, guerrillas.

JULY 24, 1959 While visiting the U.S. exhibition at a Moscow trade fair, Vice President Richard Nixon gets into a heated discussion with Soviet premier Khrushchev in a model kitchen. Khrushchev begins the **KITCHEN DEBATE** when he declares that Soviet homes also have modern conveniences. Nixon responds with an articulate defense of Western capitalism.

Life during the Cold War

JANUARY 25, 1959 American Airlines announces that it will begin **SAME-DAY SERVICE BETWEEN NEW YORK AND LOS ANGELES**. The Boeing 707 jets used by American are the same airplanes that Pan Am has been using to fly nonstop from New York to Paris. Pan Am's regular transatlantic jet service, which began last October, takes only two-thirds the time of a trip via propeller plane.

MARCH 1, 1959 Mattel introduces the **BARBIE DOLL**, which becomes the most popular toy in history. Unlike other dolls, such as Raggedy Ann [1914], Barbie looks less like a storybook character and more like a real teenage girl.

Arts & Entertainment

MARCH 11, 1959 Lorraine Hansberry's ***A RAISIN IN THE SUN*** becomes the first play by an African American ever produced on Broadway in New York City. Hansberry's script explores the difficulties faced by black families trying to escape poor, inner-city life and move to the white-dominated suburbs.

**A RAISIN IN THE SUN • Star Sidney Poitier was one of the first black actors to move past traditional and often demeaning roles.**

OCTOBER 21, 1959 The **GUGGENHEIM MUSEUM** opens in New York City. Designed by Frank Lloyd Wright [1901], the museum houses the modern art collection of copper baron Solomon R. Guggenheim. Wright's controversial design for the museum, which includes a huge spiral walkway set inside its circular structure, is a startling departure from traditional museum architecture.

Science & Technology

JULY 17, 1959 Digging in East Africa with her anthropologist husband, Louis Leakey, Mary Leakey discovers some bones that turn out to be **SKULL FRAGMENTS FROM AN EARLY ANCESTOR OF MODERN HUMANS**. The Leakeys, who believe the bones to be almost two million years old, name the species *Homo zinjanthropus*.

JANUARY 23, 1960 Swiss engineer Jacques Piccard and U.S. Navy lieutenant Don Walsh complete the deepest underwater dive ever made when they travel seven miles down into the Marianas Trench in the Pacific Ocean. The two men make the descent in the bathyscaphe ***TRIESTE***, designed by Piccard's father, Auguste, who had built the first of these deep-sea diving vessels in 1948.

APRIL 1, 1960 The U.S. launches TIROS 1, the first **WEATHER SATELLITE**. Powered by solar cells, the drum-shaped TIROS satellite includes a television camera to take pictures of weather patterns and beam them back to Earth. The information provided by TIROS satellites allows meteorologists to track and predict weather around the globe.

**FEBRUARY 13, 1960** Cuban leader Fidel Castro accepts one hundred million dollars in credits from the Soviet Union. **CASTRO'S INCREASINGLY CLOSE TIES TO THE SOVIETS** cause the United States to buy fewer sugar imports from Cuba. The Soviets increase their purchases to make up the difference in the hope that Cuba may become a base for Communism in Latin America.

**MARCH 21, 1960** South African police open fire on a crowd of blacks protesting a new law that requires them to carry identification papers at all times. Sixty-seven demonstrators are killed and 186 wounded in what comes to be known as the **SHARPEVILLE MASSACRE**. The U.S. State Department protests the killings, which focus international attention on the unjust system of apartheid [May 26, 1948].

**MAY 5, 1960** Two weeks before a summit meeting with President Eisenhower, Soviet leader Nikita Khrushchev announces that his air defense forces shot down a **U-2** high-altitude spy plane on May 1 and captured its pilot, Francis Gary Powers. Although Eisenhower agrees to end the reconnaissance flights, he refuses to apologize. As a result, Khrushchev calls off the summit.

**FEBRUARY 1, 1960** Four black college students from North Carolina Agricultural and Technical College sit down at a whites-only Woolworth's lunch counter in downtown Greensboro. Although they are refused service, they remain in the seats until closing time. Similar **SIT-IN DEMONSTRATIONS** against segregation quickly spread to seventy-seven other cities around the country.

# FEAR OF THE BOMB

DURING THE EARLY 1950s, first the United States and then the Soviet Union successfully tested hydrogen bombs. The explosive force of these weapons, which dwarfed the Hiroshima and Nagasaki bombs, made the grave nature of the nuclear arms race clear to everyone. For the first time in human history, people began to worry about starting a war that could destroy the entire planet.

Average citizens felt panicked, and the government did little to relieve their worries. The Federal Civil Defense Administration encouraged families to stockpile canned food and other essentials in case of a nuclear attack. Some people even had bomb shelters built in their backyards. These shelters ranged in price from $13.50 for a foxhole shelter to $5,000 for a deluxe suite.

In elementary and high schools, students practiced "duck and cover" drills. When teachers said "Drop," students ducked underneath their desks and covered their heads with their hands. Children were also taught to keep their eyes closed so that the flash of a nuclear explosion would not blind them. Of course, the "duck and cover" method would do nothing to protect the students from the deadly radiation produced by a nuclear blast.

**Film of the first H-bomb test in the South Pacific was shown on national television. The mushroom-shaped cloud produced by the explosion soon came to symbolize the possibility of nuclear destruction.**

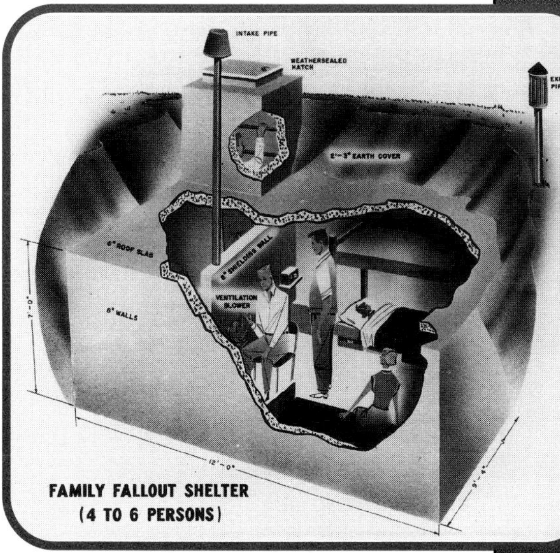


**A diagram of a backyard bomb shelter.**

AS THE 1950s ENDED, many young people began to take a deeper interest in public affairs. The civil rights movement had awakened them to the injustices of American society. John F. Kennedy's successful 1960 presidential campaign inspired many to devote themselves to the cause of social justice.

Many of those who joined the fight were white, middle-class college students eager to cast off their privileges and work for other people's rights. Some registered black voters in Mississippi. Others joined the Peace Corps. But most soon turned their attention to the Southeast Asian nation of Vietnam, where U.S. troops were helping the South Vietnamese in their civil war against Communist North Vietnam.

More than anything else, the Vietnam War radicalized 1960s America. Those young people who believed the war was pointless, unjust, and immoral staged increasingly strong protest rallies. Meanwhile, some radicals "dropped out" of mainstream society to form an alternative culture, or counterculture.

★

# The Sixties

## Politics

SEPTEMBER 26, 1960 More than seventy million people watch Senator John F. Kennedy and Vice President Richard M. Nixon meet in the first of four televised presidential debates. Both candidates speak well, but Kennedy's handsome and confident appearance swings the election his way. After the **KENNEDY-NIXON DEBATES**, television becomes an important focus in political campaigns.

AMERICAN IN SPACE • Alan Shepard waits for blastoff in the Freedom 7 capsule.

## Life in the Sixties

APRIL 29, 1961 **"WIDE WORLD OF SPORTS"** premieres on the ABC television network. This Saturday-afternoon program popularizes little-known sports such as table tennis and wrestling. Children who had once dreamed of becoming baseball stars now begin to imagine themselves as champion gymnasts or ski jumpers.

MAY 1, 1961 The first **SKYJACKING** takes place aboard a National Airlines flight bound for Key West, Florida, when an armed passenger forces the pilot to fly to Havana, Cuba, instead. When more skyjackings follow, President Kennedy asks Congress to pass a law making skyjacking punishable by death or life in prison.

## Arts & Entertainment

DECEMBER 3, 1960 The popular musical ***CAMELOT*** opens on Broadway in New York City, starring Richard Burton, Julie Andrews, and Robert Goulet. After President-elect Kennedy attends a performance, journalists begin to compare his new administration to the romantic medieval reign of King Arthur and his court at Camelot.

1960 Harper Lee publishes her first and only novel, ***TO KILL A MOCKINGBIRD***, which wins a Pulitzer Prize in 1961. The story involves a young white girl in Alabama whose lawyer father defends a black man unjustly accused of raping a white woman. Lee's tale awakens many to the deep racism faced by blacks in the South.

## Science & Technology

JANUARY 31, 1961 A Redstone rocket boosts the chimpanzee Ham 150 miles into space and returns him safely to Earth. With the success of this mission, NASA's **PROJECT MERCURY** takes an important step toward its ultimate goal: sending a human being into space. Three months later, however, an Atlas rocket carrying a dummy astronaut explodes.

APRIL 12, 1961 Twenty-seven-year-old cosmonaut Yuri Gagarin becomes the first **HUMAN IN SPACE**. His Vostok 1 mission lasts 108 minutes and includes a single orbit of Earth. Radio Moscow announces the Soviet Union's triumph in the space race while Gagarin is still in orbit.

MAY 5, 1961 Although he does not enter orbit, Alan Shepard becomes the first **AMERICAN IN SPACE** when he makes a fifteen-minute flight aboard the *Freedom 7*. The number in the capsule's name, chosen by Shepard himself, honors the original seven Project Mercury astronauts.

**NOVEMBER 8, 1960** Democrat John F. Kennedy wins the **1960 PRESIDENTIAL ELECTION**, one of the closest in history. He defeats the Republican candidate, Richard M. Nixon, by less than one percent of the popular vote. The forty-three-year-old Kennedy becomes the youngest person ever elected president.

**DECEMBER 20, 1960** In South Vietnam, opponents of President Ngo Dinh Diem join to form the **NATIONAL LIBERATION FRONT**. Although the NLF is sponsored and directed by the Communist government of North Vietnam, the organization includes non-Communists as well. The NLF wants to overthrow Diem's corrupt dictatorship and establish a single, unified Vietnam.

**JANUARY 3, 1961** The United States breaks off diplomatic relations with Cuba. The move reflects President Eisenhower's growing distrust of Fidel Castro and his revolutionary government [January 1, 1959]. **CASTRO'S NEW FRIENDLINESS TOWARD THE SOVIET UNION** leads many Americans to fear there will be a Soviet ally close to the Florida shore.

**MAY 4, 1961** The **FREEDOM RIDES** begin in Washington, D.C., when thirteen black and white volunteers board buses for the South. They intend to test a December 1960 Supreme Court ruling banning racial segregation on buses that cross state lines. On May 14, a white mob attacks one of these buses outside Anniston, Alabama, beating the Freedom Riders and setting the bus on fire.

# Folk Music

## Songs of Protest

Growing up in Minnesota, Bob Dylan's idol was folksinger Woody Guthrie.

DURING THE EARLY years of Kennedy's New Frontier, many young Americans began seeking political change. At the same time, their music changed as well. The electrifying rock'n'roll created by Elvis Presley and Chuck Berry had thrilled them as teenagers, but more serious times led them toward more earnest music. By 1963, folk music was soaring in popularity.

Folk musicians generally played acoustic guitars and sang traditional ballads, such as "The Streets of Laredo" and "On Top of Old Smoky." Woody Guthrie and Pete Seeger were among the few older folksingers who wrote their own songs. During the 1960s, however, new, young folksingers wrote many original songs, usually about social problems. Among the best known of these "protest" singers, many of whom gathered in New York City's Greenwich Village, were Bob Dylan, Joan Baez, and Phil Ochs.

Folksingers appeared regularly at civil rights and antiwar rallies, where they entertained crowds with songs like "We Shall Overcome" and Phil Ochs's "I Ain't Marching Anymore." In 1963, Peter, Paul & Mary released a recording of Bob Dylan's "Blowin' in the Wind" that became the first protest song to reach the Top Ten, reaching Number Two on the pop music charts.

Joan Baez became a political activist while attending college during the 1950s.

## Politics

**January 20, 1961** President Kennedy delivers an inspiring inaugural address, declaring that "the torch has been passed to a new generation of Americans." Outlining his New Frontier programs, the youthful Kennedy challenges other young people to work for change. **"ASK NOT WHAT YOUR COUNTRY CAN DO FOR YOU,"** he says. "Ask what you can do for your country."

**March 1, 1961** President Kennedy creates the **PEACE CORPS**, which sends more than ten thousand young volunteers to developing nations around the world during the next five years. Living in simple quarters, these volunteer health-care workers, teachers, and engineers help improve local conditions, particularly in the fields of agriculture and public health.

**April 17, 1961** A group of anti-Communist Cuban exiles, secretly trained by the CIA, lands at the **BAY OF PIGS**. These exiles plan to lead a popular revolt against the government of Fidel Castro. Instead, Castro's forces easily capture them. Although the Eisenhower administration planned the mission, President Kennedy is forced to accept blame for the disaster.

## Life in the Sixties

**1961** After buying the **MCDONALD'S** restaurant chain from brothers Mac and Dick McDonald, Ray Kroc greatly expands the fast-food business. He also founds McDonald's Hamburger University, where employees can earn a degree in Hamburger Science. For counter jobs in his restaurants, Kroc hires only young people whom he considers clean-cut, all-America types.

PEACE CORPS • A Peace Corps volunteer helps farmers in the Central American nation of El Salvador.

**February 14, 1962** First Lady Jacqueline Kennedy leads forty-seven million viewers on a **TELEVISED TOUR OF THE WHITE HOUSE**. Escorted by CBS correspondent Charles Collingwood, Mrs. Kennedy points out historical furnishings as well as recent renovations, which were carried out under her supervision. Afterward, one critic calls her "our uncrowned queen."

## Arts & Entertainment

**May 9, 1961** Calling **TELEVISION** "a vast wasteland," Federal Communication Commission chairman Newton Minow promises to hold broadcasters accountable for their programming, which he attacks as alternately boring and violent. Television sales continue to boom, however. There is now one set for every three Americans.

**January 13, 1962** Chubby Checker's recording of **"THE TWIST"** hits Number One on the *Billboard* charts. Two weeks later, Joey Dee and the Starlighters bump it from the Number One spot with another Twist song. They call theirs the "Peppermint Twist" after New York City's Peppermint Lounge, where adults dance the Twist nightly. Until now, rock'n'roll has primarily been a teen sensation.

## Science & Technology

**February 20, 1962** Astronaut **JOHN GLENN** becomes the first American in orbit, piloting the Mercury capsule *Friendship 7*. During his five-hour flight, Glenn eats a special snack designed for the weightless conditions of space. It comes packed in a tube like toothpaste.

AUGUST 12–13, 1961 During the night, the Soviet-backed government of East Germany begins construction of the **BERLIN WALL** between East and West Berlin. The barbed-wire barricade, which is later replaced by a concrete wall, cuts off the most popular escape route to the West. The wall itself becomes a symbol of the political divide between the Soviet bloc and the West.

OCTOBER 22, 1962 Speaking on national television, President Kennedy announces that U.S. spy planes have taken photographs of **SOVIET NUCLEAR MISSILE SITES UNDER CONSTRUCTION IN CUBA**. Kennedy demands that the Soviets remove the missiles immediately. Meanwhile, he orders a naval blockade of Cuba to stop Soviet ships from reaching that Caribbean island.

OCTOBER 28, 1962 The **CUBAN MISSILE CRISIS** ends when President Kennedy accepts an offer made by Soviet premier Nikita Khrushchev: The Soviets will remove their missiles from Cuba if the United States removes its missiles from Turkey and promises not to invade Cuba. The week-long emergency is probably the closest the world has ever come to nuclear war.

SEPTEMBER 30, 1962 Violence erupts at the all-white University of Mississippi after President Kennedy sends four hundred federal marshals to ensure that black air force veteran James Meredith can register there. Mississippi governor Ross Barnett had blocked Meredith's enrollment, defying a federal court order. Two people are killed in the **OLE MISS RIOTS**, and more than three hundred are injured.

**The Kennedys attend an inaugural ball at the Washington Armory with Vice President Lyndon B. Johnson.**

# The Jackie Look

IF THE KENNEDY White House indeed re-created King Arthur's court at Camelot, then much of the credit belonged to First Lady Jacqueline Bouvier Kennedy. Although Americans had once fought a revolution to overthrow a monarch, they welcomed Jackie in 1961 as an uncrowned queen. The public adored her softspoken, stylish elegance, and she used it to charm the nation and the world. The beautiful thirty-two-year-old first lady was also quite chic, and the Jackie Look soon dominated American fashion.

The classic Jackie Look featured a simple skirted suit in a bright color with a sleeveless blouse worn underneath. High-heeled shoes and bouffant, or puffed-out, hairstyles were very popular during the early 1960s, but Mrs. Kennedy toned both of these styles down. She wore her hair in a restrained bouffant and usually preferred shoes with lower heels.

Although Jacqueline Kennedy privately wore old, comfortable slacks and flat shoes, she cultivated a sophisticated public appearance because she felt it was the role of the first lady to set a high standard that other women might follow.

**One of the most memorable parts of the Jackie Look was the pillbox hat. These small, simple hats contrasted markedly with the large flowered hats that had been worn by previous first ladies.**

## Politics

MAY 25, 1963 President Kwame Nkrumah of Ghana helps found the **ORGANIZATION OF AFRICAN UNITY**. Membership in the OAU includes thirty African states that have recently won their independence [March 6, 1957]. In banding together, the OAU nations hope to increase Africa's status in world affairs.

JUNE 11, 1963 Buddhist monk Thich Quang Duc makes international headlines when he kills himself in the middle of a busy intersection in Saigon, the capital of South Vietnam. **DUC SETS HIMSELF ON FIRE** to protest the brutal behavior of South Vietnamese president Ngo Dinh Diem, who has been terrorizing his Buddhist political opponents.

**THICH QUANG DUC • Buddhist monk Thich Quang Duc sets himself on fire to protest the anti-Buddhist policies of the Catholic South Vietnamese government.**

## Life in the Sixties

MAY 3, 1963 Police chief **EUGENE "BULL" CONNOR** orders fire hoses and police dogs turned loose on civil rights marchers in Birmingham, Alabama. Television viewers are shocked by footage of black children being knocked down by jets of water and attacked by dogs. These images win even more sympathy for the civil rights movement.

JUNE 11, 1963 As he had promised, Governor George **WALLACE "STANDS IN THE SCHOOLHOUSE DOOR"** to prevent black students from enrolling at the University of Alabama. That same night, President Kennedy delivers his strongest speech yet on civil rights. Then, shortly after midnight, a gunman kills Mississippi civil rights leader Medgar Evers outside his home in Jackson.

## Arts & Entertainment

APRIL 5, 1962 Movie star and sex symbol **MARILYN MONROE** is found dead in her Los Angeles home, apparently the victim of a suicide. The autopsy report states the cause of death to be an overdose of sleeping pills. Some unusual circumstances surrounding her death, however, lead to rumors that she was murdered.

JUNE 1962 The Beach Boys release their first hit, "Surfin' Safari," which starts a nationwide craze for **SURF MUSIC**, the sport of surfing, surfing clothes, surfing lingo, and almost anything else Southern Californian.

## Science & Technology

JULY 10, 1962 The American Telephone & Telegraph Company launches **TELSTAR**, the first commercial communications satellite. Fifteen hours later, Telstar transmits live television pictures from Maine to stations in Britain and France. Television broadcasts "live via satellite" capture the popular imagination and inspire a Number One instrumental hit, also called "Telstar," by the Tornadoes.

SEPTEMBER 1962 Biologist Rachel Carson publishes ***SILENT SPRING***, one of the first books to warn people about the dangers caused by environmental pollution. Carson's controversial work emphasizes the damage caused by such chemical pesticides as DDT. As a direct result of her efforts, many of these pesticides are soon banned.

1963 Edwin Land's Polaroid Corporation introduces **POLACOLOR FILM**. Used with Land's special Polaroid cameras [November 1948], Polacolor can produce finished color prints in less than a minute. The ability of this new film to create nearly instant pictures causes a consumer sensation.

JUNE 26, 1963 President Kennedy makes a four-day trip to West Germany. In the embattled city of West Berlin [August 12–13, 1961], he delivers a speech to encourage the people there. **"ICH BIN EIN BERLINER,"** Kennedy says, meaning that in spirit he considers himself a citizen of Berlin.

AUGUST 30, 1963 In the aftermath of the Cuban Missile Crisis [October 22, 1962], the United States and the Soviet Union establish a telephone **HOT LINE** between the White House and the Kremlin. Both governments believe that a direct communications link between the U.S. president and the Soviet premier might be helpful in the event of another international crisis.

OCTOBER 7, 1963 President Kennedy signs a treaty with the Soviet Union banning nuclear testing in the atmosphere. Kennedy calls the **LIMITED NUCLEAR TEST BAN TREATY** the most important achievement of his administration. Meanwhile, environmentalists applaud the halt of above-ground testing because of the dangerous radioactive fallout it produces.

SEPTEMBER 15, 1963 Just eighteen days after the March on Washington, a **BOMB DESTROYS THE SIXTEENTH STREET BAPTIST CHURCH** in Birmingham, Alabama. The Sunday-morning explosion kills four young black girls attending Sunday School and injures seventeen more. A few hours later, police shoot a black teenager in the back.

# March on Washington

**Thirty special trains and more than two thousand chartered "Freedom buses" carried people to Washington. An eighty-two-year-old man bicycled from Ohio. Another man roller-skated from Chicago. Twelve civil rights workers from Brooklyn walked the entire way.**

**Martin Luther King, Jr. delivers his "I have a dream" speech.**

**ON AUGUST 28, 1963, MORE than 250,000 people traveled to the nation's capital for the March on Washington, the largest civil rights demonstration in U.S. history. The organizers of the march—a coalition of labor, civil rights, and church groups—wanted more job training, an end to job discrimination, and passage of the Civil Rights Act currently before Congress.**

**The highlight of the rally was the "I Have a Dream" speech delivered by Martin Luther King, Jr., from the steps of the Lincoln Memorial:**

**" . . . I have a dream that one day on the red hills of Georgia, sons of former slaves and the sons of former slave owners will be able to sit down together at the table of brotherhood. I have a dream that one day even the state of Mississippi, a state sweltering with the heat of injustice, sweltering with the heat of oppression, will be transformed into an oasis of freedom and justice. I have a dream that my four little children will one day live in a nation where they will not be judged by the color of their skin, but the content of their character. I have a dream today!"**

Politics

NOVEMBER 1, 1963 After receiving secret U.S. approval, a group of **SOUTH VIETNAMESE GENERALS LEAD A COUP** during which the dishonest President Diem is killed. With a new military government in place, the United States expands its efforts to help South Vietnam defeat the National Liberation Front [December 20, 1960].

NOVEMBER 22, 1963 While driving in a motorcade through Dallas, **PRESIDENT KENNEDY IS KILLED** by rifle shots. Two hours later, Vice President Lyndon Johnson is sworn in at the Dallas airport. Police arrest Marine Corps veteran Lee Harvey Oswald for the crime. The mentally unstable Oswald had defected to the Soviet Union in 1959 before returning to the United States in 1962.

**KENNEDY ASSASSINATION • At First Lady Jacqueline Kennedy's request, President Kennedy's funeral procession was modeled after President Lincoln's. Here it moves past the White House on its way to Arlington National Cemetery.**

Life in the Sixties

1963 Forty-two-year-old psychologist Betty Friedan publishes ***THE FEMININE MYSTIQUE***, in which she explores the dissatisfaction and boredom experienced by suburban housewives. Friedan's book attacks the cultural values that urge women to find fulfillment in their families alone. Instead, she encourages women to build identities for themselves outside the home.

Arts & Entertainment

NOVEMBER 17, 1962 *The New Yorker* magazine publishes a long article on civil rights by African-American author James Baldwin. A year later, Baldwin expands the article into a best-selling book, ***THE FIRE NEXT TIME***. In the article and book, Baldwin argues that unless the demands of the nonviolent civil rights movement are met, blacks will soon turn to violence in order to obtain justice.

1962 Charles Schultz publishes his first book, ***HAPPINESS IS A WARM PUPPY***. The collection of cartoons, which becomes a major Christmas hit, features characters from Schultz's daily comic strip "Peanuts," including Charlie Brown, Lucy, and Snoopy. *Happiness Is a Warm Puppy* soon tops the best-seller list with more than one million copies in print.

MARCH–JUNE 1963 The Guggenheim Museum in New York City sponsors the first major **POP ART** exhibit. The Guggenheim's decision to host the show adds to the growing respect being given this often-outrageous style. The works on display include Andy Warhol's painting of Campbell's Soup cans and Roy Lichtenstein's oversize comic-book panels.

Science & Technology

JANUARY 11, 1964 An expert committee appointed by Surgeon General Luther Terry releases a report directly linking smoking to lung cancer, heart disease, and other illnesses. Two days later, the Federal Trade Commission announces that tobacco companies will be required to print **HEALTH WARNINGS ON ALL CIGARETTE PACKAGES**.

JULY 31, 1964 The Ranger 7 spacecraft transmits the first **CLOSE-UP PICTURES OF THE MOON**. The probe sends back 4,316 images before crashing as planned into the lunar surface. The Ranger 7 photos show objects as small as three feet across and provide important information for the designers of the Apollo lunar module.

MARCH 18, 1965 Soviet cosmonaut Alexei Leonov becomes the first human to **WALK IN SPACE**, attached to the Voskhod 2 spacecraft by a fifteen-foot safety line. The space-suited Leonov climbs out of the capsule about ninety minutes after the launch. On June 3, Edward White becomes the first American to walk in space.

**November 24, 1963** Two days after the Kennedy assassination, a mourning nation watches nightclub owner **JACK RUBY KILL ACCUSED GUNMAN LEE HARVEY OSWALD** on television. Network cameramen had been covering Oswald's transfer from city to county jail. Ruby's links to organized crime lead many to believe that he and Oswald were both part of a larger plot to kill the president.

**January 8, 1964** In his first State of the Union message, President Johnson asks the country to wage an "unconditional **WAR ON POVERTY**." Shortly before his death, President Kennedy had introduced programs to help poor Americans, but Johnson's plans are much more ambitious. On March 16, he asks Congress for $962 million toward his goal of ending poverty in the United States.

**January 23, 1964** The ratification of the **TWENTY-FOURTH AMENDMENT** makes poll taxes illegal in federal elections. The taxes, which many poor people cannot pay, have been used throughout the South to keep blacks from voting. To get around the law, Virginia and Texas use separate state and local registration systems so they can continue to charge poll taxes in those elections.

**February 25, 1964** In a major upset, outspoken boxer Cassius Clay knocks out heavyweight champion Sonny Liston. "Liston is great, but he'll fall in eight," Clay had rhymed before the fight. At a press conference the next day, he announces that he has joined the Nation of Islam [1930]. A month later, the champ declares that his new Islamic name is **MUHAMMAD ALI**.

# Pop Art

After World War II, prosperity and the accompanying spread of television encouraged the development of a new mass culture in the United States. Painters and sculptors, for example, began creating work for a broad audience rather than a wealthy few. Instead of painting traditional landscapes or the colored shapes that had recently been popular, some artists in the early 1960s began using everyday items as subjects for their art.

Because their work used images from the popular culture, especially advertising, it was called pop art. Andy Warhol made silk-screen prints of supermarket objects, such as Campbell's Soup cans and Coca-Cola bottles. Another important pop artist, Roy Lichtenstein, painted in the style of his son's comic books. Claes Oldenburg made soft plastic sculptures of typewriters and gigantic hamburgers.

Many critics snickered at pop art and complained that it was all a bad joke. Even sympathetic critics asked the question, "Is this art?" The pop artists responded with another question: "What is art?" They argued that art could be found anywhere, even in familiar images.

Roy Lichtenstein painted *In the Car* in the style of the art found in comic books.

Pop pioneer Andy Warhol often depicted product packaging in his art works.

## Politics

**June 11, 1964** A South African court sentences civil rights activist **NELSON MANDELA** to life in prison for seeking to overthrow the country's Nationalist party government [May 26, 1948]. A month earlier, the government had strengthened its apartheid system of racial segregation by limiting the number of black Africans allowed to work in different regions of the country.

**July 2, 1964** President Johnson signs the **CIVIL RIGHTS ACT OF 1964**, which bans discrimination in public places and employment based on race, sex, religion, or national origin. An expanded version of the bill originally offered by President Kennedy, the new law is the most far-reaching civil rights legislation since the end of Reconstruction in 1877.

**August 7, 1964** After two North Vietnamese torpedo boats allegedly attack the U.S. destroyer *Maddox*, Congress passes the **GULF OF TONKIN RESOLUTION**, which gives President Johnson the power to use U.S. troops in Vietnam without a formal declaration of war or further approval from Congress. The bill passes unanimously in the House and with only two opposing votes in the Senate.

## Life in the Sixties

**June 21, 1964** Civil rights workers Andrew Goodman, Michael Schwerner, and James Chaney disappear after inspecting a bombed-out church near Philadelphia, Mississippi. The Congress of Racial Equality office in Meridian reports them missing after they fail to check in. **GOODMAN, SCHWERNER, AND CHANEY** were last seen in the custody of local police.

**August 4, 1964** The offer of a twenty-five-thousand-dollar reward produces a tip that leads FBI agents to a dam built of earth. There they find the bodies of **GOODMAN, SCHWERNER, AND CHANEY** buried in a trench. The whites, Goodman and Schwerner, were each killed with a single bullet, but Chaney, who was black, was first beaten savagely and then shot three times.

**September 14, 1964** The University of California at Berkeley bans tables set up by political groups to promote their ideas. When five students defy the ban, the dean has them report for punishment. Instead, five hundred students show up, beginning the **FREE SPEECH MOVEMENT**. Among its leaders is Mario Savio, who spent the summer in Mississippi as a Freedom Summer volunteer.

## Arts & Entertainment

**June 12, 1963** The forty-million-dollar blockbuster ***CLEOPATRA*** premieres at the Rivoli Theater in New York City. The most expensive film made to date, it stars Elizabeth Taylor as the famous Egyptian queen and Richard Burton as Marc Antony. Twentieth Century Fox later sues Taylor, claiming that her difficult behavior on and off the set led to cost overruns and the film's financial failure.

**1963** Maurice Sendak publishes the picture book ***WHERE THE WILD THINGS ARE***, which he both wrote and illustrated. Parents and teachers hail the bold and fanciful work for its attention to the feelings of very young readers, but a few critics complain about the nudity of its main character, a boy named Max.

## Science & Technology

**November 9–10, 1965** A malfunction at a generating plant near Niagara Falls leads to the largest power failure in history. The two-day **NORTHEAST BLACKOUT** affects thirty million people in seven northeastern states, plus the Canadian provinces of Quebec and Ontario. Telephones remain in service, however, and New Yorkers make more calls in one day than they usually make in two weeks.

MISSING CALL FBI

THE FBI IS SEEKING INFORMATION CONCERNING, THE DISAPPEARENCE AT PHILADELPHIA, MISSISSIPPI, OF THESE THREE INDIVIDUALS ON JUNE 21, 1964. EXTENSIVE INVESTIGATION IS BEING CONDUCTED TO LOCATE GOODMAN, CHANEY AND SCHWERNER, WHO ARE DESCRIBED AS FOLLOWS

| | ANDREW GOODMAN | JAMES EARL CHANEY | MICHAEL HENRY SCHWERNER |
|---|---|---|---|
| RACE: | White | Negro | White |
| SEX: | Male | Male | Male |
| DOB: | November 23, 1943 | May 30, 1943 | November 6, 1939 |
| POB | New York City | Meridian, Mississippi | New York City |
| AGE: | 20 Years | 21 years | 24 years |
| HEIGHT: | 5'10" | 5'7" | 5'9" to 5'10" |
| WEIGHT: | 150 pounds | 135 to 140 pounds | 170 to 180 pounds |
| HAIR: | Dark brown: wavy | Black | Brown |
| EYES: | Brown | Brown | Ligh blue |
| TEETH | | Good: none missing | |
| SCARS AND MARKS: | | 1 inch cut scar 2 inches above left ear. | Pock mark center of forehead, slight scar on bridge of nose, appendectomy scar, broken leg scar. |

SHOULD YOU HAVE OR IN THE FUTURE RECEIVE ANY INFORMATION CONCERNING THE WHEREABOUTS OF THESE INDIVDUALS YOU ARE REQUESTED TO CALL THE FEDERAL BUREAU OF INVESTIGATION. YOU MAY ALSO CALL THE COUNCIL OF FEDERATED ORGANIZATIONS, (COFO) AARON E. HENRY, CHAIRMAN. 601-624-2913. ADDRESS 213 4TH

**GOODMAN, SCHWERNER, AND CHANEY** • The FBI offered a reward for information about the missing civil rights workers.

AUGUST 22, 1964 **FANNIE LOU HAMER** of the Mississippi Freedom Democratic party asks that the integrated MFDP delegation, rather than the all-white delegation from her state, be seated at the Democratic National Convention. Speaking before the convention's Credentials Committee, the poor black sharecropper describes how she has been jailed and beaten for trying to vote.

AUGUST 30, 1964 President Johnson signs the $947-million-dollar **ECONOMIC OPPORTUNITY ACT**, which Congress has passed in response to his call for a war on poverty [January 8, 1964]. The new law funds preschool education and job training as well as loans to small businesses. It also creates the Office of Economic Opportunity to oversee these programs.

SEPTEMBER 27, 1964 The **WARREN COMMISSION**, appointed by President Johnson to study the Kennedy assassination, finds that Lee Harvey Oswald acted alone. In its report, the panel headed by Chief Justice Earl Warren dismisses the idea of a conspiracy in favor of the "lone gunman" theory. Nevertheless, many people still believe that Oswald could not have succeeded by himself.

DECEMBER 4, 1964 After Mississippi governor Paul Johnson refuses to let the state attorney general bring murder charges, the FBI arrests twenty-one men in the **GOODMAN, SCHWERNER, AND CHANEY CASE** for civil rights violations. After their conviction, Philadelphia, Mississippi, deputy sheriff Cecil Price and six others receive sentences ranging from three to ten years.

# Mississippi Freedom Summer

Black and white volunteers working together in Meridian, Mississippi.

Members of the Mississippi Freedom Democratic Party at the Democratic National Convention in Atlantic City, New Jersey.

DURING THE SUMMER OF 1964, hundreds of white college students traveled south to take part in the Mississippi Summer Project. Robert Moses of the Student Nonviolent Coordinating Committee organized the event to take advantage of the help being offered by sympathetic whites in the North.

The goal of the project was to create a new political party. Most blacks in the United States belonged to the Democratic party, but the Mississippi Democratic party didn't allow blacks to join.

Instead of fighting with the white party members, Moses and others decided to start their own party, which would represent the views of blacks and liberal whites. It was the job of Summer Project volunteers to register blacks so they could vote for Moses's new party, the Mississippi Freedom Democratic party.

Although the state was a dangerous place for civil rights workers, Moses invited white volunteers to Mississippi because he thought racist locals would be less likely to attack them. He was tragically wrong: On the first full day that white volunteer Andrew Goodman spent in Mississippi, he was murdered along with two other civil rights workers, Michael Schwerner and James Chaney.

**Politics**

OCTOBER 14, 1964 In the Soviet Union, the **CENTRAL COMMITTEE OUSTS NIKITA KHRUSHCHEV** as head of the Communist party and replaces him with Leonid Brezhnev. Khrushchev's unpredictable personality and recent attempts to modernize the Soviet system have made him unpopular and angered conservative party leaders.

MALCOLM X • This mural honoring Malcolm X was painted on the outside of the Audubon Ballroom, the site of his assassination.

**Life in the Sixties**

FEBRUARY 21, 1965 Black **GUNMEN ASSASSINATE MALCOLM X** during a speech at the Audubon Ballroom in Harlem in New York City. Malcolm first became famous as a spokesman for the militant Nation of Islam [1930], but disagreements with leader Elijah Muhammad eventually forced him out of the Black Muslim movement. Many suspect that Elijah Muhammad ordered Malcolm's death.

FEBRUARY 7, 1964 The Beatles arrive at Kennedy Airport in New York City to begin their first U.S. tour. Two days later, more than seventy million people watch their performance on Ed Sullivan's TV show, breaking the record set by Elvis Presley [September 9, 1956]. As **BEATLEMANIA** grips the nation, the Fab Four place six songs in *Billboard*'s Top Ten.

JULY 25, 1965 Purists boo **BOB DYLAN** off the stage at the Newport Folk Festival when he appears playing an electric guitar. Just two years earlier, Dylan had charmed the festival crowd with his political protest songs performed on an acoustic, or nonelectric, guitar. These same fans now call him a traitor because he wants to play rock'n'roll.

**Science & Technology**

1965 Astrophysicists Arno Penzias and Robert Wilson discover the existence of **COSMIC BACKGROUND RADIATION**. They suggest that this constant microwave radiation, which exists in all of space, may date back to the creation of the universe. In this respect, their discovery supports George Gamow and Ralph Alpher's Big Bang theory [1948].

JANUARY 27, 1967 The United States and the Soviet Union sign the **UNITED NATIONS OUTER SPACE TREATY**, which limits the military uses of space. The superpowers agree not to put nuclear weapons in orbit around Earth and not to claim ownership of celestial bodies, such as the moon or other planets.

MARCH 1, 1967 The Department of the Interior issues its first **ENDANGERED SPECIES LIST**. The list names seventy-eight species threatened with extinction. Included are the ivory-billed woodpecker, the bald eagle, and the grizzly bear. Within three years, eleven more species are added to the list.

**JANUARY 4, 1965** In his second State of the Union address, President Johnson outlines his ambitious **GREAT SOCIETY** program. Among its goals are ending poverty and racial injustice, spending more government money on education and the arts, reducing environmental pollution, and making health care available to more people.

**MARCH 2, 1965** The United States begins **OPERATION ROLLING THUNDER**, the military code name for the bombing of North Vietnam. Its purpose is to discourage the North Vietnamese from supplying the Viet Cong rebels in the south. There are currently twenty-five thousand U.S. military personnel in Vietnam, up from about one thousand when the late President Kennedy took office in 1961.

**MARCH 8, 1965** Two battalions of **MARINES LAND AT DANANG**, becoming the first U.S. combat troops to serve in Vietnam. The thirty-five hundred soldiers have been sent to guard the Danang air base against increasingly bold Viet Cong attacks. On July 28, President Johnson announces that draft calls will be doubled in order to bring U.S. troop strength in Vietnam up to 175,000 men.

**MARCH 7, 1965** In Selma, Alabama, **STATE TROOPERS ATTACK SIX HUNDRED CIVIL RIGHTS MARCHERS** with tear gas and nightsticks as they cross the Edmund Pettus Bridge. The marchers were headed for the state capitol in Montgomery to protest the February 18 killing of black voter-registration worker Jimmy Lee Jackson by a state trooper.

# The British Invasion

**The extraordinarily thin, boyish-looking Twiggy was the most popular British fashion model of the time.**

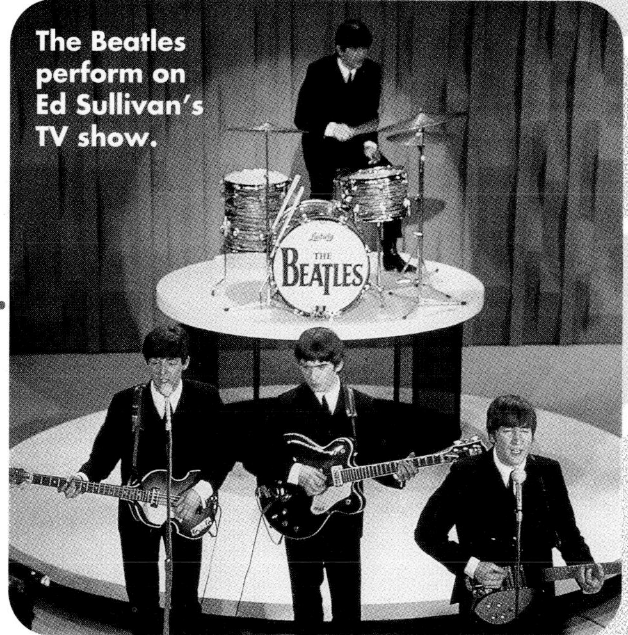

**The Beatles perform on Ed Sullivan's TV show.**

FROM THE MOMENT that the Beatles landed at Kennedy Airport, Beatlemania reigned. However, it soon became clear that England had more to offer than the Mop Tops from Liverpool. The deluge of music and fashion that followed the Beatles to America became known as the British Invasion. Suddenly, British bands were all over the pop music charts.

Beginning in February 1964, the Beatles held the Number One spot for three months with "I Want to Hold Your Hand," "She Loves You," and "Can't Buy Me Love." Other British bands with Number One hits in 1964 included Peter & Gordon ("A World Without Love"), the Animals ("House of the Rising Sun"), and Manfred Mann ("Do Wah Diddy Diddy").

The fashions that were imported along with the music came mostly from the designers along London's Carnaby Street. In 1965, Mary Quant introduced Americans to the mod look, which was then the rage of Swinging London. Quant's most important invention was the thigh-high miniskirt. London hairdresser Vidal Sassoon even devised a haircut to go with the clothes: a short, angled "bob."

**Mary Quant**

## Politics

JULY 30, 1965 At the Truman Presidential Library in Independence, Missouri, with Truman himself watching, President Johnson signs the bill establishing **MEDICARE**. The new law ends a twenty-year fight, begun by Truman, to win nationalized health insurance for the elderly. Medicare is designed to protect millions of senior citizens from being pushed into poverty by rising medical costs.

**SELMA MARCH • People from nearly every state who were concerned with the civil issue rights issue traveled to Alabama to show their support for Martin Luther King, Jr., during his march from Selma to Montgomery.**

## Life in the Sixties

MARCH 21–25, 1965 Reinforced by friends of the movement who came to Selma after the March 7 violence, Martin Luther King, Jr., leads four thousand people across the Edmund Pettus Bridge. By the time the marchers reach Montgomery, they number twenty-five thousand. Many consider King's **SELMA-TO-MONTGOMERY MARCH** to be the high-point of the nonviolent civil rights movement.

MARCH 24–25, 1965 Shortly after U.S. planes begin bombing North Vietnam [March 2, 1965], antiwar professors and students at the University of Michigan in Ann Arbor sponsor the first **TEACH-IN ON THE VIETNAM WAR**. More than thirty-five hundred people debate U.S. involvement, beginning in the late afternoon and continuing until dawn the next morning.

## Arts & Entertainment

SEPTEMBER 8, 1966 The science-fiction series **"STAR TREK"** premieres on the NBC television network. The show quickly becomes known for its plots, which treat modern-day problems in a thinly disguised way. Although "Star Trek" is canceled after only three seasons, the series becomes hugely popular in reruns.

JUNE 1, 1967 The Beatles release ***SERGEANT PEPPER'S LONELY HEARTS CLUB BAND***, the most eagerly awaited rock album ever made. Using state-of-the-art technology, the Beatles have recorded in the studio songs much too complex to ever be re-created live. The music also reflects the band's participation in the hallucinogenic drug culture.

JUNE 16–18, 1967 The three-day Monterey International Pop Festival in northern California features many of rock'n'roll's most important acts, including the Who and Jimi Hendrix, who play back to back. **MONTEREY POP** also introduces Janis Joplin, the Grateful Dead, Jefferson Airplane, and other psychedelic bands from San Francisco's happening Haight-Ashbury neighborhood.

## Science & Technology

DECEMBER 3, 1967 South African surgeon Christiaan Barnard leads a team of twenty doctors in the first successful **HUMAN HEART TRANSPLANT**. The patient, a grocer named Louis Washkansky, survives the operation but dies eighteen days later of pneumonia. The heart he received came from a fatally wounded accident victim.

1967 British astronomer Anthony Hewish and graduate student Jocelyn Bell discover pulsating neutron stars, also known as **PULSARS**. Pulsars are stars that send out short bursts of radiation at regular intervals. At first, before they discovered the source of these extraterrestrial signals, Hewish named the locations LGMs—for "little green men."

DECEMBER 21–27, 1968 The three-man **APOLLO 8** crew completes the first manned mission to the moon, which it orbits ten times before returning safely to Earth. The flight was originally scheduled to be a test of the new Saturn V rocket, but its purpose was changed after the CIA reported that the Soviets were planning their own lunar mission.

AUGUST 6, 1965 President Johnson signs the **VOTING RIGHTS ACT OF 1965**, which will make it easier for blacks to exercise their right to vote. The federal government can now prevent states from using poll taxes [January 23, 1964], literacy tests, and other unfair practices to restrict voter registration. The new law fulfills a longtime goal of the civil rights movement.

JANUARY 13, 1966 President Johnson names Robert C. Weaver to head the new Department of Housing and Urban Development. When the Senate confirms him four days later, Weaver becomes the **FIRST AFRICAN-AMERICAN CABINET MEMBER**. As the first HUD secretary, Weaver oversees Great Society [January 4, 1965] programs involving urban renewal and low-income housing.

JUNE 13, 1966 In the case of ***MIRANDA V. ARIZONA***, the Supreme Court rules that confessions can be thrown out if police do not first inform suspects of their constitutional rights, including the right to remain silent. Police complain that dangerous criminals will now be set free on technicalities. But others hail the decision as a safeguard against police misconduct.

AUGUST 11–16, 1965 In Los Angeles, **RACE RIOTS SPREAD THROUGH THE WATTS AREA**, killing thirty-four people and injuring thousands. Sparked by charges of police brutality following the arrest of a black youth for drunk driving, angry blacks loot and burn a five-hundred-square-block area until twenty thousand National Guardsmen restore order.

# THE MOON LANDING

**An Apollo 11 astronaut leaves the first human footprints on the moon.**

**More than six hundred million people around the world watched with awe as Neil Armstrong planted a U.S. flag on the moon.**

AS THE 1960s BEGAN, the United States knew it was losing the Space Race. The 1957 launch of Sputnik 1 had given the Soviets a substantial lead in space technology, and they quickly pressed their advantage. When cosmonaut Yuri Gagarin successfully orbited Earth on April 13, 1961, an embarrassed President Kennedy decided that something had to be done. On May 25 he announced that the United States was committing itself to "to land a man on the moon and return him safely to Earth" before the decade was out.

It took the National Aeronautics and Space Administration eight years to make good on Kennedy's bold promise, but NASA did indeed land astronauts on the moon by the end of the 1960s. On July 20, 1969, the lunar module Eagle landed on the surface of the moon. Aboard the Eagle were Apollo 11 astronauts Neil Armstrong and Edwin "Buzz" Aldrin. The third member of the crew, Michael Collins, stayed aboard the command module, which remained in lunar orbit. Neil Armstrong's first words as he stepped down onto the lunar surface were "one small step for a man, one giant leap for mankind."

**The Apollo 11 capsule after splashing down in the Pacific .**

## Politics

AUGUST 1966 Mao Zedong calls for a **CULTURAL REVOLUTION** to transform Chinese society. The Communist leader has become alarmed that educated people and party officials have privileges others do not. To erase this social elite, Mao expels students from the universities and organizes them into Red Guards that threaten intellectuals suspected of "counterrevolutionary" feelings.

**RALPH NADER • Nader surveys Interstate 495 near Washington, D.C. In addition to pointing out automobile safety hazards, Nader claimed that the highways were unsafe.**

## Life in the Sixties

SEPTEMBER 8, 1965 Led by labor organizer **CESAR CHAVEZ**, migrant farm workers, most of whom are Mexican American, strike grape growers in California. The demands include better wages and working conditions as well as recognition of their union. The strike gains momentum when Chavez asks college students and civil rights groups to help him organize a nationwide boycott of table grapes.

MARCH 22, 1966 During a Senate hearing, General Motors president James Roche apologizes for hiring a private investigator to spy on consumer advocate **RALPH NADER**. Nader's 1965 book, *Unsafe at Any Speed*, had exposed serious safety problems in General Motors cars, particularly the Chevrolet Corvair, and showed how the auto industry as a whole put profits ahead of passenger safety.

## Arts & Entertainment

OCTOBER 29, 1967 The hippie musical ***HAIR***, which will soon become the first Broadway show ever based on rock music, opens Off-Broadway at the Public Theater in New York City. *Hair*'s enormous popularity comes from its willingness to dramatize such controversial issues as the war in Vietnam, the draft, drug use, and free love.

NOVEMBER 1967 Twenty-one-year-old San Franciscan Jann Wenner starts a new magazine he calls ***ROLLING STONE***. Using $7,500, most of it borrowed, he prints an issue and sells six thousand copies. During the next decade, *Rolling Stone* becomes internationally famous as a journal of the counterculture and rock music in particular.

1967 Mike Nichols's film ***THE GRADUATE*** reflects young people's growing discontent with the values and life-styles of their parents. The movie stars Dustin Hoffman as a recent college graduate, with Anne Bancroft as his parents' seductive friend, Mrs. Robinson. The Simon & Garfunkel song named for her and written for the film's soundtrack tops the pop charts in June 1968.

## Science & Technology

OCTOBER 18, 1969 The Department of Health, Education, and Welfare bans the use of the artificial sweeteners called **CYCLAMATES**. HEW orders the ban on cyclamates because tests with animals have shown that these food and soft-drink sweeteners may cause cancer. The department eases the restrictions when the results of further tests are unclear.

1969 To prove his theory that Egyptians could have contacted Central Americans during prehistoric times, **THOR HEYERDAHL** [1947] sails from North Africa to the Caribbean aboard the *Ra*, an exact replica of an ancient Egyptian papyrus boat. During the fifty-seven-day journey, Heyerdahl sees garbage floating in the middle of the ocean, indicating how far pollution has spread.

JANUARY 21, 1970 Pan American Airways puts the first **BOEING 747** into service. Each of these new "jumbo jets" costs $21,400,000, but the 747's cost is easily offset by the jump in ticket sales caused by the large number of passengers wanting to fly.

FEBRUARY 10, 1967 The **TWENTY-FIFTH AMENDMENT**, ratified today, outlines what will happen should a president be killed or become disabled while in office. It sets forth the order in which various officeholders would become president. The amendment also allows the president to appoint a new vice president should the vice president die, resign, or leave office for some other reason.

JUNE 5, 1967 The **SIX DAY WAR** begins when Israeli planes attack air bases in the Arab nations of Egypt, Syria, and Jordan, nearly destroying all three air forces. Meanwhile, Israeli tanks seize the Sinai from Egypt, the West Bank from Jordan, and the Golan Heights from Syria. Shortly before the Israeli attacks, the Jewish state's three hostile neighbors had signed a military alliance.

AUGUST 30, 1967 The Senate confirms the president's appointment of **THURGOOD MARSHALL** to the Supreme Court. The renowned civil rights lawyer thus becomes the first African American to sit on the nation's highest court. Marshall's greatest victory as a lawyer came in 1954 when he convinced the Court in the *Brown v. Board of Education* case to end segregation in the public schools.

1966 *Feminine Mystique* author Betty Friedan [1963] helps to found the **NATIONAL ORGANIZATION FOR WOMEN** and becomes its first president. NOW's goals include equality for women in jobs and salary as well as an end to gender discrimination. In working to create a women's voting bloc, the group takes an important step toward an independent women's movement.

During 1968, more than half a million Americans served as soldiers in Vietnam.

# THE DRAFT

STOP THE WAR NOW

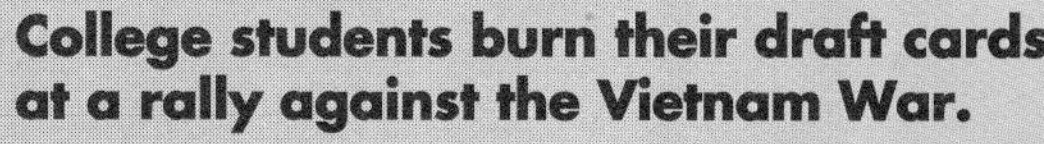

College students burn their draft cards at a rally against the Vietnam War.

**THE LANDING OF U.S. Marines in South Vietnam in March 1965 began a new phase in the Vietnam War. Before the Marines arrived, there were twenty thousand Americans in Vietnam. At the end of the year there were two hundred thousand. To provide the troops for this build-up, President Johnson announced in July that draft calls would be doubled. The army used the draft to force young men into military service. (Women were never drafted.)**

**Now that the prospect of dying in Vietnam was becoming much more real, the war became a hotly debated issue on college campuses. Students automatically received deferments, or postponements, while they remained in school. But many resisted the draft anyway, burning their registration cards, which meant breaking the law.**

**Some dodged the draft after graduation by pretending to have a variety of personal problems. Others fled to Canada, where they lived as fugitives until President Carter pardoned them in 1977. Because privileged whites often got around the draft, the burden of fighting and dying fell mostly on poor whites and racial minorities, who could not escape so easily.**

## Politics

JANUARY 30–31, 1968 During Tet, the Vietnamese New Year, North Vietnam launches a major surprise offensive, while Viet Cong guerrillas lead terrorist raids on large cities in the south. Although the attacks are eventually turned back, the **TET OFFENSIVE** makes it difficult for Americans to believe their government's claims that South Vietnam is winning the war.

MARCH 12, 1968 Campaigning against the war in Vietnam, Senator **EUGENE MCCARTHY** of Minnesota wins a surprising forty-two percent of the vote in the New Hampshire Democratic presidential primary. Although President Johnson receives seven thousand more votes, the close finish embarrasses the president, whose aides had claimed he would win easily.

## Life in the Sixties

JANUARY 14, 1967 Billed as a "Gathering of the Tribes," the **HUMAN BE-IN** draws twenty thousand hippies to San Francisco's Golden Gate Park as a prelude to the Summer of Love. Countercultural leaders such as Beat poet Allen Ginsberg and Timothy Leary, known for his experiments with drugs, speak between sets by psychedelic rock bands, including the Grateful Dead and Jefferson Airplane.

APRIL 28, 1967 Heavyweight champion Muhammad **ALI REFUSES TO BE DRAFTED** into the army because, as a member of the Nation of Islam [February 25, 1964], he opposes the Vietnam War for religious reasons. Boxing authorities strip him of his title, and ten days later the Justice Department charges him with draft evasion, claiming that his opposition is political rather than religious.

MUHAMMAD ALI • Heavyweight champion Muhammad Ali at the Armed Forces Induction Center in Houston, Texas, where he refused to be drafed into the army.

## Arts & Entertainment

JANUARY 22, 1968 The Monday-night series **"ROWAN & MARTIN'S LAUGH-IN"** premieres on the NBC television network. The show's rapid-fire, sometimes controversial political humor makes it an overnight sensation. Among its many catchphrases are "Sock it to me!" and "You bet your sweet bippy!" The show's title links it to the sit-ins, teach-ins, and be-ins sweeping the country.

1968 Director Stanley Kubrick's Oscar-winning film ***2001: A SPACE ODYSSEY*** sets a new standard for visual effects in movies. Its remarkably detailed scenes of spaceships and space travel prompt fans of psychedelia to dub it "the ultimate trip."

## Science & Technology

APRIL 1, 1970 President Nixon signs a new law **BANNING CIGARETTE ADVERTISING** on radio and television beginning January 1, 1971. The ban is followed a year later by a new Surgeon General's report showing that the health of nonsmokers may be damaged by exposure to the smoke of nearby cigarettes.

APRIL 13, 1970 An oxygen tank aboard the **APOLLO 13** spacecraft explodes, draining all the air from the capsule. The astronauts, who were expected to land on the moon, quickly move into the lunar module, which has its own oxygen supply. Using the lunar module as a lifeboat, they round the moon and return immediately to Earth, splashing down safely on April 17.

MARCH 16, 1968 Under orders to search and destroy groups suspected of helping the Viet Cong, Company C of Task Force Barker raids the South Vietnamese village of My Lai. Although no one resists them, soldiers commanded by Lieutenant William Calley massacre hundreds of civilians, including women and children. The army keeps the **MY LAI MASSACRE** secret for almost a year.

MARCH 31, 1968 During a televised speech on the war in Vietnam, President Johnson declares a partial halt to the bombing of North Vietnam and says he is willing to begin peace talks. The nation is then stunned by **LBJ'S ANNOUNCEMENT THAT HE WILL NOT RUN FOR ANOTHER TERM**. Recent polls have shown that only one in four Americans approves his handling of the war.

JUNE 5, 1968 **ROBERT KENNEDY IS SHOT AND KILLED** on the night of his victory in the California Democratic primary. The late president's brother decided to run after the New Hampshire primary [March 12, 1968] showed that Lyndon Johnson could be beaten. Kennedy's killer, a Jordanian named Sirhan Sirhan, despised the New York senator for his support of Israel.

JULY 23–30, 1967 The worst of 1967's seventy-five race riots erupts in Detroit, where many black militants are well armed. Rooftop snipers with automatic weapons control the Kercheval area for thirty-six hours, forcing the army to send in tanks to rescue soldiers trapped in police stations. Forty-three die in the **DETROIT RIOTS**, the worst violence inside the nation since the Civil War.

# THE COUNTERCULTURE

DURING THE 1960s, MANY young people pursued lifestyles that were very different from those of their conservative parents. Some were based on radical politics, while others, such as rural farm communes, developed out of the hippie ideals of unconditional love and sharing. These alternative lifestyles typically had one thing in common: a rejection of the Establishment.

The Establishment was the name given to all symbols of authority, especially the government and parents. Taken together, groups that rejected the Establishment were known as the counterculture. They all hoped to bring about ways of living that were new and better.

Perhaps the counterculture's greatest triumph came at the Woodstock Music and Art Fair, held in upstate New York on the weekend of August 15–17, 1969. Four hundred thousand people partied for three days to the music of Jimi Hendrix, Janis Joplin, Santana, and many others. To the rest of the world, the festival looked like a mess, especially after heavy rains turned the concert site into a muddy swamp. When food and medical supplies ran low, the site was declared a disaster area. But the party still went on, people shared what they had, and no one seemed to mind.

Hippies on their painted microbus at Woodstock.

At Woodstock, the counterculture's dream of a peaceful, loving community came true—for one weekend at least.

At Woodstock, Jimi Hendrix played a distorted, ear-splitting version of "The Star Spangled Banner."

## Politics

AUGUST 20–21, 1968 Much as they did in Hungary [November 4, 1956], Soviet tanks roll into Prague, Czechoslovakia, where they forcefully end the period of openness known as the **PRAGUE SPRING**. Czech leader Alexander Dubcek had been hoping to create "Communism with a human face," but Soviet authorities feared that his reforms would weaken their grip on eastern Europe.

AUGUST 26–29, 1968 Ten thousand people travel to the **DEMOCRATIC NATIONAL CONVENTION IN CHICAGO** to protest the party's support for the Vietnam War. Police respond by gassing and beating the mostly peaceful demonstrators in what is described as a "police riot." Meanwhile, members of the Youth International Party, known as Yippies, nominate a pig as their candidate for president.

NOVEMBER 5, 1968 Republican candidate Richard Nixon narrowly defeats Vice President Hubert Humphrey in the **1968 PRESIDENTIAL ELECTION**. Most observers believe that Humphrey, the Democratic nominee, lost the election because antiwar voters, who would normally have voted for him, blamed him for President Johnson's Vietnam policies.

## Life in the Sixties

OCTOBER 21, 1967 As a finale to Stop the Draft Week, antiwar groups lead a **MARCH ON THE PENTAGON**. More than seventy-five thousand people surround the building, hoping to slow the government's war effort in Vietnam. Soldiers beat about fourteen hundred protestors and arrest seven thousand, including author Norman Mailer, who chronicles the event in *The Armies of the Night* (1968).

APRIL 4, 1968 A white man, James Earl Ray, assassinates thirty-nine-year-old Martin Luther King, Jr., as the civil rights leader leans against a second-floor railing at the Lorraine Motel in Memphis, Tennessee. King had come to Memphis to help organize a garbage collectors' strike. Race riots, which break out in 124 cities, continue for more than a week after the **KING ASSASSINATION**.

OCTOBER 18, 1968 During a medals ceremony at the Mexico City Olympics, U.S. sprinters Tommy Smith and John Carlos raise their gloved fists in a **BLACK POWER SALUTE**. Like other black athletes, Smith and Carlos, who placed first and third in the two-hundred-meter dash, had been looking for a way to protest discrimination against blacks in the United States.

## Arts & Entertainment

APRIL 4, 1969 The **CBS NETWORK CANCELS "THE SMOTHERS BROTHERS COMEDY HOUR,"** despite high ratings, because of the show's repeated battles with the network censors. The Sunday-night variety program starring Tom and Dick Smothers featured many jokes on political topics. These jokes, like the show's guests, were often outspoken, liberal, and antiwar.

NOVEMBER 1969 The new Public Broadcasting Service (PBS) begins airing **"SESAME STREET,"** a daily hour-long program for children created by Joan Ganz Cooney and the Children's Television Workshop. A breakthrough in educational television, "Sesame Street" uses techniques developed for advertising to teach youngsters the alphabet as well as simple math.

**SESAME STREET • Jim Henson, creator of the Muppets, with Kermit the Frog, one of the many Muppet characters featured on Sesame Street.**

## Science & Technology

APRIL 22, 1970 Environmentalists celebrate the first **EARTH DAY** with demonstrations and rallies across the United States. Their activities call public attention to the growing environmental movement, which has been built in part on the counterculture's search for a simpler way of life.

**March 19, 1969** During his campaign last year, President Nixon claimed to have a "secret plan" to end the war in Vietnam. Today, Secretary of Defense Melvin Laird announces a new U.S. policy toward South Vietnam called **VIETNAMIZATION**. Under the Nixon plan, half a million U.S. troops in Vietnam will gradually be replaced by South Vietnamese soldiers.

**June 8, 1969** After meeting with South Vietnamese president Nguyen Van Thieu, President Nixon announces that twenty-five thousand **U.S. SOLDIERS WILL LEAVE VIETNAM** by the end of August, marking the first drop in U.S. force strength since the Marines landed at Danang [March 8, 1965]. On September 16, Nixon announces the withdrawal of thirty-five thousand more soldiers.

**February 21, 1970** National Security Adviser Henry Kissinger begins **SECRET PEACE TALKS** in Paris with Le Duc Tho of North Vietnam. The talks continue on and off for the next three years while the fighting in Vietnam also continues. Although Kissinger, a former political science professor, has little diplomatic experience, he soon becomes Nixon's most trusted foreign policy aide.

**June 28, 1969** About three in the morning, the police raid the Stonewall Inn, the most popular gay bar in New York City's Greenwich Village. For many years, gays had not resisted police beatings and harassment. This time, however, they fight back. Activists later point to the **STONEWALL RIOT** as the beginning of the gay rights movement.

# BLACK POWER

At first, the civil rights movement adhered very closely to the goals of nonviolence and integration set by Martin Luther King, Jr. By 1965, however, many blacks in the movement had become frustrated with the slow pace of change.

In May 1966, members of the Student Nonviolent Coordinating Committee (SNCC) met to elect new officers and discuss its future as a civil rights group. John Lewis, a follower of Dr. King, had served as SNCC's chairman since 1963. But this year he was challenged by Stokely Carmichael, who wanted to take SNCC in a much more aggressive direction. Like Malcolm X, he wanted change "by any means necessary," even violence.

By electing Carmichael over Lewis, SNCC reflected an important change taking place within the African-American community. Many blacks no longer believed that King's nonviolent strategy would work, and they took quickly to the "black power" that Carmichael advocated. In December 1966, SNCC's black members voted to expel all whites from the organization.

**Stokely Carmichael first made national news in Alabama in 1965, when he organized the Lowndes Country Freedom Organization to run black candidates against the all-white Republicans and Democrats. He later allied himself with the militant Black Panther party, which took its name from the black panther symbol created for Carmichael's Lowndes County group.**

**In 1966, Huey Newton and other black activists founded the Black Panther party. The Black Panthers' original purpose was to protect black neighborhoods from police brutality.**

## Politics

APRIL 30, 1970 President Nixon announces on television that he has ordered U.S. troops to cross the South Vietnamese–Cambodian border. Pointing to a map, the president indicates areas inside Cambodia where North Vietnamese troops are believed to be hiding. He insists the **INVASION OF CAMBODIA** does not represent a widening of the war.

MIRACLE METS • Fans at Shea Stadium celebrate the Mets' 1969 World Series victory.

## Life in the Sixties

OCTOBER 8–11, 1969 The Weathermen, a violent offshoot of Students for a Democratic Society, begin the **DAYS OF RAGE** in Chicago. On the first day, six hundred men and women in leather boots and helmets storm the Drake Hotel, where Judge Julius Hoffman, the presiding judge in the Chicago Eight trial, lives. The Weathermen hope to trigger mass violence that will bring down the government.

OCTOBER 16, 1969 The New York Mets win the World Series just seven years after coming into the league as an expansion team. Beating the powerful Baltimore Orioles in five games, the **MIRACLE METS** complete an improbable season in which they struggled in third place until late August. Violinist Isaac Stern declares, "If the Mets can win the Series, anything can happen—even peace."

## Arts & Entertainment

DECEMBER 6, 1969 Unable to play at Woodstock in August, the Rolling Stones stage their own music festival at the **ALTAMONT** Speedway outside San Francisco. Unfortunately, as the Stones begin to play "Sympathy for the Devil," members of the Hell's Angels motorcycle gang, who had been hired as security guards, stab and kill a young black man holding what looked like a gun.

1969 Twenty-year-old Yale student Garry Trudeau begins distributing his antiwar comic strip **"DOONESBURY"** to twenty-five newspapers nationwide. Trudeau began the strip in 1968 in the *Yale Daily News* under the title "Bull Notes." "Doonesbury" surges in popularity after 1972, when it begins satirizing the growing Watergate scandal.

1969 Although studios have been making exploitation movies about hippies, bikers, and drug users for years, ***EASY RIDER*** is the first major film made by people inside the counterculture. It tells the story of two motorcycle-riding drug dealers, played by director Dennis Hopper and producer Peter Fonda, who ride from Los Angeles to New Orleans, experiencing the country.

## Science & Technology

JULY 1970 President Nixon signs an executive order establishing the **ENVIRONMENTAL PROTECTION AGENCY**. On December 2, the day the EPA becomes active, the Senate confirms William Ruckelshaus as its first director. Nixon's action follows his February 4 executive order that federal agencies stop polluting the air and water.

NOVEMBER 18, 1970 Chemist Linus Pauling, winner of a 1954 Nobel Prize for his research into chemical bonding, reports that large doses of **VITAMIN C CAN PREVENT THE COMMON COLD**. Doctors are not convinced, but much of the public accepts Pauling's controversial claim.

1971 Three Intel Corporation engineers build the first commercial **MICROPROCESSOR**: the Intel 4004. This revolutionary integrated circuit [September 12, 1958], or microchip, contains a tiny computer processor, which forms the basis for the computer revolution that follows.

JUNE 13, 1971 The *New York Times* begins publishing a history of the Vietnam War written secretly for the government. Daniel Ellsberg, a consultant to the military, leaked the study to reporter Neil Sheehan, who has been working with a team of thirty colleagues to digest the material. The **PENTAGON PAPERS** reveal that the government has consistently lied about events in Vietnam.

JUNE 30, 1971 In the **PENTAGON PAPERS CASE**, the Supreme Court rules that the *New York Times* may continue to publish the secret documents. The Justice Department had sued to stop publication, claiming risks to national security, but the Court decides that the public's right to know is more important. An angry President Nixon approves formation of a "plumbers" unit to "fix leaks" to the press.

JUNE 30, 1971 Ratification of the **TWENTY-SIXTH AMENDMENT** lowers the voting age to eighteen. The constitutional change extends an act passed by Congress in 1970 giving eighteen-year-olds the vote in national elections. Many college students had complained that if they were old enough to fight for their country in Vietnam, they should also be old enough to vote for its leaders.

NOVEMBER 15, 1969 The New Mobilization Committee to End the War in Vietnam hosts the **LARGEST DEMONSTRATION EVER HELD IN WASHINGTON**. Estimates of the number of protesters range as high as eight hundred thousand. The organizers of the march, an umbrella organization known as the Mobe, represent eighty-four antiwar groups, from the Quakers to the Communists.

# CHICAGO EIGHT

**FOLLOWING THE VIOLENCE OUTSIDE the 1968 Democratic National Convention, eight radical antiwar leaders were arrested and charged with conspiring to start the riots there. The defendants, who claimed they were being tried for their political beliefs and not their actions, included Abbie Hoffman and Jerry Rubin of the Youth International Party (or Yippies), Tom Hayden of Students for a Democratic Society, and Black Panther chairman Bobby Seale.**

**From the beginning, the trial of the Chicago Eight was theatrical. The seventy-four-year-old judge, Julius Hoffman, made clear his distaste for the defendants. They responded by showing their disrespect for him, his court, and the government that controlled it. The eight defendants sang, read poetry, and shouted insults at the judge, who ordered Bobby Seale bound and gagged for his disruptive behavior. Shortly afterward, the government decided to try Seale separately, and the Chicago Eight became the Chicago Seven.**

**The trial, which began in September 1969, ended on February 18, 1970, when the seven remaining defendants were found not guilty of the conspiracy charges. Five of the seven were convicted of lesser riot-related charges, but these convictions were all overturned on appeal, in part because Judge Hoffman displayed such bias against the defendants.**

**Abbie Hoffman jokingly told reporters that Judge Julius Hoffman was his father.**

**Bobby Seale**

**The defendants hold a press conference.**

## Politics

OCTOBER 25, 1971 After expelling the Chinese Nationalists based on Taiwan, the **UNITED NATIONS RECOGNIZES THE PEOPLE'S REPUBLIC** as the true government of China. The United States reversed its opposition to this move after Henry Kissinger made a secret trip to mainland China, during which Premier Zhou Enlai promised not to take military action against Taiwan.

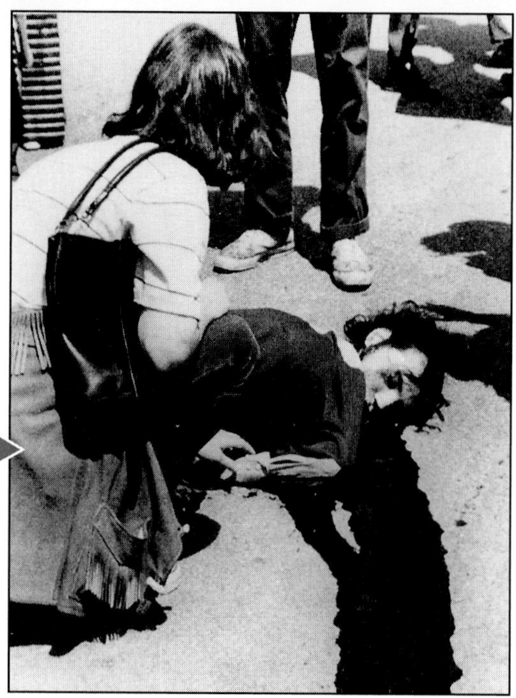

**KENT STATE • A student tries to help one of twelve people shot by National Guardsmen during a rally on campus protesting the Vietnam War.**

## Life in the Sixties

MAY 4, 1970 National Guardsmen fire on student demonstrators at **KENT STATE** University in Ohio, killing four and wounding eight. Most students had mistakenly believed that the jittery guardsmen were using rubber bullets. The soldiers were called in after students protesting the bombing of Cambodia [April 30, 1970] set fire to an army ROTC building on May 2.

SEPTEMBER 21, 1970 **"MONDAY NIGHT FOOTBALL"** debuts on the ABC network with a game featuring the New York Jets and brash quarterback "Broadway" Joe Namath, who had guaranteed the Jets' victory in Super Bowl III. ABC's announcing team includes Keith Jackson, Don Meredith, and Howard Cosell, whose fancy language and forceful opinions make the show a hit.

## Arts & Entertainment

SEPTEMBER 18, 1970 The **DEATH OF JIMI HENDRIX** from drug-related causes shocks the counterculture, especially when it is followed two weeks later by Janis Joplin's fatal heroin overdose. The premature deaths of these popular musicians, both twenty-seven years old, mark the end for many of the optimism associated with the 1960s.

SEPTEMBER 19, 1970 **"THE MARY TYLER MOORE SHOW"** premieres on the CBS network, presenting Moore in an unusual role for a lead actress on television. She plays Mary Richards, an ambitious, career-minded single woman living in the midwestern city of Minneapolis, Minnesota. Moore's character soon comes to symbolize the independent career woman of the 1970s.

1970 ***ARE YOU THERE GOD? IT'S ME, MARGARET*** sets Judy Blume apart as one of the country's leading modern children's authors. Blume's first book, *The One in the Middle Is the Green Kangaroo* (1969), established her concern with the middle child in families. *Are You There God? It's Me, Margaret*, however, takes on more universal questions of religious belief.

## Science & Technology

1971 In an isolated region of the Philippines, anthropologists discover the **TASADAY**, a tribe of people who live in caves, dress in loincloths, and use crude tools, much as people did during the Stone Age. The find generates worldwide attention. In 1986, however, investigators charge that the Tasaday were a publicity stunt created by Philippine president Ferdinand Marcos.

1971 Harvard biologist Edward O. Wilson publishes *The Insect Societies*, in which he describes the behavior of ants and other insects that live in groups. Wilson soon applies this knowledge to other animals, including humans, founding the study of **SOCIOBIOLOGY**. Wilson assumes that genetic traits determine how animals behave.

JUNE 14, 1972 The Environmental Protection Agency bans **DDT**, a chemical widely used by farmers to protect their crops from insects. The use of DDT first became controversial after the publication of Rachel Carson's *Silent Spring* [September 1962].

FEBRUARY 21–28, 1972 President Nixon travels to China. His historic visit is the first by any U.S. president to the Communist People's Republic. Many regard Nixon's **"OPENING THE DOOR" TO CHINA** as the greatest success of his career. Television coverage of Nixon's visit provides Americans with their first glimpse of life in a country hidden from the West for more than twenty years.

MARCH 22, 1972 After it passes both houses, Congress sends the proposed Twenty-seventh Amendment to the states for ratification. Known as the **EQUAL RIGHTS AMENDMENT**, the new law calls for complete legal equality between the sexes, including equal pay for equal work. At first, it appears that the amendment will be easily ratified, but support for the ERA soon dwindles.

MAY 26, 1972 During a visit to Moscow, President Nixon and Soviet premier Leonid Brezhnev sign the **SALT** strategic arms limitation treaty. The SALT agreement limits nuclear defense systems and freezes the number of missiles for each nation. Nixon's friendliness to China and the Soviet Union is particularly remarkable given his lifelong attacks against Communism [January 21, 1950].

MARCH 8, 1971 Less than six months after a federal judge orders Muhammad Ali's boxing license renewed, the flamboyant Ali meets Joe Frazier in a showdown of unbeaten champions. The first **ALI-FRAZIER FIGHT** goes the full fifteen rounds, with the shy but determined Frazier winning a unanimous decision. Three months later, the Supreme Court finds Ali not guilty of draft evasion [April 28, 1967].

# THE SILENT MAJORITY

**BECAUSE POLITICAL protesters and other activists were so visible during the 1960s, it was sometimes tempting to conclude that all Americans were pacifists, hippies, Black Panthers, or feminists. If that were the case, however, Richard Nixon would never have won the 1968 presidential election. But he did, and he deeply resented the constant attacks on his policies now that he was president. Nixon believed that his opponents were only a small minority of Americans and that most people supported him.**

**In late 1969, as antiwar rallies grew in number and size, Nixon's handling of the Vietnam War came under increasingly heavy attack. Demonstrators demanded that Nixon withdraw all U.S. troops from South Vietnam, yet the president feared that South Vietnam would collapse if the troops were pulled out right away.**

**On November 3, 1969, Nixon gave a speech in which he asked for support from the "silent majority" of Americans who shared his goal of "peace with honor." In response to the speech, the White House received nearly one hundred thousand letters and telegrams backing the president's policy, and his approval rating soared to seventy percent.**

**The outpouring of support from the Silent Majority for Nixon's policies allowed the president to continue his pursuit of "peace with honor" in Vietnam. As a result, U.S. troops continued to fight there for another three years.**

# The Seventies

DURING THE EARLY 1970s, Americans learned that the U.S. government had been withholding information from them—about Vietnam, about FBI harassment of political groups, about the morals of their leaders. They discovered that President Richard Nixon had broken the law when he attempted to cover up his knowledge of the Watergate break-in. These disclosures destroyed the trust most Americans had in their government. Disillusioned and frustrated, many 1960s activists turned inward. They jogged and ate health foods to make themselves fit. They practiced yoga and transcendental meditation to relieve their stress. The Me Generation, journalists called them.

Meanwhile, important changes were taking place in the U.S. economy. The Arab oil embargo, imposed in 1973, doubled gasoline prices from an average of thirty cents per gallon during the 1960s to nearly sixty cents per gallon by 1975. Americans had been accustomed to buying big cars and cheap gasoline. Now "gas guzzlers" were too expensive to drive, and middle-class families found themselves buying small foreign-made cars instead.

★

## Politics

**June 17, 1972** District of Columbia police catch former FBI agent James McCord and four others breaking into the offices of the Democratic National Committee in the **WATERGATE** building. The burglars were fixing electronic bugs planted in the committee's telephones during a previous break-in. Papers found on the men show that they work for the Committee to Reelect the President.

**August 12, 1972** The **LAST U.S. COMBAT TROOPS LEAVE VIETNAM**, completing President Nixon's Vietnamization policy [March 19, 1969]. The burden of fighting the ground war now rests on the South Vietnamese. However, nearly fifty thousand Americans—including civilian office workers, military advisers, and bomber crews—remain behind to provide advice and assistance.

## Life in the Seventies

**June 19, 1972** In a case involving St. Louis Cardinals outfielder **CURT FLOOD**, the Supreme Court upholds baseball's reserve clause, which keeps players bound to their teams. The dispute began in the spring of 1970 when the Cardinals traded Flood to the Phillies and Flood refused to report to his new team. Flood had sued for the right to play for any team he liked.

**January 23, 1972** Gloria Steinem and thirteen other women put out the first issue of ***MS.* MAGAZINE**. The three-hundred-thousand-copy press run sells out in just nine days. Highlighting feminist issues, *Ms.* enjoys a wide readership among supporters of women's liberation.

**MS. MAGAZINE • *Ms.* began as a pull-out supplement to *New York* magazine. The first cover showed all the roles women were expected to fill, including mother, housewife, nurse, and businesswoman.**

## Arts & Entertainment

**1973** ***AMERICAN GRAFFITI*** tells the nostalgic story of four young men in 1962 on the night before two of them leave for college. The film, written and directed by George Lucas, wins Academy Award nominations for best picture, best director, and best screenplay. Meanwhile, the soundtrack album of early rock'n'roll classics spurs a 1950s revival.

**1973** The Public Broadcasting Service airs **"AN AMERICAN FAMILY,"** a twelve-part documentary series about the well-to-do Louds of Santa Barbara, California. The documentary's portrayal of intimate family details arouses a great deal of controversy, some calling it brilliant television and others an invasion of privacy.

## Science & Technology

**1972** At Koobi Fora in northern Kenya, paleontologist **RICHARD LEAKEY** discovers the skull of a human ancestor more that two million years old. The skull dazzles the scientific community because it lacks the pronounced brow of related fossils and has nearly twice the brain capacity.

**1972** At 1,350 feet, New York's **WORLD TRADE CENTER** becomes the tallest building in the world. Built at a cost of $750 million, the Twin Towers each rise 110 stories into the air. Two years later, however, the Sears Tower in Chicago becomes the world's tallest structure at 1,454 feet.

**1972** Computer pioneer Nolan Bushnell develops Pong, the world's first commercial **VIDEO GAME**. An electronic version of Ping-Pong, Bushnell's game allows two players to control rectangular "paddles" on a video screen, while the game's microprocessor [1971] controls the "ball."

SEPTEMBER 5, 1972 **ARAB TERRORISTS INTERRUPT THE MUNICH OLYMPIC GAMES** when they raid the Israeli team's quarters, killing two coaches and taking nine athletes hostage. After a day of difficult negotiations, the eight terrorists and their captives are flown by helicopter to a nearby airport, where five of the terrorists and all nine hostages die in a shootout with German police.

OCTOBER 26, 1972 Just two weeks before the presidential election, National Security Adviser Henry Kissinger announces at a press conference that **"PEACE IS AT HAND"** in Vietnam. President Nixon's top foreign policy aide has just returned from talks in Paris with representatives of North Vietnam [February 21, 1970]. The next day, Nixon orders a halt to the bombing of Hanoi.

NOVEMBER 7, 1972 Richard Nixon wins a second term with a landslide victory over Democratic antiwar candidate George McGovern in the **1972 PRESIDENTIAL ELECTION**. Reports that Nixon might be linked to the Watergate burglary seem not to have had any effect on the voters. In fact, polls show that most people have never heard of the break-in [June 17, 1972].

FEBRUARY 28–MAY 8, 1973 Members of the American Indian Movement led by Dennis Banks and Russell Means occupy the South Dakota town of **WOUNDED KNEE**. They want to call attention to the government's poor treatment of Indians. AIM's leaders chose Wounded Knee for symbolic reasons: In 1890, the Seventh Cavalry massacred a band of defenseless Sioux there.

# Gloria Steinem

Gloria Steinem at the 1972 Democratic National Convention.

**IN THE APRIL 1969 ISSUE of *New York* magazine, journalist Gloria Steinem published an openly feminist essay called "After Black Power, Women's Liberation." In this article Steinem pointed out that many women from the civil rights and antiwar movements were now taking up an even more personal cause: women's rights.**

**Steinem quickly became one of the leading supporters of what became known as women's liberation. In 1971, she joined with *Feminine Mystique* author Betty Friedan and New York congresswomen Bella Abzug and Shirley Chisholm in founding the National Women's Political Caucus. The NWPC promoted such issues as equal pay for equal work and a woman's right to have an abortion. Steinem's writings in *Ms.* magazine, which she helped found, and her personal appearances soon built feminism into a national movement.**

**The success of *Ms.*, in particular, made Steinem famous, and she used her fame and money to promote her cause. During the late 1970s, she worked hard to win ratification of the Equal Rights Amendment. In 1978, she helped organize the July 9 Women's March on Washington, which drew one hundred thousand marchers and convinced Congress to extend the deadline for ERA ratification by another four years.**

Women in Springfield, Illinois, march in support of the Equal Rights Amendment.

## Politics

DECEMBER 18, 1972 When the Vietnam peace talks being held in Paris stall once again, President Nixon orders the renewed bombing of Hanoi and nearby Haiphong harbor. Nixon believes that around-the-clock air raids will convince North Vietnam to reduce its demands. The president halts the **CHRISTMAS BOMBING** on December 30 when the North Vietnamese offer to return to the peace table.

JANUARY 22, 1973 In the case of ***ROE V. WADE***, one of the most controversial in U.S. history, the Supreme Court rules that every woman has the right to obtain an abortion during the first three months of pregnancy. The Court's decision overturns state laws that deny women abortions during these months. Antiabortion groups protest the decision, claiming that abortion is murder.

JANUARY 27, 1973 President Nixon announces that National Security Adviser Henry Kissinger and Le Duc Tho of North Vietnam have agreed to a **CEASE-FIRE IN THE VIETNAM WAR**. The agreement calls for the return of U.S. prisoners in exchange for the withdrawal of U.S. forces. Refusing to admit defeat, the president claims he has achieved "peace with honor."

## Life in the Seventies

SEPTEMBER 20, 1973 In the **BATTLE OF THE SEXES TENNIS MATCH**, Wimbledon champion Billie Jean King defeats Bobby Riggs, an aging former champion and outspoken opponent of feminism. King wins the match, televised nationally from the Houston Astrodome, in three straight sets. With her victory, she captures the one-hundred-thousand-dollar winner-take-all purse.

DECEMBER 15, 1973 Reversing its century-old stand on the matter, the American Psychiatric Association announces that it no longer considers **HOMOSEXUALITY** to be an illness. This action comes in response to the growing gay liberation movement [June 28, 1969].

1973 California chef Alice Waters uses a ten-thousand-dollar loan to open her Chez Panisse restaurant in Berkeley. Waters's imaginative cooking style features fresh ingredients, many grown in her own garden. Chez Panisse soon popularizes this healthful new way of eating, which the media dubs **CALIFORNIA CUISINE**.

## Arts & Entertainment

JANUARY 15, 1974 Hoping to ride the wave of 1950s nostalgia, ABC television begins broadcasting a situation comedy set in mid-1950s Milwaukee, Wisconsin. The weekly series stars Ron Howard as high school student Richie Cunningham and Henry Winkler as the Fonz, a motorcycle-riding dropout. In just two years, **"HAPPY DAYS"** becomes the most popular show in all of television.

FEBRUARY 12, 1974 The KGB, or Soviet secret police, arrests Nobel Prize–winning author **ALEXANDER SOLZHENITSYN** after his account of the Soviet prison system, *The Gulag Archipelago*, is published in the West. Charged with treason, he is stripped of his citizenship and deported the following day. Eventually, he settles in Vermont, where the climate reminds him of his homeland.

**ALEXANDER SOLZHENITSYN • Solzhenitsyn became internationally famous after he wrote *One Day in the Life of Ivan Denisovich* (1962), about life in a forced-labor camp during the Stalin era.**

## Science & Technology

MAY 14, 1973 NASA launches the **SKYLAB** space station. The mission runs into trouble, however, when a malfunction destroys one of the two main solar panels. After a ten-day delay, during which mission controllers ponder the situation, NASA launches the Skylab crew, which docks with the station and repairs most of the damage.

JUNE 25, 1973 Former White House counsel **JOHN DEAN** begins five days of testimony before a Senate committee investigating the Watergate burglary [June 17, 1972]. Dean tells the committee that President Nixon knew of the break-in and helped to cover it up. Dean also claims that top Nixon aides H.R. Haldeman and John Ehrlichman were involved.

JULY 16, 1973 Testifying before the Senate Watergate committee, deputy White House chief of staff Alexander Butterfield reveals that President Nixon taped conversations in the Oval Office. On July 23, special prosecutor Archibald Cox issues a legal demand, or subpoena, for the **WHITE HOUSE TAPES**. Nixon refuses, claiming reasons of national security and executive privilege.

OCTOBER 6, 1973 The **YOM KIPPUR WAR** begins when Egypt and Syria jointly attack Israel on the most sacred Jewish holiday. Both Egypt (the Sinai) and Syria (the Golan Heights) invade through lands seized by Israel during the Six Day War [June 5, 1967]. Although surprised Israeli troops suffer losses at first, they soon push into Syria and Egypt, redrawing the map of the Middle East.

FEBRUARY 5, 1974 The Symbionese Liberation Army, a small band of radicals, kidnaps **PATTY HEARST**, the nineteen-year-old daughter of wealthy publisher Randolph Hearst. On February 12, the SLA demands a ransom of seventy dollars' worth of food for every needy Californian. In response, the Hearsts begin a two-million-dollar food giveaway.

**Carl Bernstein (left) and Bob Woodward retraced their investigations in the best-selling book *All the President's Men,* published in 1974. Their experience encouraged future generations of reporters to pursue corruption much more vigorously.**

# WATERGATE

THE WATERGATE SCANDAL not only forced the first resignation of a president but also shook Americans' faith in their government. For at least a year after the June 17, 1972, break-in at the Democratic party headquarters in the Watergate office complex, most Americans refused to accept that there were criminals in the White House. Even President Nixon's political enemies found it difficult to believe that he had ordered illegal phone taps, burglaries, and FBI investigations.

Although most other reporters let the story drop, Bob Woodward and Carl Bernstein of the *Washington Post* followed the trail of hundred-dollar bills found on the Watergate burglars. The money led them directly to the Committee to Reelect the President, known as CREEP. Woodward and Bernstein eventually discovered that the break-in was only one of many "dirty tricks" carried out by Nixon's staff.

**Richard Nixon delivers his resignation speech.**

In the spring of 1973, articles in the *Post* pushed the Senate to appoint a special committee to investigate the growing scandal. Testimony by witnesses at the hearings threatened the trust Americans had in their public servants. The disillusionment produced by the Watergate scandal can still be found in the popular attitude that all politicians are crooks.

## Politics

**OCTOBER 10, 1973** Vice President Spiro **AGNEW RESIGNS** after making a deal with prosecutors to avoid going to jail. Agnew had been charged with failure to pay income tax on bribes he allegedly took while governor of Maryland. Although Agnew's crimes have nothing to do with Watergate, his plea bargain deepens public distrust of the Nixon administration.

**PATTY HEARST • Hearst, who renamed herself Tanya, poses with a rifle in front of a Symbionese Liberation Army flag. This photograph was used as evidence of her radical conversion.**

## Life in the Seventies

**MARCH 4, 1974** Hoping to reach the people who once subscribed to *Life* magazine, which ceased publication two years ago, Time, Inc. launches ***PEOPLE***. The success of the new gossip-oriented weekly leads to a broad expansion in the field of celebrity journalism. Some critics attack the magazine for the shallowness of its stories, but sales at supermarket checkout counters remain high.

**APRIL 8, 1974** Atlanta Braves slugger **HANK AARON** hits his 715th home run. Hammerin' Hank's shot breaks the career record set by Babe Ruth nearly forty years earlier. Aaron, who began his career in the Negro leagues [February 13, 1920], received hate mail from white fans who did not want to see a black break Ruth's record.

**APRIL 15, 1974** After claiming in an April 3 message that she has joined her kidnappers [February 5, 1974], **PATTY HEARST** helps them rob a San Francisco bank. While friends and family claim that she has been brainwashed, Hearst remains on the run from the FBI until her capture on September 18, 1975. A year later, a jury convicts her of bank robbery, and she gets seven years in jail.

## Arts & Entertainment

**1974** Former British diplomat John Le Carré publishes ***TINKER, TAILOR, SOLDIER, SPY***, a spy novel about Secret Service agent George Smiley. The opposite of James Bond [1953], Smiley is overweight, dull, and uncomfortable with people. Le Carré's novels are read worldwide because they precisely capture the Cold War fear of not knowing whom to believe or trust.

**OCTOBER 11, 1975** The premiere of NBC's ***"SATURDAY NIGHT LIVE"*** features comedy sketches by the Not Ready for Prime Time Players. The program soon launches such comic stars as Chevy Chase, John Belushi, Dan Aykroyd, Bill Murray, and Gilda Radner. Guest hosts range from comedian George Carlin, the first host, to consumer advocate Ralph Nader [March 22, 1966].

**1975** ***ONE FLEW OVER THE CUCKOO'S NEST*** becomes the first film since *It Happened One Night* (1934) to sweep the top five Academy Awards. One goes to Jack Nicholson for his portrayal of a prisoner who fakes insanity to avoid a work detail. Another goes to Lawrence Hauben and Bo Goldman for their adaptation of Ken Kesey's 1962 novel about a sane man in an insane world.

## Science & Technology

**JUNE 1974** In an article in *Emergency Medicine* magazine, Cincinnati surgeon Henry Jay Heimlich describes a new method for saving choking victims. The technique, which comes to be known as the **HEIMLICH MANEUVER**, uses sharp upward thrusts just below the rib cage to dislodge the blockage. It has since been credited with saving thousands of lives.

**1974** During the Arab oil embargo [October 19–21, 1973], the Department of Transportation approves the use of motorized bicycles, called **MOPEDS**. Half motorcycle and half bicycle, mopeds have a top speed of 35 miles per hour, but they get 150 miles to a gallon of gas. More than 250,000 Americans buy the inexpensive, economical mopeds during the next three years.

**1974** Universal Product Code labels, or **BAR CODES**, begin appearing on food packages across the United States. The labels help speed customers through supermarket checkout lines because they can be read by electronic scanners. At first, supermarkets are reluctant to invest in the scanners, but they eventually welcome the new technology.

OCTOBER 19–21, 1973 The Arab states that control the Organization of Petroleum Exporting Countries stop oil shipments to the United States to punish Americans for their support of Israel during the ongoing Yom Kippur War [October 6, 1973]. The **ARAB OIL EMBARGO** soon leads to soaring prices, shortages, rationing, and long lines at the gas pump.

OCTOBER 20, 1973 After Archibald Cox refuses to give up his fight for the White House tapes [July 16, 1973], President Nixon orders Attorney General Elliot Richardson to fire him. Both Richardson and his deputy, William Ruckelshaus, resign rather than fire the special prosecutor. Finally, Solicitor General Robert Bork carries out the president's order, ending the **SATURDAY NIGHT MASSACRE**.

JANUARY 4, 1974 South Vietnamese president Nguyen Van Thieu admits that the cease-fire in Vietnam has not held. **"THE WAR HAS RESTARTED,"** he declares. About sixty thousand soldiers have died in battle since the signing of the Paris peace accord one year ago [January 27, 1973]. On April 4, Congress rejects a struggling President Nixon's request for more aid to South Vietnam.

JUNE 12, 1974 League officials announce that **GIRLS CAN PLAY LITTLE LEAGUE BASEBALL**. They admit that the "changing social climate" has led them to reconsider their longstanding opposition to letting girls play. Two years later, a popular film comedy, *The Bad News Bears*, tells the story of one girl, played by actress Tatum O'Neal, who becomes a pitching star for a Little League team.

**During the energy crisis of the 1970s, long lines and rationing at gas stations encouraged many Americans to buy foreign cars, which used much less fuel than large American "gas guzzlers."**

# THE ENERGY CRISIS

IN JUNE 1973, PRESIDENT Nixon warned Americans that the days of cheap, plentiful energy might soon be over. He pointed out that the United States, with six percent of the world's people, was consuming more than thirty percent of its energy output. Three months later, the danger of this reliance on foreign oil became dramatically clear when Arab oil-producing nations cut off shipments to the United States because it supported Israel.

The immediate effects of this cut-off, or embargo, included factory closings and long lines at gas stations, where prices nearly doubled. Meanwhile, President Nixon ordered temperatures lowered in federal buildings to save heating fuel. He also signed a law calling for a national fifty-five-miles-per-hour speed limit to save gas.

The Arab nations ended the embargo in March 1974, but prices remained high. In April 1977, President Carter delivered a major speech in which he compared the energy crisis to a war. He proposed reducing dependence on foreign oil in three ways: 1) by raising the price of oil through tax increases; 2) by urging conservation; and 3) by developing other energy sources, such as nuclear and solar power.

**Cars line up for gasoline in California.**

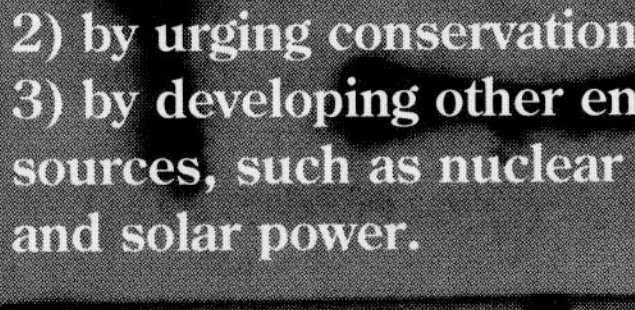

## Politics

JULY 24, 1974 Deciding unanimously in the case **U.S. V. NIXON**, the Supreme Court rules that the president must immediately turn over the White House tapes subpoenaed by the Watergate special prosecutor [October 20, 1973]. That night on the network news programs, Nixon attorney James St. Clair announces that the president will hand them over, thus avoiding a constitutional crisis.

AUGUST 8, 1974 During a televised speech, Richard **NIXON ANNOUNCES THAT HE WILL RESIGN** the presidency at noon the following day. Vice President Gerald Ford, who was appointed by Nixon to replace Spiro Agnew [October 10, 1973], will succeed him. Although Nixon thought he could survive the Watergate scandal, the recently released White House tapes leave little doubt that he broke the law.

## Life in the Seventies

SEPTEMBER 12, 1974 On the first day of classes, violence shakes the Boston school system. White parents and students riot rather than accept black students at their schools. A federal judge had ordered Boston to equalize its public schools by **BUSING** some black students into white neighborhoods and white students into black neighborhoods.

DECEMBER 15, 1974 Arbitrator Peter Seitz frees star pitcher Jim "Catfish" Hunter from his contract with the Oakland Athletics because owner Charles O. Finley has failed to honor all its clauses. Seitz's decision makes Hunter the first **FREE AGENT**, meaning that he can sign with any team. Hunter thus wins the battle that Curt Flood had lost [June 19, 1972].

**BUSING • Mounted police enforce a federal court order that Boston's Charlestown High School be integrated.**

## Arts & Entertainment

1975 Director Steven Spielberg's record-breaking thriller ***JAWS*** becomes the first movie ever to sell more than one hundred million dollars' worth of tickets. Trouble with the huge mechanical shark built for the film tripled the time it took to shoot and doubled the budget. But Spielberg's care in making the man-eating shark seem realistic pays off at the box office.

JANUARY 10, 1976 C.W. McCall's song "Convoy" tops the *Billboard* pop music charts, reflecting a growing national fascination with citizen's band, or **CB**, radio. Americans begin talking like truckers, calling police officers "smokies" and names "handles." First Lady Betty Ford soon admits to broadcasting on CB from the White House using the handle First Mama.

## Science & Technology

DECEMBER 11, 1975 Congress calls for a voluntary switch to the **METRIC SYSTEM** within ten years. Schoolchildren are particularly encouraged to learn this international system, which uses meters instead of yards and kilometers instead of miles. But most adults resist the change, and the conversion fails.

JANUARY 21, 1976 The **CONCORDE**, the first civilian jet to break the sound barrier, makes its first commercial flights from London to the Arab nation of Bahrain and Paris to Rio de Janeiro, Brazil. Produced jointly by the British and the French, the sleekly designed supersonic transport (SST) carries up to 139 passengers at a maximum speed of 1,448 miles per hour.

JULY 20, 1976 Almost a year after its launch, NASA's **VIKING 1** spacecraft lands softly on Mars. A few minutes later, mission controllers switch on the probe's television cameras, which return the first images from the surface of another planet. The pictures show a rock-strewn red landscape beneath a pink sky.

APRIL 17, 1975 Phnom Penh, the capital of Cambodia, falls to Communist **KHMER ROUGE** guerrillas, who topple the U.S.-backed regime of Lon Nol. Their victory ends five years of fighting and begins the brutal reign of French-educated revolutionary Pol Pot. Under his rule, the Khmer Rouge murder hundreds of thousands of Cambodians, especially teachers and other intellectuals.

APRIL 29–30, 1975 As North Vietnamese troops surround the South Vietnamese capital of Saigon, U.S. helicopters rescue the last Americans still trapped there. On April 30, General Duong Van Minh announces the **SURRENDER OF SOUTH VIETNAM**. The country's reunification comes twenty years after it was divided by an agreement with the French in Geneva [July 21, 1954].

JUNE 16, 1976 The township of **SOWETO** endures the worst race riots in South Africa's troubled history. An estimated ten thousand black students storm through the streets, looting and burning in protest of a requirement that Afrikaans, the language spoken by whites, be taught in the public schools. It takes police five days to restore order, during which time 176 people die.

1974 Students in California start a new fad when they run naked through surprised college classrooms. Because they run quickly, the students become known as streakers. Soon, **STREAKING** finds its way into middle-class culture. A fifty-year-old college dean, for example, streaks his own birthday party, and Robert Opel streaks the live telecast of the Academy Awards.

# Health Craze

**DURING THE 1970s, many people who were frustrated with politics turned inward. The growing environmental movement taught them to be concerned with the health of the earth, and this concern naturally led them to improve their own health as well.**

**Many Americans began to pay attention to chemical additives in the processed foods they ate as well as the quality of the air they breathed. Whole-wheat bread appeared more frequently in supermarkets alongside bleached white breads. Meanwhile, the number of health-food stores multiplied. Many former hippies opened up natural-food restaurants, which served unusually healthful dishes made with tofu, alfalfa sprouts, seaweed, and carob.**

**Americans also began to exercise more. Jogging, in particular, became a popular way of staying in condition while reducing one's risk of heart disease. Sneaker companies made a fortune catering to the footwear and fashion needs of the new joggers, bikers, and hikers. Even people who did not exercise began to wear running shoes as part of their everyday attire.**

**James F. Fixx's best-selling *The Complete Book of Running* helped popularize jogging in the United States.**

## Politics

JULY 3–4, 1976 A daring Israeli commando raid rescues 104 hostages from an Air France flight hijacked to the African nation of Uganda. Pro-Palestinian terrorists had ordered the pilot to fly the plane to Entebbe Airport because they knew Ugandan dictator Idi Amin would treat them sympathetically. During the **RAID ON ENTEBBE**, which saves all the hostages' lives, only one Israeli soldier dies.

**BARBARA WALTERS • Walters chats with her co-anchor, Harry Reasoner, on the set of the "ABC Evening News" after their first broadcast together.**

## Life in the Seventies

1975 The American appetite for fads and useless goods takes on a new dimension when sales of **MOOD RINGS AND PET ROCKS** skyrocket. The five-dollar Pet Rock, marketed to people who think dogs and cats require too much care, is a rock in a box. Yet people buy five million of them as well as twenty million mood rings, which are supposed to change color to reveal the wearer's mood.

1975 *Time* and *Newsweek* publish cover stories on the **TRANSCENDENTAL MEDITATION** craze sweeping the country. The 370 TM centers nationwide serve an estimated six hundred thousand people who have taken up the meditation-and-relaxation program to relieve stress. Celebrities flock to TM, and some corporations hire instructors to teach TM to their staffs.

APRIL 22, 1976 **BARBARA WALTERS** becomes the first woman hired to anchor a network television news program. Her five-year, five-million-dollar contract with ABC News makes her the highest-paid journalist in the country.

## Arts & Entertainment

OCTOBER 1976 EMI Records releases the Sex Pistols' first single, "Anarchy in the U.K.," which launches the **PUNK ROCK** movement. Although the violence associated with punk convinces EMI to drop the band, the Sex Pistols quickly become the most influential rock group since the Beatles, inspiring many unemployed and unhappy youths on both sides of the Atlantic to form their own bands.

1976 The release of his *Rastaman Vibration* album on Jamaican-based Island Records makes Bob Marley, already well known in Britain and Europe, a star in the United States. Marley and his band, the Wailers, popularize **REGGAE**, a style of music unique to the Caribbean island of Jamaica. Reggae combines rock, soul, and rhythm'n'blues with Jamaican folk music.

1976 Conceptual artist **CHRISTO** erects a twenty-four-mile-long sculpture in the hills of Northern California. His *Running Fence* consists of nylon sheeting that blows in the breeze and accents, Christo believes, the beauty of the environment. Christo pays for the two-million-dollar project by selling plans and drawings of his sculpture.

## Science & Technology

JULY 21–24, 1976 During an American Legion convention in Philadelphia, nearly two hundred people contract a mysterious illness, later called **LEGIONNAIRE'S DISEASE**. Their symptoms include pneumonia, a high fever, and a persistent cough. Twenty-nine people die while doctors remain baffled as to the cause.

MAY 2, 1977 The Clamshell Alliance of antinuclear activists sponsors a protest at the site of a planned nuclear power plant near **SEABROOK**, New Hampshire. More than two thousand demonstrators respond and occupy the site, where they pledge to remain until plans for the reactor are abandoned. Police sent to clear the site arrest fourteen hundred people.

JULY 2, 1977 Medical researcher Raymond Damadian obtains the first pictures of the human body using magnetic resonance imaging. Damadian's **MRI SCANNER** soon allows doctors to look inside a patient's body without exposing that person to harmful X-rays. The Food and Drug Administration approves the sale and use of MRI scanners in 1984.

**OCTOBER 1976** After Chinese Communist leader Mao Zedong dies on September 9, China's new leaders imprison his widow, Jiang Qing, and three of his close associates. The prisoners, who become known as the **GANG OF FOUR**, are blamed for the cruelty and repression of the Cultural Revolution [August 1966].

**FEBRUARY 24, 1977** Secretary of State Cyrus Vance announces that the United States will be cutting back its foreign aid to three nations accused of repeated **HUMAN RIGHTS** violations. Vance's action, which comes only one month into the new Carter administration, redeems the president's campaign pledge to make human rights a priority of his foreign policy.

**SEPTEMBER 7, 1977** President Carter and Panamanian leader Omar Torrijos sign a treaty today returning the Panama Canal to Panama by the year 2000. The president now faces a difficult fight in the Senate, which must approve the agreement. The new **PANAMA CANAL TREATY** would replace the Hay-Bunau-Varilla Treaty [November 18, 1903], which gave the United States the Canal Zone forever.

**JULY 4, 1976** The United States celebrates its **BICENTENNIAL**, marking the two hundredth anniversary of the Declaration of Independence with celebrations all over the country. The Liberty Bell rings in Philadelphia, musicians play a jazz marathon in New Orleans, and New York City hosts a fleet of "tall ships" that recalls ships used during colonial times.

# CAMP DAVID

**FOR TWELVE DAYS BEGINNING on September 6, 1978, President Jimmy Carter hosted a Middle East peace conference at the Camp David presidential retreat in Maryland. The principal negotiators were Carter, Egyptian president Anwar el-Sadat, and Israeli prime minister Menachem Begin. Carter had called the meeting to work out differences that had arisen since Sadat's courageous visit to Israel in November 1977.**

**Several times, the talks between Begin and Sadat nearly broke down. But each time Carter found a way to resolve the problems. Finally, on September 17, the three men came out of their secret negotiations to announce that they had agreed to a "framework for peace" between Israel and Egypt. The two treaties became known as the Camp David Accords. As part of these agreements, Egypt became the first Arab nation to recognize Israel's right to exist.**

**At the press conference announcing the agreements, Sadat and Begin both thanked Carter for providing the persistence and patience necessary to bring them together. Negotiating the Camp David Accords was the high point of Carter's presidency.**

## Politics

NOVEMBER 19, 1977 Just four years after the Yom Kippur War [October 6, 1973], Egyptian president Anwar **SADAT MAKES A HISTORIC TRIP TO ISRAEL** at the invitation of Israeli prime minister Menachem Begin. During his visit, Sadat addresses the Israeli parliament, or Knesset. Many credit the diplomacy of President Carter with urging both sides toward peace.

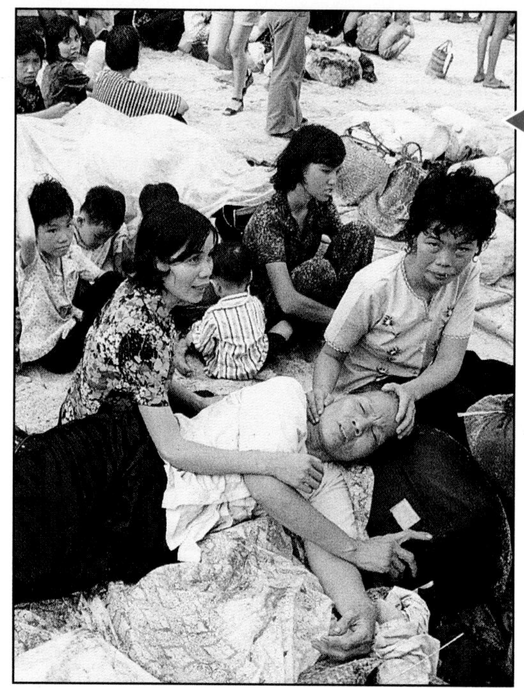

DECEMBER 3, 1977 The State Department agrees to admit ten thousand Vietnamese on an emergency basis. The refugees are called **BOAT PEOPLE** because most of them have fled the Communist government of Vietnam on small boats and rafts. Since the fall of South Vietnam two years ago [April 29–30, 1975], the United States has admitted nearly two hundred thousand Southeast Asian refugees.

**BOAT PEOPLE • Vietnamese boat people comfort each other after landing in Malaysia. They were among forty-two thousand refugees who sailed to Malaysia in overcrowded, unsafe boats.**

## Life in the Seventies

SEPTEMBER 18, 1976 Fifty thousand followers of the Reverend Sun Myung Moon, known as **MOONIES**, travel to Washington, D.C., for a God Bless America rally sponsored by Moon's Unification Church. The controversial South Korean minister has been attacked by other clerics for distorting Christian teachings as well as by parents for brainwashing their children.

## Arts & Entertainment

JANUARY 23–30, 1977 An estimated 130 million viewers watch ***ROOTS***, which airs on eight consecutive nights. Based on the best-selling book by Alex Haley, which tells the story of his family's history from slavery to modern times, the twelve-hour ABC miniseries transforms the portrayal of African Americans on television. Before *Roots*, most blacks on TV were maids, chauffeurs, or baseball players.

AUGUST 16, 1977 Forty-two-year-old rock pioneer **ELVIS PRESLEY DIES** from drug-related causes at his Graceland mansion in Memphis, Tennessee. All over the world, television stations interrupt their programming to announce the news. In Santiago, Chile, newspapers stop their presses, and radio stations put on marathon tributes to "El Rey de Rock and Roll."

1977 ***SATURDAY NIGHT FEVER*** captures the national mania for disco dancing. The film stars John Travolta as a Brooklyn hardware store clerk whose life revolves around going to the local disco on Saturday nights. The movie's soundtrack album, featuring the Bee Gees, spawns three Number One hits: "How Deep Is Your Love," "Stayin' Alive," and "Night Fever."

## Science & Technology

JULY 28, 1977 The first barrels of oil arrive in Valdez, Alaska, at the southern end of the 799-mile **TRANS-ALASKA PIPELINE**. Pumping had begun at the northern end near the Prudhoe Bay oil field on June 20. The project, which cost eight billion dollars, became a strategic necessity after the OPEC oil embargo [October 19–21, 1973] exposed U.S. dependence on foreign oil.

AUGUST 20, 1977 NASA launches the first of two **VOYAGER** spacecraft, the second taking off two weeks later. These probes are designed to explore the farthest reaches of the solar system. In March 1979, Voyager 1 arrives at Jupiter, where it discovers thin rings around the planet before flying on to Saturn (November 1980), Uranus (January 1986), and Neptune (August 1989).

MAY 1977 Apple Computers introduces the **APPLE II**, its first commercial personal computer. Founders Steve Jobs and Stephen Wozniak, both college dropouts, built prototypes for the machine in their own garage with just $1,300 in working capital. The Apple II uses a television set for a monitor and an audiocassette recorder for data storage.

**June 6, 1978** Californians approve by a vote of nearly two to one a citizen-initiated measure that will dramatically reduce property taxes in the state. Organizer Howard Jarvis claims **PROPOSITION 13** will benefit suburban property owners who resent paying for social welfare programs that benefit poor city residents.

**June 28, 1978** In the **BAKKE CASE**, the Supreme Court rules that racial quotas have unfairly kept white student Allan P. Bakke out of medical school, making him a victim of reverse discrimination. The Court's decision permits schools to give extra consideration to minorities, a practice known as affirmative action, but it rules out quotas that set aside a specific number of places for them.

**January 16, 1979** As the **ISLAMIC REVOLUTION IN IRAN** gains strength, Shah Mohammed Raza Pahlavi flees his country after nearly four decades in absolute power. On February 1, the Ayatollah Ruhollah Khomeini, a Muslim clergyman who directed the uprising from his exile in Paris, returns to Tehran, Iran's capital, where he is greeted by more than one million admirers.

**January 17, 1977** A Utah firing squad kills convicted murderer **GARY GILMORE**, making him the first prisoner executed in the United States since 1967. After trying twice to kill himself in prison, Gilmore made headlines when he demanded that his death sentence be carried out. Gilmore's story is soon told by Norman Mailer in *The Executioner's Song*, based on interviews with Gilmore.

**At four o'clock in the morning on March 28, 1979, workers at Pennsylvania's Three Mile Island nuclear power plant made a mistake. Confused by some misleading gauges, they shut down equipment that was pumping water into the Unit 2 reactor to cool it. As a result, the reactor's core overheated.**

**During the crisis, dangerous radioactive gases were released into the air. Governor Richard Thornburgh quickly ordered the removal of pregnant women and children from a five-mile area around the plant. Investigators later learned that the core came within thirty minutes of melting down completely, which would have caused a huge explosion, the deaths of many thousands of people, and the contamination of southeastern Pennsylvania.**

**There had been scattered protests against nuclear power before 1979—most notably in Seabrook, New Hampshire—but the antinuclear movement snowballed after Three Mile Island. In May, more than sixty thousand demonstrators traveled to Washington, D.C., for a huge No Nukes rally that reminded many people of the massive antiwar demonstrations of the 1960s.**

**In the aftermath of Three Mile Island, the Nuclear Regulatory Commission closed down several plants for testing, and utility companies across the country canceled plans to build eleven new reactors.**

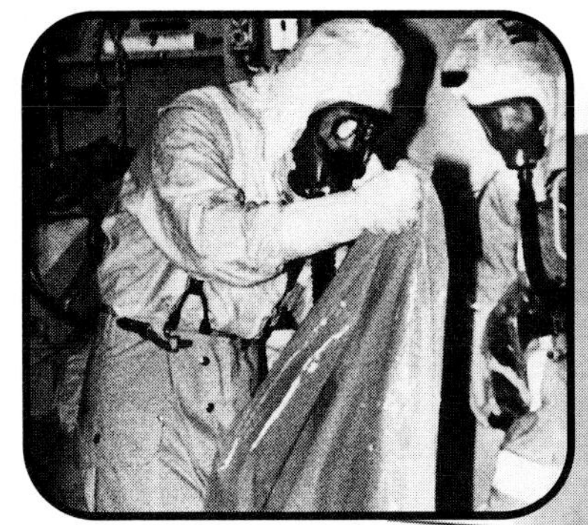

**This Three Mile Island engineer was one of the first to enter the plant after the accident.**

## Politics

**May 3, 1979** With her Conservative party's decisive victory in the British parliamentary elections, **MARGARET THATCHER** becomes the first woman prime minister in British history. The Iron Lady, as she is known, promises to cut taxes, social welfare programs, and the role of government in the lives of ordinary citizens. Thatcher's conservative rule reshapes British politics.

**June 18, 1979** After five years of negotiations, President Carter and Soviet premier Leonid Brezhnev sign the **SALT II** strategic arms limitation treaty [May 26, 1972]. SALT II limits the number of nuclear missile launchers that each side can have. Senate ratification proves difficult, however, because pro-military "hawks" think the agreement gives the Soviets too good a deal.

**July 17, 1979** With Sandinista rebels closing in, Nicaraguan strongman Anastasio Somoza abandons his presidency and escapes to Miami. The **SANDINISTAS** represent a coalition of groups, both democratic and Communist, that banded together to oppose Somoza's brutal rule. At first, President Carter offers U.S. aid to the Sandinista government to prevent its alliance with the Soviet Union.

## Life in the Seventies

**April 26, 1977** Steve Rubell and Ian Schrager open **STUDIO 54**, which sets a new standard for flamboyant celebrity nightlife in New York City. Thousands of eager patrons line up outside the disco each night, hoping to mingle with the club's rich and famous clientele.

**1977** In *The Complete Book of Running*, author James F. Fixx urges Americans to take up jogging in order to improve their health. His best-seller sparks a fitness movement that turns **JOGGING** into one of the country's most popular participator sports. Fixx writes that jogging has helped him lose weight and reduce his risk of heart disease.

**March 26, 1979** Michigan State defeats Indiana State, 75–64, in the finals of the NCAA college basketball tournament. The stars of the game, Michigan State's Earvin **"MAGIC" JOHNSON** and Indiana State's **LARRY BIRD**, both become first-round picks in that year's NBA draft. NBA officials later credit these two stars with turning around the league's falling attendance figures.

## Arts & Entertainment

**1977** The science-fiction adventure ***STAR WARS*** sets a new standard for visual effects in film, easily surpassing *2001: A Space Odyssey* [1968]. Writer-director George Lucas paid for the project with money he made from *American Graffiti* [1973]. Lucas says he intends his *Star Wars* fable for the new generation of teenagers that has grown up without fairy tales.

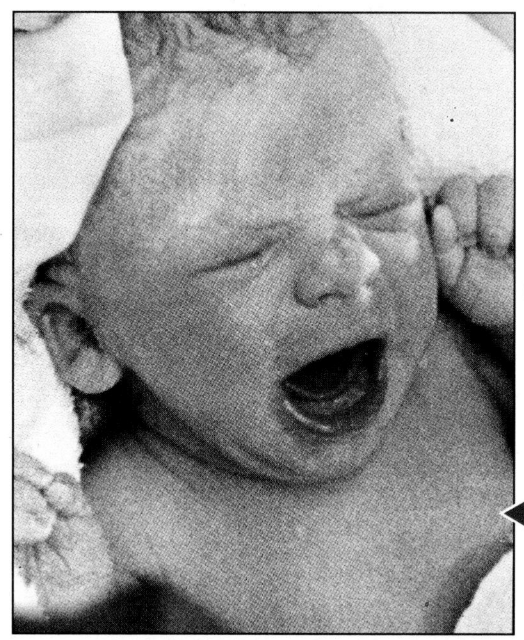

TEST TUBE BABY • Louise Brown, shortly after her birth.

**1978** The hit comedy ***ANIMAL HOUSE*** stars John Belushi and Tim Matheson as members of a rowdy college fraternity during the early 1960s. The film sparks a craze for toga parties, which spoof ancient Rome. Young people attend them wearing sheets draped around themselves. Toga parties become so popular that national department stores report record-breaking sales of white sheets.

## Science & Technology

**June 15, 1978** The Supreme Court halts the hundred-million-dollar Tellico Dam project in Tennessee because its construction threatens the only known habitat of the **SNAIL DARTER**, a tiny fish protected by the Endangered Species Act of 1973. The Court rules that continued work on the project might cause the snail darter's extinction.

**July 25, 1978** British doctors Patrick Steptoe and Robert Edwards supervise the birth of Louise Brown, the world's first **TEST TUBE BABY**. About nine months earlier, Steptoe and Edwards had removed an egg from Louise's mother, who was having difficulty becoming pregnant. They fertilized the egg in a test tube and then placed it in her womb.

DECEMBER 27, 1979 When a Muslim rebellion seems ready to topple the Soviet-dominated government of Afghanistan, Soviet premier Leonid Brezhnev orders combat troops across their common border. The **SOVIET INVASION OF AFGHANISTAN** enrages President Carter, who withdraws the SALT II treaty [June 18, 1979] and halts wheat exports to the Soviets.

1979 Evangelist Jerry Falwell, whose weekly television program airs on three hundred stations nationwide, forms the **MORAL MAJORITY** to give the Religious Right a voice in politics. Falwell's group champions small government, a strong military, laws against abortion, and legalized prayer in public schools. He opposes homosexuals and the Equal Rights Amendment [March 22, 1972].

AUGUST 14, 1980 Union activist Lech Walesa, an electrician by trade, convinces his fellow workers at the Lenin Shipyards in Gdansk, Poland, to strike against rising meat prices. The strike soon spreads to other factories in the Gdansk area. On August 31, the Polish government agrees to the formation of **SOLIDARITY**, the first independent trade union in a Soviet-bloc country.

MAY 17–19, 1980 Miami endures the country's worst rioting since 1967 [July 23–30, 1967] when an-all white jury in Tampa acquits four white policemen in the beating death of a black businessman. The trial was moved from Miami when the presiding judge ruled that the case was "a racial time bomb." Eighteen die in the **MIAMI RIOTS**, which cause one hundred million dollars in property damage.

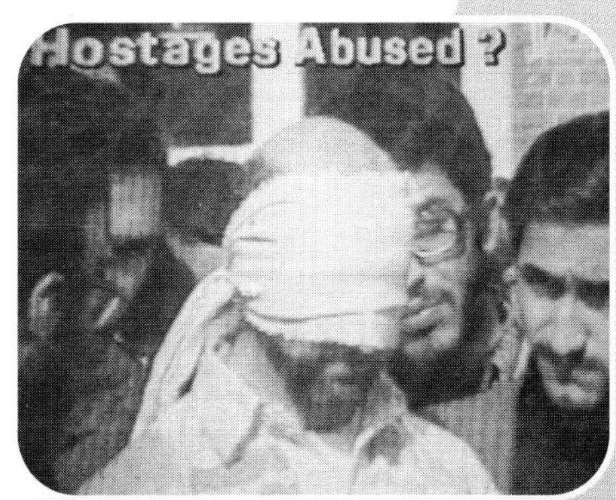


# The Iranian Hostage Crisis

**ON NOVEMBER 4, 1979, thousands of revolutionaries stormed the U.S. embassy in Tehran, Iran, taking about ninety people hostage. They demanded that the United States arrest the former shah, or king, who was receiving medical treatment in New York City. When President Carter refused the Iranian demands, the hostage crisis began.**

**Early on, the twenty-four hostages who were not Americans were released along with fourteen others, including several ill hostages, women, and blacks. Remaining in captivity were fifty-two embassy workers, who were often blindfolded and paraded in front of television cameras while so-called "students" chanted "Death to America!" and "Death to Carter!"**

**President Carter immediately seized eight billion dollars' worth of Iranian deposits in U.S. banks and ordered the navy to send warships to international waters near Iran, but neither action convinced the Iranians to release any of the hostages. As the crisis dragged on, Carter approved plans for a rescue attempt. On April 25, 1980, the rescue mission ended in disaster when a transport plane collided with a helicopter in the Iranian desert, killing eight servicemen. President Carter never recovered from this failure, and it contributed greatly to his loss in the 1980 presidential election.**

**Islamic fundamentalists led by the Ayatollah Ruhollah Khomeini wanted the shah returned to Iran so that he could be punished for his many years of harsh rule.**

# The Eighties

AS THE 1980s BEGAN, Americans wanted to regain their sense of unlimited opportunity. President Jimmy Carter had faced many frustrations during his first term in office. The economy had performed badly, and he had been unable to win the release of the American hostages being held in Iran.

During the 1980 presidential campaign, Republican candidate Ronald Reagan presented himself as a clear alternative. Where Carter had been weak, Reagan said, he would be strong. Whereas Carter had occasionally criticized the nation and told the public that resources were limited, Reagan always talked about how great the United States was. He promised to cut taxes and raise defense spending to make the United States strong again. People voted for him overwhelmingly.

As president, Reagan indeed cut taxes on the rich and raised defense spending, but his policies had unfortunate consequences. They produced the largest budget deficits in U.S. history and set the mood for the country during the Reagan years, which many called the Greed Decade.

★

## Politics

NOVEMBER 4, 1980 Former actor and California governor Ronald Reagan trounces Jimmy Carter in the **1980 PRESIDENTIAL ELECTION**. Although President Carter's campaign was often sidetracked by the ongoing foreign policy crisis in Iran, Reagan's most successful attacks concerned economic issues. "Are you better off than you were four years ago?" he asked Americans during one debate.

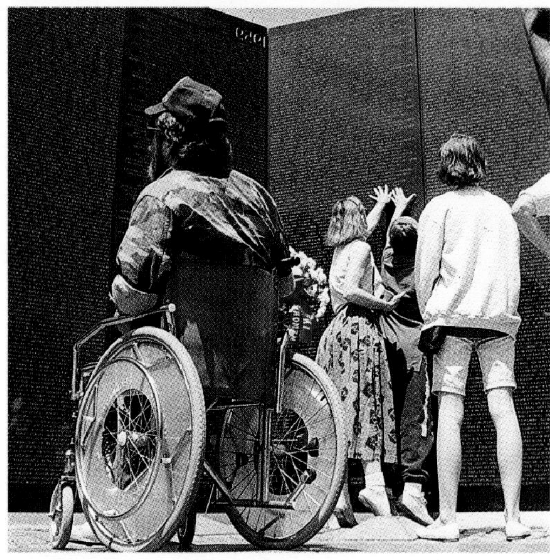

**VIETNAM WAR MEMORIAL • A veteran of the Vietnam War visits the Vietnam War Memorial in Washington, D.C.**

JANUARY 20, 1981 Just minutes after Ronald Reagan takes the oath of office as president, **IRAN RELEASES THE FIFTY-TWO AMERICANS** it has held hostage for 444 days. Former president Carter flies to West Germany to meet them. He is dismayed that they have been so poorly treated.

## Life in the Eighties

JUNE 12, 1981 A strike called by the players halts games two months into the baseball season. The most important issue dividing the players and the owners involves compensation to teams that have lost free agents [December 15, 1974]. By the time the two sides settle the **BASEBALL STRIKE** on July 31, more than one-third of the season has been lost.

JANUARY 8, 1982 American Telephone & Telegraph agrees to break up its twenty-two local **BELL TELEPHONE** companies in order to settle a suit filed by the Justice Department in 1974. The suit accused AT&T of operating a monopoly on telephone service in the United States. The breakup helps other telephone companies compete for customers.

## Arts & Entertainment

DECEMBER 8, 1980 A crazed **FAN MURDERS JOHN LENNON** outside his New York City apartment building as Lennon and his wife, Yoko Ono, return from a recording session. The former Beatle had just released a new album, *Starting Over*, his first in five years. Killer Mark David Chapman, a former mental patient, explains that he shot Lennon so he could become famous.

JUNE 6, 1981 Yale student Maya Yang Lin wins a national contest to design a **VIETNAM WAR MEMORIAL** in Washington, D.C. Her proposal features two low granite walls in the shape of a V. Inscribed on them will be the names of every U.S. soldier who died in the war. Her unusual design offends some people who wanted a more traditional monument, but many veterans defend Lin's approach.

AUGUST 1, 1981 **MTV**, the first all-music network, begins serving cable subscribers nationwide. Hosted by "veejays," MTV airs videos of rock'n'roll acts performing their music. Its remarkable success leads to more "narrowcasting," in which cable networks aim programs at small parts of the viewing audience, such as teenagers or fans of old movies.

## Science & Technology

JANUARY 8, 1981 An article in the *New England Journal of Medicine* reports that people who eat foods high in **CHOLESTEROL** are much more likely to develop heart disease than those who do not. News coverage of this twenty-year study prompts many Americans to stop eating high-cholesterol foods, such as butter and beef.

APRIL 12–14, 1981 The world's first reusable spacecraft, the **SPACE SHUTTLE** *Columbia*, completes its first voyage in space. The shuttle's orbiter takes off like a rocket, maneuvers like a spaceship, and lands like an airplane. NASA believes that the *Columbia* can be refitted for another flight in just six months.

AUGUST 12, 1981 The International Business Machines Corporation, the largest computer company in the world, introduces its long-awaited personal computer: the **IBM PC**. Because of IBM's powerful position in the marketplace, the IBM PC quickly becomes the international standard for personal computers.

**February 18, 1981** In his first State of the Union address, President Reagan proposes budget cuts of forty-one billion dollars, mostly from programs that aid poor people. He also asks for a thirty percent cut in income tax rates and seven billion dollars more in defense spending. During the next few months, Congress passes **REAGAN'S ECONOMIC PLAN** with very few changes.

**March 30, 1981** President Reagan receives a severe bullet wound during an **ASSASSINATION ATTEMPT** in Washington, D.C. In an effort to reassure the nation, aides report that, before entering surgery, Reagan joked to his wife, Nancy, "Honey, I forgot to duck." Gunman John W. Hinckley, Jr., is later found not guilty by reason of insanity and sent to a mental hospital.

**May 13, 1981** John Paul II barely survives emergency surgery after twenty-three-year-old Turk Mehmet Ali **AGCA SHOOTS THE POPE** in Rome's St. Peter's Square. An international investigation points to the involvement of the Bulgarian secret police and through them the Soviet Union. The Soviets object to the pope's active support for Poland's Solidarity movement [August 14, 1980].

**October 5, 1982** Johnson & Johnson announces a complete recall of Extra Strength Tylenol capsules after pills containing cyanide kill seven people in the Chicago area. The killer is never found, but the crime leads to the development of tamper-proof packaging as well as government regulations that will prevent **PRODUCT TAMPERING** in the future.

# The Computer Generation

During the 1980s, developments in technology brought about dramatic changes in the way people lived. The introduction of the personal computer changed the way people went about their business. As PCs dropped in price, they became standard equipment in most offices and even appeared in homes. Along with fax machines and overnight delivery services, they made it possible for some people to work at home. The practice of sending work over the telephone lines came to be known as telecommuting.

Computers were also purchased for schools, where children of the 1980s became the first generation to grow up knowing how to use them. In many families, children became the technology experts. As they learned more, however, some teenagers and college students began to carry out computer pranks. One favorite sport was to break into large networks of computers that were linked together.

Young, mischievous computer experts were known as hackers. The 1983 movie *War Games* told the fictional story of one hacker who nearly started a nuclear war after he broke into one government network. In 1988, a real hacker named Robert Morris made news when he launched a computer virus that shut down thousands of university and government computers.

## Politics

AUGUST 3, 1981 Despite a law against strikes by its members, the Professional Air Traffic Controllers Organization orders a walkout after turning down the government's latest contract offer. President Reagan demands that the **PATCO** controllers return to work by August 5 or face dismissal. When thousands remain on strike, Reagan fires them.

AUGUST 4, 1981 A coalition of Republicans and conservative Democrats pushes the president's **INCOME TAX CUTS** through Congress. Although less than he originally requested [February 18, 1981], the cuts are still the largest in history, lowering rates by twenty-five percent. Reagan believes that the rich, who benefit most, will create a prosperity that "trickles down" to the poor.

## Life in the Eighties

DECEMBER 22, 1984 Bernard Goetz shoots four young men on a New York City subway train, later claiming they tried to rob him. After disappearing down a tunnel, Goetz flees to New Hampshire before turning himself in. When New Yorkers, weary of crime, learn that Goetz's victims all have criminal records, many rally behind the **SUBWAY VIGILANTE**.

**MICHAEL JACKSON • Other hit songs from Michael Jackson's *Thriller* album include "Beat It" and "Wanna Be Startin' Somethin'."**

## Arts & Entertainment

1982 Director Steven Spielberg releases ***E.T.—THE EXTRATERRESTRIAL***, a fantasy about a child-sized alien stranded in the suburbs of Southern California. The most successful movie made to date, *E.T.* brings in nearly one billion dollars in ticket sales worldwide. Like *Star Wars* [1977], *E.T.* also spawns a huge number of toys based on the movie's characters.

FEBRUARY 28, 1983 The **FINAL EPISODE OF "M*A*S*H"** attracts 125 million viewers, by far the largest audience ever to watch a single television program. Although set during the Korean War, "M*A*S*H" reflected the antiwar sentiment of the 1960s. Earlier TV war comedies, such as "McHale's Navy" and "Hogan's Heroes," avoided the realism of "M*A*S*H."

MAY 16, 1983 Michael Jackson introduces his moonwalk dance step during a television special honoring Motown Records. Jackson performs the move while singing "Billie Jean" from his new ***THRILLER*** album. Topping the pop music charts for a record thirty-seven weeks, *Thriller* sells more than forty million copies worldwide, making it the best-selling album of all time.

## Science & Technology

DECEMBER 2, 1982 Severely ill retired dentist Barney Clark becomes the first human patient to receive an **ARTIFICIAL HEART**. Dr. William De Vries performs the operation using a mechanical heart developed by Dr. Robert Jarvik. The device, known as the Jarvik 7, keeps Clark alive for an additional 112 days.

MARCH 30, 1983 The first **CALIFORNIA CONDOR CHICK** born in captivity hatches at the San Diego Zoo. This endangered bird has proved difficult to breed because condors lay just one egg every two years. Among the world's largest and rarest birds, the California condor now struggles for survival in the San Rafael mountains, where fewer than fifty birds remain in the wild.

JUNE 13, 1983 The Pioneer 10 probe, launched in March 1972, becomes the first **SPACECRAFT TO LEAVE THE SOLAR SYSTEM** when it crosses the orbit of Neptune. Although Pioneer 10 does not carry a television camera, it does send information back to Earth using radio signals that take almost a day to reach mission control.

SEPTEMBER 25, 1981 Chief Justice Warren Burger swears in Sandra Day O'Connor, who becomes the **FIRST WOMAN TO SIT ON THE SUPREME COURT**. President Reagan nominated the fifty-one-year-old Arizona judge in July to replace retiring justice Potter Stewart. Reagan chose O'Connor because of her firmly conservative views, even though she has supported a woman's right to have an abortion.

OCTOBER 6, 1981 During a military parade in Egypt, five soldiers break formation and attack the presidential stand of **ANWAR EL-SADAT** with grenades and machine-gun fire. The soldiers, all Islamic fundamentalists, kill Sadat because he signed the Camp David peace accords with Israel, a country the fundamentalists consider their greatest enemy.

JUNE 30, 1982 The deadline set by Congress for ratification of the **EQUAL RIGHTS AMENDMENT** [March 22, 1972] passes with the amendment falling three states short of approval. In 1978, when Congress extended the deadline, thirty-five of the necessary thirty-eight states had already ratified the ERA, but no others had joined them during the last four years.

JULY 21, 1985 Treasure hunter Mel Fisher's sixteen-year search ends when he discovers the **WRECK OF THE SPANISH GALLEON *NUESTRA SEÑORA DE ATOCHA*** off the coast of Key West, Florida. The *Atocha*, which sank during a hurricane in 1622, carried gold, silver, and other valuables worth nearly four hundred million dollars today.

# JESSE JACKSON

JESSE JACKSON For PRESIDENT in '88

**In 1988, Jackson finished second in the Democratic primaries to nominee Michael Dukakis, who considered him for the vice-presidential nomination before choosing conservative senator Lloyd Bentsen of Texas.**

IN NOVEMBER 1983, forty-two-year-old Baptist minister Jesse Jackson announced that he would run for president. Jackson was a well-known civil rights leader, but his announcement was still remarkable because no African-American had even run a major campaign for president before.

Jackson grew up in a segregated town in South Carolina, where he learned firsthand the cruelty of racial prejudice: Because the state kept whites and blacks apart, young Jesse had to walk five miles to school each day, because the school two blocks away was for white children only.

After his college graduation, Jackson enrolled at the Chicago Theological Seminary, but he dropped out in 1966 to work full-time with Martin Luther King, Jr., and his Southern Christian Leadership Conference. Later, Jackson formed his own civil rights organization called People United to Save Humanity, or simply PUSH, which worked to inspire black students in city high schools.

In 1984 and again in 1988, Jackson tried to win the Democratic nomination for president by building a Rainbow Coalition of the poor, minorities, and other people who had little say in the way the government was being run.

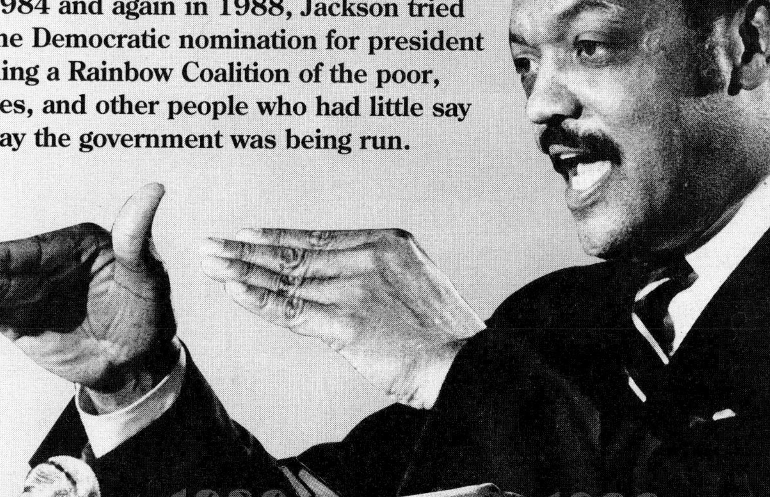

## Politics

MARCH 23, 1983 In a televised speech to the nation, President Reagan proposes a **STRATEGIC DEFENSE INITIATIVE**, which would use lasers and other technology to shoot down Soviet nuclear missiles before they could reach their targets. Critics mock Reagan's proposal, which they call Star Wars, as hugely expensive and foolishly unrealistic.

AUGUST 21, 1983 After three years of exile in the United States, Filipino opposition leader Benigno Aquino ignores several death threats and returns to Manila. As he leaves the airplane, a gunman sidesteps military guards and shoots Aquino in the head, killing him instantly. Many suspect **PHILIPPINE DICTATOR FERDINAND MARCOS** of murdering his most vocal opponent.

SEPTEMBER 1, 1983 Controllers lose contact with **KOREAN AIR LINES FLIGHT 007** during a flight from New York to Seoul, South Korea. The Soviet Union eventually admits that one of its fighters shot down the 747 when it strayed over Soviet airspace, killing 269 people. Although the Soviets insist that Flight 007 was on a spy mission, investigations confirm that the plane was just off course.

## Life in the Eighties

MAY 25, 1986 More than six million people join hands to form a human chain as part of **HANDS ACROSS AMERICA**. The 4,150-mile-long chain stretches from New York City to Long Beach, California, with only a few breaks in desert areas. The event raises thirty-two million dollars to fight hunger and homelessness in the United States.

**HANDS ACROSS AMERICA • Participants join hands in Long Beach, California.**

## Arts & Entertainment

NOVEMBER 11, 1983 More than one hundred million Americans watch ***THE DAY AFTER***, an ABC television movie that attempts to picture life after a nuclear war. The film provokes heated public debate about the dangers and benefits of nuclear weapons.

1983 The **TEENAGE MUTANT NINJA TURTLES** first appear in an underground comic created by newspaper illustrator Peter Laird and Kevin Eastman, a twenty-year-old working as a cook. The turtles soon become a merchandising sensation, generating hundreds of millions of dollars in licensing fees from companies that sell everything from Turtle skateboards to Turtle breakfast cereal.

1983 The Japanese Sony and Dutch-based Philips corporations begin marketing music on **COMPACT DISCS**, or CDs, which they have developed jointly. At first, record companies are slow to make albums available in the new high-quality digital format. But CDs catch on quickly, and by 1991 CDs outsell vinyl records and tapes.

## Science & Technology

APRIL 23, 1984 Federal researchers announce that they have found the virus thought to cause Acquired Immune Deficiency Syndrome, or **AIDS**. This fatal disease first appeared in the United States three years ago. Since then, it has infected four thousand Americans. Doctors predict that the illness will become an epidemic, affecting many people within the population, by 1990.

MARCH 1985 British scientists report the discovery of a large **HOLE IN THE OZONE LAYER** over Antarctica. The ozone layer filters out the sun's harmful ultraviolet rays. Although no one knows what has caused the hole, many scientists believe that chlorofluorocarbons, or CFCs, have eaten away at the upper atmosphere. CFCs have been widely used in refrigerators and aerosol cans [1941].

SEPTEMBER 1, 1985 A joint U.S.-French deep-sea exploration team finds the wreck of the ***TITANIC***, the luxury liner that sank during its first voyage in 1912. The explorers mark the site of the discovery in the middle of the North Atlantic but keep it secret to discourage treasure hunters.

**October 9, 1983** Public outrage forces the **RESIGNATION OF INTERIOR SECRETARY JAMES WATT** after he belittles the members of an advisory panel as "a black, a woman, two Jews, and a cripple." The outspoken cabinet member has been under attack from environmental groups for allowing private business interests to develop public resources, including oil, on public lands.

**October 23, 1983** After speeding through security barriers, a truck loaded with dynamite causes an **EXPLOSION INSIDE THE U.S. MARINES HEADQUARTERS IN BEIRUT**, Lebanon. The blast, which kills 241 sleeping soldiers, leaves a crater thirty feet deep. The Marines had been sent to Lebanon by President Reagan as part of an international peacekeeping force.

**October 25, 1983** The United States invades the tiny Caribbean island of Grenada, where "left-wing thugs have violently seized power," according to President Reagan. U.S. forces easily subdue the Grenadans and a few Cubans who have been building an airport on the island. As an excuse for the **GRENADA INVASION**, Reagan uses his concern for Americans attending medical school there.

**June 19, 1986** Drug abuse among college athletes becomes national news when University of Maryland **BASKETBALL STAR LEN BIAS DIES OF A HEART ATTACK BROUGHT ON BY COCAINE USE.** Bias reportedly took the cocaine at a party held to celebrate his signing a professional contract with the Boston Celtics two days earlier.

# GORBACHEV

**When seventy-three-year-old Konstantin Chernenko died in March 1985, Mikhail Gorbachev succeeded him as leader of the Soviet Union. The fifty-four-year-old Gorbachev, an agricultural specialist with little experience in international relations, was a new kind of Soviet leader.**

**As Gorbachev took over, the Soviets were having a difficult time keeping up with the United States. At President Reagan's insistence, Congress had drastically increased U.S. defense spending. During his first few years in office, Reagan often referred to the Soviet Union as "the evil empire."**

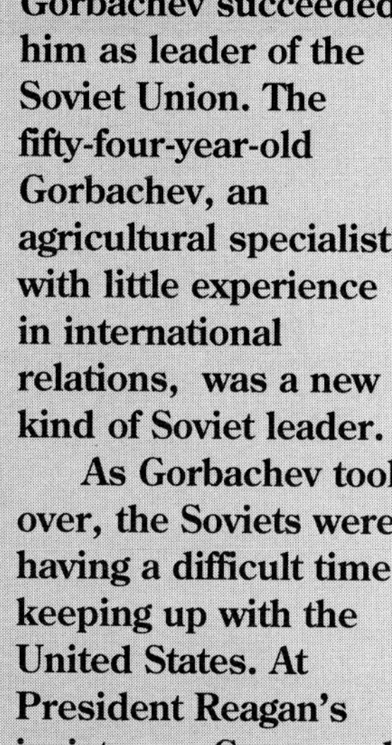

**Gorbachev knew the government-controlled Soviet economy could not compete with the free-market system in the United States. So he decided to cooperate instead. Two years after coming to power, Gorbachev developed a plan to overhaul the Soviet system. He called it *perestroika*, or restructuring.**

**Because of his liberal policies and relaxed, friendly manner, Gorbachev enjoyed among Americans a popularity that was remarkable for a Soviet leader. At one point during a trip to Washington, D.C., Gorbachev unexpectedly left his motorcade. "Hello," he told the passersby, "I'm glad to be in America."**

## Politics

MARCH 1, 1985 After Nicaraguan leader Daniel Ortega offers to improve relations with the United States, President Reagan attacks the Sandinista government and praises Nicaragua's **CONTRA REBELS**, whom he calls "freedom fighters" and "the moral equal of our Founding Fathers." Worried that Reagan may draw the country into war, Congress bans military aid to the contras on July 18.

SEPTEMBER 9, 1985 The growing outcry against apartheid [May 26, 1948] forces the United States to reverse its tolerant policy and instead support **ECONOMIC SANCTIONS AGAINST SOUTH AFRICA**. These sanctions, or penalties, are intended to force the white minority government to share power with South Africa's black majority.

SEPTEMBER 16, 1985 The Department of Commerce reports that, for the first time since 1914, the **UNITED STATES HAS BECOME A DEBTOR NATION**, owing more than it is owed. Economists blame the national debt, which has ballooned since passage of the Reagan tax cuts [August 4, 1981]. Reagan's policies have reduced government income and boosted defense spending, producing huge deficits.

## Life in the Eighties

JULY 27, 1986 Greg LeMond becomes the **FIRST AMERICAN TO WIN THE TOUR DE FRANCE**, the most famous bicycle race in the world. The annual month-long event covers twenty-five hundred miles of French countryside in daily stages. LeMond finishes in 110 hours, 35 minutes, 19 seconds, beating his nearest rival by just over 3 minutes.

NOVEMBER 14, 1986 Admitting to illegal **INSIDER TRADING**, Wall Street tycoon Ivan Boesky agrees to pay a fine of one hundred million dollars. The following April, he pleads guilty to a criminal charge in exchange for a reduced prison sentence. Boesky also agrees to help the government prosecute other insider traders, who used nonpublic information to make money in the stock market.

JANUARY 16, 1987 San Francisco's KRON becomes the first major-market television station in the United States to broadcast **ADVERTISEMENTS FOR CONDOMS**. KRON decides to air the commercials as a public service because San Francisco's large gay population has been severely affected by AIDS [April 23, 1984].

## Arts & Entertainment

SEPTEMBER 20, 1984 **"THE COSBY SHOW"** premieres on NBC, featuring Bill Cosby as a well-to-do New York City doctor. Cosby's first success in television came in 1965, when his appearance in "I Spy" made him the first black actor to star in a dramatic series. "The Cosby Show" quickly climbs the ratings, becoming the country's most popular show for the rest of the decade.

JULY 13, 1985 British musician Bob Geldof organizes **LIVE AID** concerts that are held simultaneously in London and Philadelphia and feature the biggest stars in the music business. Broadcast to 152 countries, the rock'n'roll extravaganza raises seventy million dollars to feed starving Africans threatened by famine.

MAY 1986 Profile Records, an independent rap-dance label, releases Run-D.M.C.'s ***RAISIN' HELL***. The album features the white band Aerosmith joining the black rap group Run-D.M.C. on a new version of Aerosmith's 1977 hit "Walk This Way." The album, which goes platinum, helps bring rap music into the American mainstream as "Walk This Way" reaches Number Four on the *Billboard* charts.

## Science & Technology

JANUARY 28, 1986 Seventy-three seconds after launch, the **SPACE SHUTTLE *CHALLENGER* EXPLODES** above Florida's Kennedy Space Center. All seven astronauts die. A special commission later blames the explosion on a leak caused by extremely cold weather before liftoff.

**CHALLENGER EXPLOSION • The space shuttle Challenger exploded seventy-three seconds after launch. Among the victims of the disaster is Christa McAuliffe, chosen from eleven thousand applicants to be the first teacher in space.**

DECEMBER 10, 1985 President Reagan signs the **GRAMM-RUDMAN-HOLLINGS ACT** designed to eliminate deficits and balance the federal budget by reducing government spending. The law calls for automatic budget cuts if Congress fails to make specific cuts in a particular year. Seven months later, the Supreme Court declares the law unconstitutional.

FEBRUARY 7, 1986 Philippine authorities announce that dictator Ferdinand Marcos has been elected president over Corazon Aquino, widow of Benigno Aquino [August 21, 1983]. Because of widespread voter fraud, however, Mrs. Aquino refuses to accept the results, beginning the **PEOPLE POWER REVOLUTION**. Marcos flees to Hawaii on February 27.

APRIL 15, 1986 A surprise **U.S. AIR STRIKE HAMMERS TRIPOLI**, Libya. The warplanes, flying from bases in Great Britain, bomb military targets as well as the home of Libyan leader Muammar el-Qaddafi. President Reagan ordered the attack after he learned that Libyan terrorists were involved in the April 5 bombing of a West German disco that killed one U.S. soldier and injured sixty more.

MARCH 22, 1987 A barge carrying thirty-two hundred tons of garbage leaves Long Island, New York, beginning a six-month search for a place to unload. Other states and three foreign countries turn the barge away before the ship returns to Long Island. The **GARBAGE BARGE** calls attention to the growing waste-disposal problem in the United States.

# THE GREED DECADE

**Michael Milken being sworn in for a Congressional hearing on Wall Street fraud.**

**The 1980s saw the gap between rich and poor Americans grow much wider. By 1989, the year President Reagan left office, the richest one percent of Americans (among them Michael Milken, shown at right) owned forty-eight percent of the country's wealth.**

**WHEN HE TOOK OFFICE IN 1981, President Ronald Reagan had two important goals: One was to spend more money on national defense. The other was to cut taxes. He argued that giving rich people and corporations more money to spend and invest would benefit the entire economy. Another important part of Reagan's economic plan was deregulation, or a reduction in the rules governing business and industry.**

**As a result of these policies, business on Wall Street prospered. With little to hold them back, investors speculated wildly. Deal-maker Michael Milken soon became famous for his high-interest, high-risk "junk" bonds, which paid for the takeovers of many corporations. While tens of thousands of people lost their jobs, Milken personally earned as much as five hundred million dollars in a single year.**

**Driven by greed, many financial professionals crossed over into illegal activities. Some bank owners took advantage of deregulation by stealing money from their depositors or investing it illegally, creating the savings-and-loan crisis. Milken himself pled guilty in 1990 to using inside information to make illegal investments.**

## Politics

NOVEMBER 3, 1986 A magazine in Lebanon reports that the United States has been secretly selling arms to Iran. The shipments were authorized by President Reagan, who sought Iran's help in freeing U.S. hostages being held by Muslims in Lebanon. On November 12, Reagan admits that he knew of the arms sales but denies that he was **TRADING ARMS FOR HOSTAGES**.

NOVEMBER 25, 1986 The **IRAN-CONTRA SCANDAL** becomes public knowledge when the White House admits that profits from the Iranian arms sales have been used to pay for weapons for the Nicaraguan contras [March 1, 1985]. This use clearly violates Congress's ban on military aid to the Nicaraguan rebels. National Security Advisor John Poindexter resigns, and his aide Oliver North is fired.

JANUARY 27, 1987 Soviet premier Mikhail Gorbachev begins calling for changes in the way his Communist government manages the Soviet economy. His reforms, announced June 25, are known as **PERESTROIKA**, a Russian word meaning "restructuring." Gorbachev also introduces *glasnost*, or "openness," which promises less censorship and more freedom to express different points of view.

**IRAN-CONTRA SCANDAL • Security guards escort Lieutenant Colonel Oliver North into his lawyer's office building.**

## Life in the Eighties

OCTOBER 19, 1987 Just two months after a record-setting high, the **STOCK MARKET PLUNGES** 508 points in a single day. Shareholders lose more than five hundred billion dollars. The panic breaks records set on Black Tuesday [October 29, 1929]. However, a similar nationwide financial collapse does not follow, partly because of safeguards put in place during the Great Depression.

## Arts & Entertainment

FEBRUARY 24, 1987 Paul Simon's **GRACELAND** wins the Grammy for Album of the Year. Simon began the project in 1985 when he traveled to South Africa to record with black musicians there. At first, anti-apartheid activists attacked him for breaking the boycott of South African products and culture. The finished album, however, popularizes African music and the musicians who perform it.

NOVEMBER 11, 1987 At the Sotheby's auction house in New York, Vincent van Gogh's *Irises* sells at auction for $53.9 million, the highest price ever paid for a work of art. The record sale begins a **SURGE IN THE ART MARKET**, during which investors take money out of bonds and place it in paintings, hoping for a better return. Van Gogh painted *Irises* in 1889, shortly before killing himself.

## Science & Technology

MARCH 6, 1986 The Soviet Vega 1 probe, the first of four spacecraft sent to investigate **HALLEY'S COMET** [May 18, 1910], passes within six thousand miles of the comet's nucleus. Eight days later, the more ambitious Giotto probe, developed by the European Space Agency, flies through the head of the comet.

APRIL 26, 1986 At the Soviet Union's Chernobyl nuclear power plant, Reactor Number Four explodes, releasing huge clouds of radiation. More than thirty emergency workers die in a heroic and successful effort to prevent an even more catastrophic core meltdown. The **CHERNOBYL DISASTER** confirms many people's fears about the safety of nuclear power.

**October 23, 1987** By a vote of 58–42, the **SENATE REJECTS SUPREME COURT NOMINEE ROBERT H. BORK**, currently a federal appeals court judge. During his Senate confirmation hearings, liberal groups attacked Bork for his extremely conservative views on civil rights and privacy. Also, as the U.S. solicitor general, Bork had played a role in the Saturday Night Massacre [October 20, 1973].

**December 8, 1987** President Reagan and Soviet leader Mikhail Gorbachev sign the Intermediate-Range Nuclear Forces treaty. Unlike previous arms control agreements, which limited the number of weapons each side could have, the **INF TREATY** actually orders cuts. About two thousand nuclear warheads based in Europe will be destroyed, three-quarters of them belonging to the Soviet Union.

**February 5, 1988** A **GRAND JURY IN MIAMI INDICTS MANUEL NORIEGA**, the military dictator of Panama, for illegal drug smuggling. The Justice Department accuses Noriega of accepting bribes from drug dealers in exchange for protection and the use of Panamanian airports. It is reported that the CIA ignored Noriega's drug activities because he provided the agency with information.

**June 21, 1989** In the case of *Texas v. Johnson*, the Supreme Court reverses the conviction of Gregory Johnson, who was sentenced to a year in prison for burning the U.S. flag during a political protest. The Court rules that **FLAG BURNING** is a form of political speech and therefore is protected by the First Amendment.

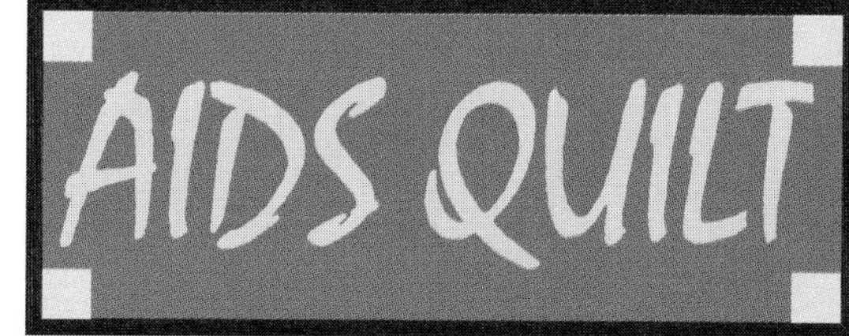

Each of the unique and colorful panels of the AIDS Memorial Quilt symbolizes an individual whose life was lost to AIDS.

In 1987, the number of deaths in San Francisco caused by Acquired Immune Deficiency Syndrome (AIDS) topped one thousand. To dramatize this milestone, gay rights activist Cleve Jones asked people to write on placards the names of loved ones who had died of AIDS. These signs were then taped to a downtown federal office building. Together, they formed a patchwork design that reminded Jones of a quilt.

Soon Jones organized the Names Project Foundation to carry out an even greater task: the creation of a huge quilt made up of individual panels, each one commemorating a victim of AIDS. The result was the AIDS Memorial Quilt. Its handmade panels used fabrics of every color, and some even contained personal mementoes, such as Barbie dolls, stuffed animals, and champagne glasses.

As news of the quilt spread, people from every state and many foreign countries contributed panels. On October 11, 1987, the quilt was displayed on the Capitol Mall in Washington, D.C. At that time, there were two thousand panels. Since then, the quilt has grown to include nearly thirty thousand, with special panels dedicated to tennis champion Arthur Ashe and artist Keith Haring.

The Aids Memorial Quilt on display on the Mall across from the White House in Washington, D.C.

## Politics

JULY 5, 1988 Attorney General **EDWIN MEESE**, who is being investigated by a special prosecutor, announces his resignation. Meese claims that the special prosecutor's soon-to-be-released report will "vindicate" him, showing him to be blameless. The July 18 report actually condemns Meese's activities as unethical but admits that there is not enough evidence to charge him with a crime.

JULY 20, 1988 Iran's Ayatollah Khomeini agrees to a UN-sponsored cease-fire in the eight-year-old **IRAN-IRAQ WAR**. The fighting, which has killed more than one million people, began with the Iraqi invasion of Iran on September 15, 1980. When both sides began attacking neutral oil tankers, the United States, Great Britain, and other nations sent warships for escort duty in the Persian Gulf.

AUGUST 18, 1988 **"READ MY LIPS, NO NEW TAXES!"** promises Vice President George Bush as he accepts the Republican nomination for president. Campaigning, Bush pledges to carry on the policies of Ronald Reagan and attacks the Democratic candidate, Massachusetts governor Michael Dukakis, as too liberal. Dukakis, for his part, says that a tax hike may be necessary.

## Life in the Eighties

AUGUST 30, 1989 A jury convicts hotel tycoon **LEONA HELMSLEY** of tax fraud for claiming personal expenses as business deductions. The case drew national attention after her remark that "only the little people pay taxes" was widely reported. Helmsley's greed, her starring role in splashy ads for her hotels, and her blatant disregard for the law all win her little sympathy.

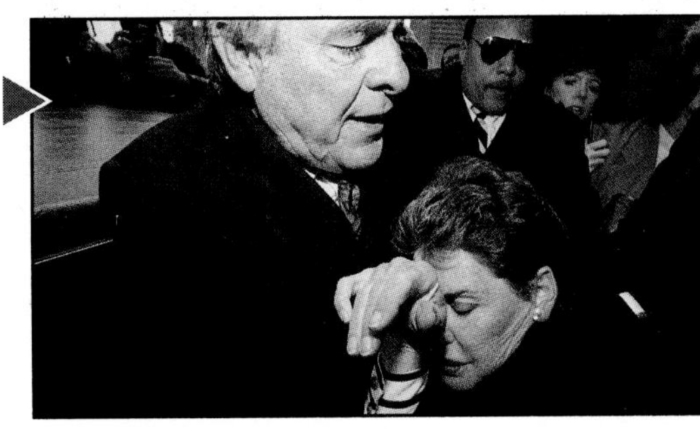

**LEONA HELMSLEY • Helmsley collapses after receiving a sentence of four years in jail for tax fraud.**

## Arts & Entertainment

1987 Tom Wolfe's first novel, ***THE BONFIRE OF THE VANITIES***, attacks the morality of New York's rich elite. The book becomes an instant best-seller, in part because so many of its characters bring to mind real people. Wolfe himself became famous during the 1960s, when he helped create the New Journalism, a style of writing that used the techniques of novelists to report true stories.

FEBRUARY 14, 1989 Iranian religious leader Ayatollah Ruhollah Khomeini offers three million dollars as a reward for the killing of author Salman Rushdie. Khomeini orders this *fatwa*, or death sentence, because Rushdie's latest novel, ***THE SATANIC VERSES***, describes the prophet Mohammed in ways that offend many Muslims. Rushdie goes into hiding immediately.

1989 Young African-American director Spike Lee completes his film ***DO THE RIGHT THING***, set in a Brooklyn neighborhood during the hottest day of the summer. The movie examines the conflict between white Italians who run a local pizzeria and their black customers. Lee's film, which ends with a riot, appears to mirror much that is happening every day on America's city streets.

## Science & Technology

OCTOBER 22, 1986 "The silence must end," says **SURGEON GENERAL C. EVERETT KOOP** in his official report on AIDS [April 23, 1984], released today. Amid a storm of controversy and despite strong opposition from other Reagan administration officials, Koop advises parents to be frank with their children about sexual matters in order to stop the spread of the disease.

SEPTEMBER 16, 1987 A scientific conference in Montreal, Canada, drafts an international agreement calling for a **FREEZE IN CHLOROFLUOROCARBON (CFC) PRODUCTION**, followed by a gradual decrease. Motivated by growing fears about the thinning ozone layer [March 1985], the U.S. Senate ratifies the treaty on March 14, 1988, by a vote of 83–0.

JUNE 23, 1988 NASA researcher James Hansen warns a Senate committee that the so-called **GREENHOUSE EFFECT** may be causing temperatures to rise worldwide. He suggests the cause may be increased levels of carbon dioxide in the atmosphere that trap the sun's warmth. He warns that global warming may eventually lead to huge floods caused by melting polar ice.

JUNE 4, 1989 Chinese troops fire at a crowd of protesters, mostly students, gathered in Beijing's Tienanmen Square. The students have been camping out in Tienanmen, the largest open space in the Chinese capital, since April 15, when they began demonstrating for greater democracy. Perhaps as many as two thousand protesters die in the **TIENANMEN MASSACRE**.

AUGUST 9, 1989 President Bush commits $166 billion in public funds to pay for closing down the nation's many failed savings-and-loans. Many observers blame former president Reagan for the **SAVINGS-AND-LOAN BAILOUT**. They accuse his administration of carelessness and neglect in allowing banks to risk their depositors' money in reckless stock and real estate deals.

AUGUST 24, 1989 After forty years, **COMMUNIST RULE ENDS IN POLAND** when a new parliament makes Solidarity nominee Tadeusz Mazowiecki prime minister. Mazowiecki has the support of both Lech Walesa, founder of the Solidarity movement, and Catholic leader Jozef Cardinal Glemp. The Communists, however, remain in control of the interior and defense ministries.

OCTOBER 17, 1989 An earthquake measuring 7.1 on the Richter scale [1935] rocks San Francisco's Bay Area. It is the nation's most powerful since the one that destroyed San Francisco earlier in the century [April 18, 1906]. Highways and bridges collapse in Oakland, killing nearly one hundred people. The **BAY AREA EARTHQUAKE** stops a World Series game being played at Candlestick Park.

# EXXON VALDEZ

DURING THE EARLY-morning hours of March 24, 1989, the *Exxon Valdez* ran aground on Bligh Reef off the coast of Alaska. The thousand-foot supertanker had just left the port of Valdez at the southern end of the Trans-Alaska Pipeline. The accident punctured the tanker's hull, causing the worst oil spill in U.S. history. Before the damage could be contained, more than eleven million gallons of crude oil had poured into Prince William Sound.

Under extreme public pressure, Exxon began a clean-up operation. But the oil company's efforts fell apart when a storm hit the area on March 27. The storm's high winds turned the spill into a forty-mile-long oil slick, which currents carried even farther away. As a result, the spill coated hundreds of miles of Alaskan coastline, creating an ecological disaster area.

The accident cost Exxon more than two billion dollars in clean-up costs as well as a record hundred million dollars to settle victims' lawsuits. Even that much money, however, could not erase the damage done to the environment.

**An investigation into the accident revealed that the captain of the *Exxon Valdez* was below deck, and probably drunk, when his ship hit Bligh Reef, which was well marked on nautical charts. He had left an inexperienced third mate in charge.**

Clean-up workers spray the beach of an island in Prince Williams Sound

# The Nineties

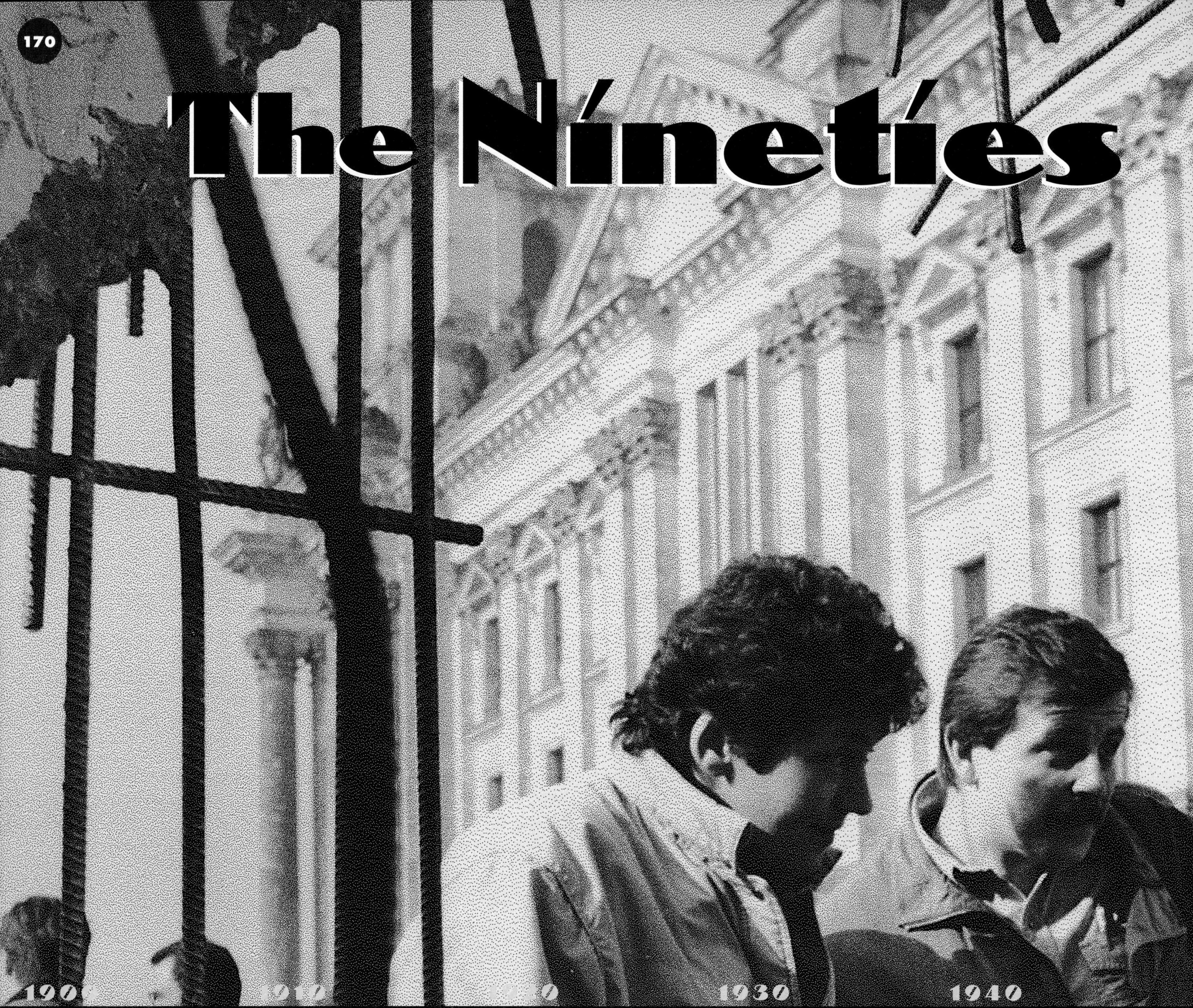

DURING THE COLD WAR, the Soviet Union focused on keeping up with the United States in the race for larger and more powerful weapons. Because the state-controlled Soviet economy was far less productive than the capitalist U.S. economy, the Soviets regularly sacrificed the everyday needs of their people to build more weapons. They did not have enough factories to produce both bombs and refrigerators at the same time.

During the early 1970s, tensions relaxed a bit under President Richard Nixon's policy of detente. But there was little cooperation between the two nations until Mikhail Gorbachev came to power in 1985. Gorbachev believed that the Soviet Union had to change. He called his policies glasnost (meaning "openness") and perestroika (meaning "restructuring"). Although Gorbachev's reforms were meant to be gradual, the pace of change quickly overwhelmed him. Democratization followed—and then, almost before anyone noticed, the Cold War was over. Taking its place, President George Bush announced, would be a "new world order."

★

## Politics

NOVEMBER 9, 1989 Jubilant Germans begin to **TEAR DOWN THE BERLIN WALL** after East German chancellor Egon Krentz allows free travel between East and West Berlin. Previously, East Germany's Communist government had tightly controlled movement across its borders. Krentz's decision comes in response to political reforms sweeping the Warsaw Pact nations [May 4, 1955].

DECEMBER 10, 1989 More than forty years of Communist rule end in Czechoslovakia when a new cabinet with Communists in the minority takes power. The peaceful transfer of government becomes known as the **VELVET REVOLUTION**. On December 29, the new cabinet elects playwright Vaclav Havel president of the country's new Western-style democracy.

DECEMBER 20, 1989 President Bush orders the **INVASION OF PANAMA**, where twenty-four thousand U.S. troops overthrow the dictatorship of General Manuel Noriega. A Miami grand jury had earlier indicted Noriega on drug-trafficking charges [February 5, 1988]. At first, Noriega takes refuge in the Vatican embassy. But after two weeks of negotiations, he surrenders on January 4.

## Life in the Nineties

JANUARY 31, 1990 The first Soviet **MCDONALDS OPENS IN MOSCOW**. The fast-food chain's decision to invest in the Soviet Union follows Mikhail Gorbachev's attempts to reform his country's economy [January 27, 1987]. Crowds of Muscovites wait in long lines to buy Big Macs, called *Bolshoi Macs* in Russian, despite their cost, which is high by Soviet standards.

MARCH 22, 1990 President **BUSH BANS BROCCOLI FROM THE WHITE HOUSE MENU** because he does not like its taste. "I'm the president of the United States," Bush says, "and I'm not going to eat any more broccoli." Broccoli farmers protest the president's action, which they say harms their public image, especially with children.

**EARTH SUMMIT • President George Bush and First Lady Barbara Bush add their signatures to the environmental Earth Pledge at the Earth Summit in Rio de Janeiro, Brazil.**

## Arts & Entertainment

DECEMBER 17, 1989 A new cartoon series called **"THE SIMPSONS"** debuts on the new Fox television network. Its instant success helps establish Fox as a legitimate fourth network. The weekly show, created by Matt Groening, is the first animated series since "The Flintstones" to become a hit in prime time.

1989 **MADONNA** makes a multimillion-dollar deal to promote the soft drink Pepsi with her new video, "Like a Prayer." The song reaches Number One on the pop charts, where it remains for three weeks. But Pepsi cancels the contract after religious groups object to Madonna's use of Christian imagery in the video. She gets to keep Pepsi's money, though.

## Science & Technology

JUNE 26, 1990 The Environmental Protection Agency places the **NORTHERN SPOTTED OWL** on its Endangered Species List. This action leads to limits on logging in some forests of the Pacific Northwest, where the spotted owl lives. When logging companies object, the bird comes to symbolize the potential conflicts between environmental protection and jobs.

OCTOBER 2, 1991 **IBM AND APPLE** announce that they have joined together to develop a new generation of computers. The two companies have agreed to the alliance because their sales have been falling. The new chips, or microprocessors, are introduced in 1994 as part of the PowerPC and Power Mac lines, making the two brands compatible.

JUNE 14, 1992 Meeting at the first **EARTH SUMMIT** in Rio de Janeiro, Brazil, representatives of 153 countries sign treaties designed to protect the environment. They address global warming caused by the greenhouse effect [June 23, 1988] and biodiversity. The goal of the biodiversity treaty is to protect the diversity of living things from extinction.

FEBRUARY 7, 1990 Following Mikhail Gorbachev's recommendation, the Central Committee of the **COMMUNIST PARTY ENDS ITS MONOPOLY ON POLITICAL POWER IN THE SOVIET UNION**. In free elections held in May, Boris Yeltsin becomes president of Russia, the largest of the Soviet republics. In June, Yeltsin resigns from the Communist party but keeps his presidency.

FEBRUARY 11, 1990 Pressured by riots in black townships, South African president F.W. de Klerk has Nelson **MANDELA FREED FROM JAIL**, ending Mandela's twenty-seven years as a political prisoner [June 11, 1964]. De Klerk wants Mandela to help him negotiate a peaceful end to apartheid, which has allowed South Africa's white minority to control the country's wealth and government.

JUNE 26, 1990 Less than two years after promising not to raise taxes [August 18, 1988], President Bush admits that the rising federal budget deficit has forced him to consider **TAX INCREASES**. The change in policy draws particularly harsh attacks from conservatives, who contributed to his election because they believed his repeated pledge, "Read my lips, no new taxes!"

MARCH 15, 1991 A Los Angeles grand jury indicts four white police officers in the March 3 **BEATING OF BLACK MOTORIST RODNEY KING**. The incident became national news after TV stations began airing a videotape of the beating shot by an amateur. The tape, which shows the motionless King being repeatedly clubbed, has called attention to police brutality against blacks.

**Making matters worse, cutbacks in federal housing aid during the Reagan years limited the number of units available in low-rent public housing projects.**

# The Homeless

DURING THE 1980s, THE United States suffered its worst housing crisis since the Great Depression. Record numbers of homeless people appeared at emergency shelters. Others, who considered the shelters dangerous, lived on the streets. By 1991, the National Alliance to End Homelessness estimated that three hundred thousand Americans did not have a place to call home. This number included many families with children as well as single men and women.

Several trends contributed to the crisis. During the 1970s, patients at psychiatric hospitals who were not considered dangerous were released. Some people thought the government had no right to keep these patients locked up; others wanted to save money. In any case, many of the former patients could not hold jobs and often ended up on the street. Increased drug and alcohol abuse also contributed to the street population.

But the greatest cause of homelessness, by far, was poverty. Despite media portrayals of the homeless as drug addicts and mental patients, more than forty percent were members of families headed by parents who had lost their jobs and could not afford to pay rent.

## Politics

AUGUST 2, 1990 Iraqi leader Saddam Hussein orders the **INVASION OF KUWAIT**, a tiny but oil-rich nation on the northern coast of the Persian Gulf. The Iraqi army easily seizes oil fields that Hussein has claimed belong to his country. On August 8, President Bush sends U.S. troops to protect Saudi Arabia, drawing "a line in the sand" and warning Hussein not to cross it.

JANUARY 17, 1991 The United States and its allies begin **OPERATION DESERT STORM**, attacking Iraq from the air two days after Iraqi leader Saddam Hussein ignores a United Nations deadline to withdraw his troops from Kuwait [August 2, 1990]. On February 28, four days after the allies launch their ground attack, President Bush announces that Kuwait has been liberated.

AUGUST 19, 1991 A group of Communist hard-liners tries to take control of the Soviet government in order to reverse Mikhail Gorbachev's reform policies, particularly his surrender of monopoly power [February 7, 1990]. The **SOVIET COUP** fails after President Boris Yeltsin of the Russian Republic calls for a general strike, and workers in Moscow take to the streets.

## Life in the Nineties

NOVEMBER 7, 1991 L.A. Lakers star Earvin **"MAGIC" JOHNSON SAYS HE HAS TESTED POSITIVE FOR HIV**, the virus that causes AIDS. At a press conference announcing his retirement from basketball, Johnson claims he contracted HIV through sex with a woman. His disclosure stuns many Americans who had believed that only homosexuals and drug users could get AIDS.

AUGUST 9, 1992 The U.S. men's basketball team, which includes professional players for the first time, wins the gold medal at the Summer Olympics in Barcelona, Spain. Known as the **DREAM TEAM**, the twelve-man squad easily dominates the competition. NBA stars on the team include Michael Jordan, Larry Bird, and Magic Johnson, who plays despite being infected with the virus that causes AIDS.

SEPTEMBER 25, 1992 A judge in Florida grants twelve-year-old Gregory Kingsley a **DIVORCE FROM HIS BIOLOGICAL MOTHER** so that he can be adopted by his foster parents. Gregory had charged his mother with neglect and abuse. The state judge's decision marks the first time in U.S. history that a child has won a legal action to separate himself from his biological parents.

## Arts & Entertainment

1989 Amy Tan makes the best-seller list with ***THE JOY LUCK CLUB***, her novel about Chinese-American life in San Francisco. Tan's story, which features four Chinese-American women and their daughters, captures the conflict between immigrant Chinese parents and their children who have grown up as Americans.

孩子

SEPTEMBER 23–27, 1990 Nearly forty million Americans watch ***THE CIVIL WAR***, an epic documentary series created for public television by Ken and Ric Burns. The eleven-hour program, airing on five consecutive nights, wins critical praise for its inventive blend of still images, music of the period, and excerpts from the diaries and letters of ordinary people.

**DREAM TEAM • Earvin "Magic" Johnson rejoices after receiving his 1992 Olympic gold medal.**

## Science & Technology

OCTOBER 24, 1993 The *New York Times* reports that scientists at George Washington University Medical Center in Washington, D.C., have successfully cloned human embryos. **CLONING** involves copying genes from one cell to another. The article provokes a debate on whether it is moral to engineer human genes. Meanwhile, the Roman Catholic Church calls for an immediate halt to cloning research.

**OCTOBER 15, 1991** By the narrow margin of 52–48, the Senate confirms the nomination of **CLARENCE THOMAS** to the Supreme Court, making him the second black justice. Law professor Anita Hill had challenged Thomas's nomination, accusing him of sexually harassing her while she had worked for him. Thomas himself called the televised hearings on Hill's charges a "high-tech lynching."

**FEBRUARY 20, 1992** Appearing on Larry King's CNN show, billionaire **ROSS PEROT** announces that he will run for president as an independent candidate if supporters place his name on the ballot in all fifty states. Although this condition is met, Perot drops out of the race in July, then resurfaces in October when his television commercials focus voter attention on the federal budget deficit.

**NOVEMBER 3, 1992** In the **1992 PRESIDENTIAL ELECTION**, Bill Clinton wins a close three-way race. The Democrat from Arkansas takes forty-three percent of the popular vote, compared to thirty-eight percent for incumbent president George Bush and nineteen percent for independent candidate Ross Perot.

**FEBRUARY 26, 1993** An **EXPLOSION SHAKES THE WORLD TRADE CENTER** in New York City, killing five people and injuring more than a thousand. The bomb, hidden inside a van parked in an underground garage, leaves a crater seven stories deep. A week later, the FBI begins arresting members of a radical Muslim group for the crime, the worst terrorist attack on U.S. soil.

# L.A. RIOTS

**ON APRIL 29, 1992, THE jury in the Rodney King case delivered its verdict in the trial of four white police officers accused of beating King because he was black. The case had been moved from Los Angeles to the suburb of Simi Valley because the lawyers for the policemen had convinced a judge that the mostly black Los Angeles jurors would not give their clients a fair trial.**

**Instead, the Simi Valley jury, which included no blacks, found the policemen not guilty. The jury members accepted the officers' explanation that King was drunk, high on drugs, and dangerous. They believed the police despite an amateur videotape that showed King being beaten as he lay motionless on the ground.**

**When the verdict was announced, rioting broke out in the poor black neighborhood of South Central Los Angeles. Outnumbered police retreated, while frustrated, rampaging youths broke windows, looted stores, and burned buildings to the ground. That evening, Mayor Tom Bradley declared a state of emergency, and California governor Pete Wilson called in the National Guard. After martial law was declared, Rodney King himself appeared on television to plead for calm.**

**The rioting, which went on for three days, killed thirty-seven people, injured more than fifteen hundred, and destroyed six hundred million dollars' worth of property.**

**On May 2, Koreans in Los Angeles attended a rally to promote peace between Koreans and blacks. That same day, Rodney King went on television to plead for peace.**

## Politics

DECEMBER 9, 1992 **MARINES LAND IN SOMALIA**, where President Bush has sent them to restore order. A long drought has produced a famine in this East African country, where rival warlords control different armed clans. Relief agencies have been airlifting food and other humanitarian aid, but these shipments are being seized by the warlords before they reach Somalis dying of starvation.

JANUARY 22, 1993 **ZOË BAIRD**, President Clinton's nominee for attorney general, withdraws her name from consideration after she apologizes for failing to pay the required social security tax for two household employees. Baird, the first cabinet nominee to withdraw in 120 years, eventually pays sixteen thousand dollars in back taxes, interest, and fines.

NOVEMBER 17, 1993 In a major victory for President Clinton, the House narrowly approves the **NORTH AMERICAN FREE TRADE AGREEMENT**, which removes the trade barriers among Mexico, Canada, and the United States. Tariffs currently charged have added to the cost of imported goods. The removal of these taxes will ease the flow of products across North American borders.

## Life in the Nineties

APRIL 26, 1993 The **HOLOCAUST MEMORIAL MUSEUM**, dedicated to the victims of Nazi Germany, opens in Washington, D.C. The museum's exhibits portray life inside a concentration camp. Visitors watch video interviews with people who survived the camps and walk through replicas of sleeping quarters as well as one of the original railroad cars used to transport Jews to these camps.

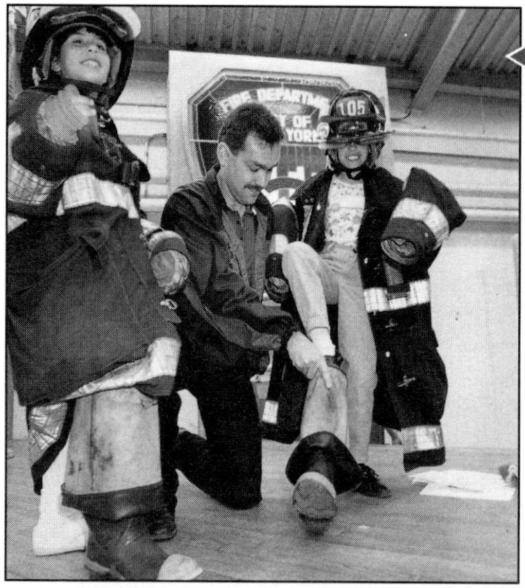

APRIL 28, 1993 On **TAKE OUR DAUGHTERS TO WORK DAY**, hundreds of thousands of girls accompany their parents to work, where they learn about jobs and the workplace. The event, originally sponsored in New York City by the Ms. Foundation, picked up nationwide support after founder Gloria Steinem mentioned the idea in a *Parade* magazine article.

**TAKE OUR DAUGHTERS TO WORK DAY • A New York City fireman helps his daughter and niece try on protective clothing at the New York Fire Academy.**

## Arts & Entertainment

1991 The huge success of Nirvana's *Nevermind* album convinces record companies to sign up other Seattle-based "grunge" rock bands. Taking its name from the sloppy appearance of band members, **GRUNGE** spawns a new fashion style as teenagers all over the country begin wearing worn flannel shirts, loose dirty jeans, ripped T-shirts, and ski caps.

1994 ***ZLATA'S DIARY***, written by a young Bosnian girl living under siege in Sarajevo, dramatizes the ongoing war in the former Yugoslavia. The book's thirteen-year-old author, Zlata Filipovic, tells of her experiences escaping Serbian shelling by hiding in basement shelters. She also recounts her family's difficulties coping with shortages of food, water, and heating fuel.

## Science & Technology

DECEMBER 5–9, 1993 Astronauts aboard the space shuttle *Endeavour* repair the $1.5-billion **HUBBLE SPACE TELESCOPE**. Soon after NASA launched the telescope in April 1990, it discovered flaws in the telescope's mirrors that prevented its cameras from focusing. The *Endeavour* crew successfully replaces these elements so that the Hubble now works properly.

JANUARY 4, 1994 A World Health Organization report estimates that over fifteen million people, including more than one million children, have contracted the HIV virus that causes **AIDS** [April 23, 1984]. According to WHO estimates, that total may reach forty million by the year 2000.

MARCH 29, 1994 Vice President Albert Gore presents the Clinton administration's plan to develop an **INFORMATION SUPERHIGHWAY** in the United States. The telecommunications network will link personal computers in people's homes with libraries, universities, and other sources of information worldwide.

MAY 10, 1994 Former political prisoner Nelson Mandela is sworn in as the **FIRST BLACK PRESIDENT OF SOUTH AFRICA** [February 11, 1990]. Mandela's election followed a September 1993 power-sharing agreement between the African National Congress and the ruling white Nationalist party, which gave black South Africans the right to vote.

JULY 1, 1994 Palestine Liberation Organization chairman and former terrorist Yasir Arafat returns to his homeland in the Gaza Strip on the West Bank of the Jordan River. Arafat's return follows secret PLO negotiations with Israel. The talks produced an agreement allowing **PALESTINIAN SELF-RULE** in territory seized by the Israelis during the Six Day War [June 5, 1967].

NOVEMBER 8, 1994 For the first time since 1954, the Republicans win control of both the House and the Senate. The president's party usually loses seats in Congress during midterm elections, but the **1994 ELECTIONS** represent a much more significant defeat for the Democrats. New speaker of the House Newt Gingrich of Georgia pledges to scale back the federal government and balance the budget.

AUGUST 12, 1993 President Clinton signs a $6.2-billion relief bill to help victims of the **GREAT FLOOD OF 1993**, the second worst in U.S. history. The disaster began when midwestern soil, already soaked by melting snow, could not absorb heavy spring rains. Fifty people have died in states along the Mississippi River, including Iowa and Illinois, where seventy thousand are now homeless.

# HILLARY CLINTON

**During the 1992 campaign, Mrs. Clinton often told voters, "If you elect Bill, you get me, too." Her professional achievements qualified her to serve in a presidential administration, but President Clinton still received criticism for including her in so many policy decisions.**

MANY FIRST LADIES, including Eleanor Roosevelt and Nancy Reagan, were known to have influenced their husbands' policies. But no first lady had ever advised her husband in an important official capacity. That is, not until January 25, 1993, when President Clinton named his wife, Hillary Rodham Clinton, to head the presidential Task Force on National Health Care Reform.

Mrs. Clinton and her husband met while they were both students at Yale University Law School. During the years that Bill Clinton served as governor of Arkansas, Hillary worked as a full-time lawyer at one of the state's leading firms. She also became a nationally recognized advocate for children's rights and served on the boards of several large corporations. In 1988 and again in 1991, the National Law Journal named her one of the country's most influential lawyers.

# Glossary

**acquittal** A judgment of not guilty in a court of law.

**allies** Nations that fight on the same side during a war.

**anarchy** The belief that the best form of government is no government at all.

**annex** To take control of a region belonging to another country.

**antitrust laws** Laws that regulate the formation of trusts (see trust).

**appeasement** Giving in to the demands of an aggressor in the name of peace.

**armistice** An agreement that suspends or ends the fighting during a war.

**Aryan** A term used by the Nazis to describe northern Europeans who share certain physical traits, including blond hair, fair skin, and blue eyes.

**avant-garde** The leading, often controversial edge of an art form, known for its new ideas and styles.

**bankrupt** Unable to pay one's debts.

**bathyscaphe** A spherical deep-sea diving vessel.

**blacklist** To deny work or membership in a group, usually secretly, to people with unpopular political views.

**bloc** A group of nations under the control of a superpower or otherwise allied for a common purpose.

**bootlegging** The sale of illegal alcohol during the era of Prohibition.

**boycott** The refusal to take part in an activity or buy particular goods as a form of protest.

**budget deficit** The debt created when a government spends more than it takes in.

**capitalism** An economic system based on the ownership of private property.

**cease-fire** An often temporary agreement to suspend fighting during wartime.

**censorship** The denial of free speech.

**charter** The formal document that establishes a group.

**circumstantial evidence** Proof used in a legal case that does not rely on eyewitness testimony.

**civil disobedience** Nonviolent protest against the government that challenges its authority or policies.

**civil libertarian** A person who believes the government should not limit its citizens' thoughts or actions.

**civil rights** Rights guaranteed to individuals by the Constitution.

**collectivization** The transfer of the ownership of property from an individual to a group.

**colony** A territory settled and controlled by another country.

**commando** A member of a small force trained to conduct raids in enemy territory.

**commune** A group of people living together who share everything.

**Communism** A form of government based on the ideas of Karl Marx that advocates the elimination of private property.

**Communist** A member of the Communist party.

**concentration camp** A prison in which people are held because of their ethnicity or political associations.

**conservationist** A person concerned with protecting the environment.

**conservative** A person who favors a reduced role for government in solving society's problems.

**conspiracy** A secret plan carried out by a group of people.

**corollary** A statement that naturally follows from a proposition or doctrine.

**cosmonaut** The Soviet term for astronaut.

**counterrevolutionary** A person or thing working against a political revolution.

**coup** The quick, often violent overthrow of a government.

**defect** To leave one's country for political reasons and seek asylum in another.

**delegation** A group of people representing a place or organization, as at a convention.

**dissent** To argue or protest against an established opinion.

**doctrine** A statement of beliefs or principles.

**dole** The name given to government financial aid for the poor and unemployed during the Great Depression.

**dove** A person who opposes war as a means of solving problems between nations.

**embargo** A governmental ban on trade with another country, often used as a form of protest or punishment.

**emigrate** To leave one country to live in another.

**empire** A colonial power and the territories it controls.

**epidemic** The rapid spread of a disease.

**espionage** The practice of spying.

**ethnicity** The racial, cultural, or national group to which a person belongs.

**evolution** The scientific theory that all life developed from earlier, more primitive forms.

**fallout** Dangerous radioactive particles that fall to the earth after a nuclear explosion.

**fascism** The political philosophy that advocates a strong central government controlled by a single political party and headed by a powerful dictator.

**feminist** A person who believes that women should have the same rights and opportunities as men.

**guerrilla** A member of a small, unofficial force fighting against an invading army.

**hallucinogens** Drugs that produce hallucinations, or sights or sounds that are not actually present.

**hawk** A person who favors war as a means of solving problems between nations.

**hemisphere** One half of the earth—either northern and southern or eastern and western.

**immigrate** To settle in one country after leaving another.

**improvisational jazz** Jazz music performed spontaneously without a written score.

**incumbent** The person currently holding a particular political office.

**individualism** The practice of self-reliance.

**integrate** To bring together people who were formerly segregated, or kept apart.

**integrated circuit** The path taken by an electric current through a number of different but interconnected components.

**International Style** A style of architecture popular during the 1920s and 1930s characterized by skyscrapers made of concrete, steel, and glass.

**interracial** Involving members of different races.

**Islamic fundamentalist** A person who believes in an extremely strict form of Islam.

**isolationism** The belief that a nation should not become involved in the affairs of other nations.

**juvenile delinquent** A young person, often a teenager, who has committed a crime.

**kaiser** The German emperor.

**labor union** A group of workers who act together for better pay and working conditions.

**land speculation** The buying of land with the hope that its value will go up, so that it can be sold for a profit.

**laser** A highly concentrated beam of light.

**legislate** To enact a law.

**liberal** A person who believes the government should play an important role in solving society's problems.

**literacy** The ability to read and write.

**lynch** To hang a person without a trial.

**mass culture** Art and information created for a broad audience.

**mass hysteria** A public panic based on an irrational fear.

**meteorologist** A person who studies the earth's atmosphere and predicts the climate and weather.

**microprocessors** Tiny computers that process information.

**migrant workers** Farm workers who move from place to place as different crops become ready to harvest.

**militant** A person who is extremely aggressive or violent in support of a cause.

**missionary** A member of a religious group who travels to another country to convert people holding different beliefs.

**monopoly** The complete control of an industry.

**multinational** Involving more than one nation.

**nationalism** Extreme loyalty and support for one's nation.

**nationalize** The act of a government taking control of a private business.

**nuclear fission** The splitting apart of an atomic nucleus.

**nuclear fusion** The forcing together of two atomic nuclei.

**nuclear reactor** The container in which nuclear fission takes place.

**pacifism** The belief that war and violence are morally wrong under all circumstances.

**pension** Money paid to people after they retire from a fund in which they invested during their working years.

**poll tax** A fee paid by people in order to vote in an election.

**populism** A political movement intended to advance the needs of common people.

**prefabricated** Constructed from parts that have been mass-produced and assembled in advance.

**primary election** An election held by a political party to determine its candidates for office.

**progressive** A person who believes that government action can improve the quality of life for people in a nation.

**propaganda** Biased information that promotes a particular group or cause.

**protocol** A document written by diplomatic negotiators.

**psychedelic** Relating to hallucinogenic drugs and the effects associated with them.

**putsch** A secret and sudden attempt to overthrow a government.

**Quaker** A member of a Christian religious group committed to pacificism.

**quota** The percentage of a whole that is reserved for a specific person or group.

**racketeer** A person who obtains money illegally as part of a criminal conspiracy, often by threatening people with violence.

**radiation** Energy given off by an object in the form of particles or waves.

**radical** A person who holds extreme political views.

**ration** To limit the amount of goods and food people can buy because of shortages.

**Reconstruction** The historical period immediately following the Civil War during which the federal government controlled southern state governments.

**repeal** To reverse the passage of a law.

**repress** To put down and keep down, often by force.

**Reserve Officers Training Corps (ROTC)** A group established by the U.S. armed forces to train students on college campuses.

**satellite** An object that orbits a celestial body such as a planet, or a country dominated by a more powerful nation.

**segregate** To separate people, usually according to their race or ethnicity.

**settlement houses** Organizations that helped poor immigrants adapt to life in the United States during the early 1900s.

**sexual harassment** Unwelcome or threatening sexual advances made in the workplace.

**sharecroppers** Farmers who paid landlords rent not with money but with a share of the crops they grew.

**socialism** A form of government that advocates common ownership of a community's land and economic resources.

**sociobiology** The study of animal societies.

**storm trooper** A member of a private Nazi political army known for its ruthlessness.

**strike** The refusal by employees to work until their demands for more pay or better working conditions are met.

**subversive** A term used to describe a person suspected of acting against the common good for political reasons.

**sweatshop** A cramped factory in which people work long hours for little pay under dangerous and often illegal conditions.

**tariffs** Taxes on imported and exported goods.

**terrorist** A person who uses violence against civilians to draw attention to and promote his or her political goals.

**treaty** A formal agreement between national governments.

**tribunal** A court of law.

**trust** A group that takes complete control of an industry in order to set the price of its goods.

**tsar** The Russian emperor.

**ultimatum** A final warning signaling the end of negotiations.

**unconstitutional** Not lawful under the Constitution.

**vaccine** A substance taken to prevent infection by a particular disease.

**vaudeville** The name given during the early 1900s to popular stage entertainments that featured musical acts, dancers, comedians, and acrobats.

**xenophobia** The fear or hatred of foreigners.

# Index

## TIMELINE VEHICLES:

| | |
|---|---|
| 1900–1906 | Wright brothers' *Flyer I* |
| 1906–1920 | Model T Ford |
| 1920–1929 | Charles Lindbergh's *Spirit of St. Louis* |
| 1929–1939 | Dirigible LZ 129 *Hindenburg* |
| 1939–1946 | Sherman tank |
| 1946–1960 | Soviet satellite Sputnik |
| 1960–1972 | Apollo 11 lunar module *Eagle* |
| 1972–1980 | AMC Gremlin economy car |
| 1980–1989 | Space shuttle *Columbia* |
| 1989–1994 | F 117-A Stealth fighter |

HOOVER ELEMENTARY SCHOOL
INSTRUCTIONAL MATERIAL CENTER
WAYNE COMMUNITY SCHOOL DISTRICT